Louis Althusser and the
Traditions of French Marxism

Louis Althusser and the Traditions of French Marxism

William S. Lewis

LEXINGTON BOOKS

A division of
ROWMAN & LITTLEFIELD PUBLISHERS, INC.
Lanham • Boulder • New York • Toronto • Oxford

LEXINGTON BOOKS

A division of Rowman & Littlefield Publishers, Inc.
A wholly owned subsidiary of The Rowman & Littlefield Publishing Group, Inc.
4501 Forbes Boulevard, Suite 200
Lanham, MD 20706

PO Box 317
Oxford
OX2 9RU, UK

British Library Cataloguing in Publication Information Available

Library of Congress Cataloging-in-Publication Data

Lewis, William S., 1971-
  Louis Althusser and the traditions of French Marxism / William S. Lewis.
    p. cm.
  Includes bibliographical references and index.
  ISBN 0-7391-0983-9 (cloth : alk. paper)—ISBN 0-7391-1307-0 (pbk. : alk. paper)
  1. Althusser, Louis. 2. Philosophy, Marxist—France. I. Title.
B2430.A474L49 2005
194—dc22   2005015852

Printed in the United States of America

♾™ The paper used in this publication meets the minimum requirements of American
National Standard for Information Sciences—Permanence of Paper for Printed Library
Materials, ANSI/NISO Z39.48–1992.

For Julianne

Parts of this book have appeared in the following journals: an extended version of the argument for maintaining Althusser's science/ideology distinction from chapters 6 and 7 is given in "Knowledge versus 'Knowledge': Louis Althusser on the Autonomy of Science and Philosophy from Ideology." *Rethinking Marxism*, vol. 17, no. 3 (July 2005); and part of the discussion of contradiction and overdetermination from chapter 6 is taken from "The Under-theorization of Overdetermination in the Political Philosophy of Ernesto Laclau and Chantal Mouffe." *Studies in Social and Political Thought*, no. 11 (May 2005). The cover image is used by permission of the French Communist Party and is copyright ©1961.

Contents

Acknowledgments

There are many persons and institutions whose help was invaluable to me in the research and writing of this book and to whom I wish to extend my profound thanks. These include first and foremost my mentors at the Pennsylvania State University: Dan Conway, Vincent Colapietro, Allan Stoekl and, especially, John Stuhr. All were extremely helpful in turning a vague idea into a (hopefully) coherent narrative and philosophic argument. In France, the direction of my work was greatly influenced by conversations with Rainer Rochlitz, Jacques Léenhart, Étienne Balibar, and Geoffrey Goshgarian. Each in his own way corrected my rather naive notions about the role Marxism and Althusser played in twentieth-century French philosophical and political debates. Also in France, my research into Althusser and into PCF theory was aided immeasurably by Olivier Corpet and Sandrine Samson at the Institut Mémoire de l'Édition Contemporaine, and by Catherine Bensadek at the Bibliothéque Marxiste de Paris. Jacques Amsellem and Lili Zeller made these trips to France a pleasure. Pascal Carreau and the Parti Communiste Francais were extremely gracious in allowing me to use the propaganda image selected for the book's cover. I would also like to recognize the careful eyes of Matthew Bohenek and Daisy Larom who helped proof the manuscript during its final stages. Finally, I would like to recognize the institutional support received from the Pennsylvania State University, Georgetown University, and Skidmore College in the form of grants and fellowships without which this work would have proved impossible to accomplish.

Introduction

Why Marxism?
Why French Marxism?

Why Marxism?

In the 1990s the argument was often popularly advanced that with the fall of the Berlin Wall in 1989 and the collapse of the Soviet System we have witnessed not only the fall of Marxist-inspired governments but also, concomitant with this failure, the disproof of Marx's philosophy. China's increasing liberalization, at least in the area of free trade, has likewise been recognized as signaling such a proof. As this argument or narrative usually proceeds, the history of the twentieth century functioned something like a grand laboratory experiment in which two competing systems were allowed to run their course. Capitalism, already the norm at the start of the century and earlier justified and explained theoretically by Smith and Ricardo among others, was taken as the control group. Communism, the arriviste alternative, became the experimental system. Quarantined after 1923, it was allowed to play itself out just as capitalism was allowed to continue with its established patterns. When in the late 1980s Communism definitively "failed to thrive," the experiment was concluded and the theory which supported it, Marxist philosophy, was discarded as false because such a system was proven not to work in the "real" world.

One can of course find many other arguments justifying a rejection of Marx's philosophy. Some of these, such as those which would critique Marx's philosophy as necessarily demanding a totalitarian political practice or those identifying it as a well-disguised and always in practice harmful utopian idealism are quite sophisticated. Others, like the vulgar

Darwinian "survival of the fittest" argument, lack this subtlety. Nonetheless, many of these arguments are similar to the crude "lab experiment" contention in that they draw their rhetorical strength or, at the very least, their impetus and proof from the unfortunate history of Marxist inspired movements and not from close reading or consideration of Marx's work. Not to offer an apology for Stalin's famines and gulags, for Mao's Cultural Revolution, or for the terrorism of the Shining Path, however, each of these arguments that would jettison Marx's philosophy into the dustbin of history along with the failed communist projects it inspired often neglect the facts of history, the subtlety, originality, and provisional nature of Marx's work as well as the current and insistent realities of the global economy. Ignored also is the fact that history is messy and that "actually existing communism" was never a pure distillation of Marx's philosophy (if ever there could be such a thing). Also overlooked is the fact that while this "lab experiment" was going on, the global economy continued to run its course much as Marx had theorized that it would, characterized by the progressive upward transfer of capital, interspersed with periodic, if now "managed," crises.

Given that the "lab experiment" and its more sophisticated rhetorical brethren might be looked upon with suspicion and that—at least on the surface—Marx's economic theory still appears to have some value, might it also be the case that Marx's philosophy also retains some worth? This is the question that animates this book: "What remains of Marx's philosophy which is of philosophical and—as the two cannot be separated for Marx—political value?" As the question of whether or not Marx even had a philosophy is one that has been much debated, this is necessarily a very difficult question to answer. However, if a response can be given to this question it must be one that goes beyond a close reading and consideration of Marx's texts and examines the history of their interpretation, appropriation, and use. This is so not only because Marx's philosophy—if it includes or permits a science of history—demands such an account but also because this past is inextricably tied to the way in which Marx can now be read. This point should not be taken as primarily a hermeneutic one. Our interpretation of Marx will no doubt be marked by our place in history and in society. However, and more importantly, it is only by taking account of the relationship between Marxist theory and Marxist practice as it has unfolded through history that we can begin to discern this theory's contemporary value and relevance.

What should we think of Marx and Marxist philosophy today, keeping in mind Marxism's history? Must we now treat Marxism as a lamentable curiosity, as one of a number of Left Hegelian philosophies that happened to have a bit more influence than that of Bruno Bauer but whose projects and concerns remain those of nineteenth-century German radicals? Or, if convinced by our examination of society and of history that there is some lasting worth in Marxism we reject this diminution and choose to champion Marxism as a political philosophy with contemporary relevance, then how do we avoid and correct the theoretical and practical errors which have marked prior interpretations of Marxism? Is this avoidance and emendation even possible?

To answer these questions, this book will not engage in simply another reading of Marx. Rather, it will examine the actual history of and actual problems with Marxist philosophical and political practice. By examining a specific history of attempts to instantiate and (usually only when instantiation failed) to understand the philosophy of Marx, it is hoped that this work will avoid the methodological errors of treating Marx's philosophy either ahistorically or solely in regard to a history of ideas. The former mistake is most obvious in the treatment of Marx by philosophers who seek to apply analytic methods and "ratiocinative rigor" to determine which of Marx's claims retain philosophical value. Not surprisingly for a critical project that takes for granted the validity of rational choice theory and the universality of formal logic,[1] most of these projects conclude that Marx's individual arguments do not hold up and that there is not enough left of them to consider that today "Marxism exists as a systematic collection of substantive claims."[2] In their ahistoricism, what these accounts miss is any critical analysis of their own projects. Such an analysis might reveal the ideological production of their own assumptions and thereby confirm the philosophical value of Marxism in a different fashion. However, their methodology precludes such introspection. Though this study is not totally averse to the treatment of Marx and Marxism as a development in the history of ideas, all too often this approach leads to the diminution of Marx's originality and a tendency to equate Marxism with its influences. This is especially evident in classic works like Robert Tucker's *Philosophy and Myth in Karl Marx* (1972), where Marx is shown to be nothing but a German Rationalist, but it is also present in works like Ernesto Laclau and Chantal Mouffe's *Hegemony and Socialist Strategy* (1985), where the history of Marxist thought becomes a history of its necessary theoretical diminution at the hands of its principal theorists. All too often, what is lost in these histories is an account of the social and political backgrounds that motivated these concepts and their revisions, a consideration that is necessary if one is to understand Marx and Marxism as anything more than the development of an idea. If this work succeeds in avoiding the errors of ahistorical and "history of ideas" approaches to the evaluation of Marxist philosophy and if it is consistent in its method of looking at the actual history of and actual problems associated with Marxist philosophical and political practice, then what will hopefully be gained in this approach is a better understanding of the limits and strengths of Marxist philosophy.

Though it can be roughly distinguished as existing within a single culture and is contained within a single nation, the specific and often overlooked tradition drawn upon in this work's historical analysis is not a singular one. This plural and rarely univocal tradition is the one shared by French Intellectual Marxism and the French Communist Party. This history stretches from their hopeful inaugurations in the wake of the Great War and on through the crises each faced in the 1950s and 1960s when it became apparent that both the theory and practice of Marxism were badly in need of reconsideration. After tracing this trajectory and detailing the various problems that French Intellectual Marxism and French Communism encounter, some time will be spent considering one philosopher who, instead of offering a eulogy or a curse over the corpse of Marxist theory and practice, attempts to offer solutions to the problems which were produced in the process of reading and instantiating Marx's philosophy. Not coincidentally, this philosopher is wholly a part and product of those problematic practices he wishes to critique and save. Nonetheless, in the course of providing this critique, he offers original solutions which not only suggest ways in which French Marxism might work its way out of the crises it found itself in during the 1960s, but his work may also suggest ways to understand Marxism that have contemporary relevance. This philosopher is Louis Althusser.

When Althusser first offered his rereadings of Marx in the mid-1960s, Marxist philosophy and communist practice were in shambles. After Khrushchev's revelations of Stalinist atrocities at the Twentieth Congress of the CPSU and the invasion of Hungary in 1956, it became very difficult to understand Marx's philosophy as a guide for political practice. This is not just because Marxists like Lenin, Stalin, and (as it later became apparent) Mao had "betrayed" Marx, but also because there seemed to be something inherent to Marxism that created, encouraged, and allowed the authoritarian excesses of Lenin, Stalin, and Mao. Today, however, it may be even harder to conceive of Marxism as a viable political philosophy. This same history still casts a long shadow and now, added to this darkening, is the near total recession of global Communism, a seeming testament to the total failure of Marxist philosophy to realize itself as true. The result: although no one can deny its historical importance and influence, Marx's philosophy—at least in North America and in Western Europe—is by academic philosophy either ignored, deconstructed, treated as an anachronism, assimilated into idealism, or used piecemeal as a theoretical tool when it seems to fit the rhetorical needs of an author. All this is particularly true of Marx's status vis-à-vis contemporary political philosophy where his insights are often incorporated without acknowledgment or mind to context, bracketed off as untenable speculation, or relieved of their revolutionary and deterministic baggage as well as any pretenses to scientific status.[3] This consideration of the history of French Marxism wishes to suggest that, as an alternative to this thoughtless appropriation, it might be a wise idea to carefully consider the history of Marxist thought in its interpretations and instantiations in order that we may better understand what resources it may hold both for political philosophy and for political action today.

Why French Marxism?

France seems a strange choice for a country in which to locate and identify a tradition of reading Marx that would serve to reignite interest in him as a political philosopher and to suggest his work's contemporary relevance. Despite its history as the country whose political philosophy and tradition of social revolution in large part engendered, inspired, and directed Marx's own philosophy, French Marxism in both its intellectual and political manifestations has made few significant and lasting contributions to Marxist theory and practice. This lack of contribution is particularly ironic given that France's politics from the 1880s up until very recently have been strongly influenced by Marxist inspired movements and that its intellectuals have likewise found themselves consumed with problems inspired by Marxist philosophy. Thus while one can trace a continuous and at times domestically influential political tradition of French Marxism from its origins with Blanqui to its formative years with Guesde and Jean Jaurés, through its popular apex with Blum and Thorez, and finally on to the contemporary diluted Socialism of François Hollande as well as the anachronistic Communism of Marie-George Buffet, one does not find in this political tradition anything near a Lenin, a Mao, or even an Allende. Likewise, though one can follow a distinct tradition of French Intellectual Marxism that stretches from Georges Sorel and Benoît Malon in the 1890s to Gérard Duménil and Étienne Balibar in the 2000s, with perhaps one exception, France has not, produced a theorist who has had the type of widespread and international influence on Marxist thought as have had Adorno, Lukács, and Gramsci.

That France has not produced such theorists despite an enduring and serious concern with Marxist issues both theoretical and practical may be due to the fact that the intellectual tradition of reading Marx in France can from a certain point of view be categorized as regressive. From the time when Marx began to be taken seriously in limited French academic circles in the 1880s, the dominant characteristic of French Intellectual Marxism has been its tendency to provide idealist interpretations of Marx's philosophy, concentrating on the rational and cognitively creative aspects of the dialectic and paying little attention to the primacy of the material. Looked at from the perspective of those who would see Marx's philosophy as inaugurating a decisive shift in philosophy away from German Idealism and towards a radically materialist philosophy as well as towards a philosophy of political practice, such a proclivity seems decidedly retrograde.

Despite this inclination, the tepid reception abroad of French Intellectual Marxism and its now almost total domestic eclipse probably have less to do with these factors than with its tendency to hermeticism, its lack of originality, and its relative isolation from the debates of Western Marxism. Global political changes, no doubt, have also played a significant role in its diminution. With the possible exceptions of Georges Sorel, who was mostly ignored in his own country when he was active and whose philosophy has only recently been somewhat rehabilitated, and of Louis Althusser, who enjoyed a brief international vogue in the 1960s and early 1970s, the impact of French Marxist Philosophy, while overwhelming in French post-World War II academic circles, has had little direct and lasting impact outside the hexagon.[4] Since the end of the 1970s, it also has had little influence within it.[5] Furthermore, the limited appeal of a philosophical tradition that has seemingly run its course on the world historical stage would seem to consign what is generally regarded as a minor variant within this tradition to a legacy of neglect. This is especially true outside the country which originated it and for whom French Intellectual Marxism might still retain at least historical interest. Given all this, the idea of looking to the tradition of French Intellectual Marxism as a body of thought which might yield new insights about the way in which Marxism might be understood as a political philosophy with contemporary relevance seems less than promising.

If the history of French Academic Marxist Philosophy is a decidedly unlikely place to look for a tradition that might suggest and reveal the contemporary relevance of Marx's philosophy, then the tradition of theoretical Marxism practiced by the Parti Communiste Français (PCF) seems an even more unlikely one. The generally held view of the PCF is that, unlike the Italian Communist Party which maintained relative theoretical autonomy, the PCF owed the sum of its interpretations of Marx (just as it owed the rest of its initiatives) to the directives of the Soviet Union, never differing significantly from the Soviet-directed lines of the Cominform nor from the Cominform's pre-World War II predecessor, the Comintern. Adding to this external constraint was the internal constraint that the PCF could not and would not desire to make any significant independent contributions to Marxist philosophy or, acting autonomously, to revolutionary political practice. This was because the history of the PCF, from its inception at the Congress of Tours in 1920 to its Twenty-second Congress in 1976, was characterized by the firm belief that correct Communist revolutionary practice demanded that it follow the theoretical and practical lead of Moscow.

That the official Marxist philosophy of the Soviet Union as it was exemplified and defined by Stalin's *Short Course* and known by the pejorative "diamatics" was, in general, execrable should attest to the impoverished and derivative philosophy produced by the PCF, an organization whose theoretical output in large part consisted of justifications and defenses of this dogmatic form of Marxism-Leninism. Generally speaking, for most of its history, the role of PCF philosophers was only to explain and disseminate the theory "originated" by the CPSU. Sometimes, though, they would risk the acceptable deviation of lending to this theory a Gallic "tint," harking back to French Utopian Socialism or implying that Communism somehow uniquely fit the French national character or that France had a special role to play in the development of international Communism. Adding to the poverty (in quality if not at all in quantity) of Marxist theory produced by the PCF was the reliance by party theorists and educators on the few Marxist texts deemed canonical by the CPSU, such as *The Communist Manifesto*, Engels's *Anti-Dühring*, Stalin's *Le Léninisme théorique et pratique*, and the aforementioned *Short Course*. Likewise, as the theoretical branch of a political movement, party theorists and party intellectuals often found their role forcibly limited to that of apologist for the actions of the CPSU and PCF. Rarely, if ever, did party intellectuals question the philosophical foundations of their party's political practice or entertain the diverse interpretive possibilities suggested by Marx's work and demanded by the march of history such as were explored in Hungary, Germany, Italy, and in various Latin American countries. In the mid-1960s when party philosophers were belatedly and finally forced by the revelations of the Communist Party of the Soviet Union's Twentieth Congress to start entertaining alternatives to a rigid Stalinism, their speculative efforts often resulted in bizarre theoretical miscegenations, such as attempts to force Marx's political philosophy to cohabitate with the Christian cosmology of Teilhard de Chardin.[6]

This analysis of the poverty of the PCF's theoretical contribution to Marxism is shared by the majority of historians and philosophers who deal with Communism and Marxism in France. This includes both the preponderance of histories following in the wake of Annie Kriegel's classic studies which are biased against Communism and Marxism as well as the minority of studies like Claude Willard's and Maxwell Adereth's which are sympathetic to it. If there is a difference between the two types of histories, it is that while they both deplore the forms that Communism and Marxist theory have historically taken in France, the anti-Communist historians provide a narrative in which Communism appears as a foreign cancer imposed on the French population which must be explained, vilified, and excised, preferably so that neo-liberalism might take root.[7] Those historians sympathetic to Communism see its roots and its future in France's native traditions of revolutionary reform and utopian socialism and view the era from 1920 to the 1970s as aberrant or, most charitably, as a well-intentioned mistake.[8] Almost without exception, no scholar and certainly no philosopher looks to the theoretical output of the PCF for original insights into the reading of Marx. It is far too derivative of other dogmatic readings of Marx to allow for this. As such, PCF philosophy would seem an even more unlikely place than the tradition of French Intellectual Marxism to suggest fruitful ways in which Marx might be read, understood, and utilized today.

In addition to the mainstream of French Intellectual Marxism and to the theoretical output of the French Communist Party, there is yet a third area where France attempted and failed to make a significant and original contribution to Marxist philosophy. This contribution was "Existential Marxism," a philosophy which surfaced in the wake of World War II and endured in various permutations into the 1970s. As a jury-rigged combination of French Hegelianism, pre-war German Phenomenology, and of Communist (and therefore Marxist in its expositors' minds) inspired resistance action during the war, Existential Marxism represented an attempt on the part of French Intellectuals to cast Marxism as a humanism and as a philosophy of personal choice and political action. Though popular both domestically and embraced by foreign intellectuals at the time of its appearance, the general consensus now is that French Existential Marxism was a philosophy rife with internal contradictions. Principal among these was the impossibility of consistently maintaining an ontology specifying radical cognitive and ethical autonomy while simultaneously arguing for historically determination by socioeconomic factors. This looming internal contradiction made it very difficult for Existential Marxists to develop a coherent ethical or political philosophy. It is hard to maintain both that we are all autonomous beings capable of free ethical choice and political action while simultaneously trying to preserve and prove ethical and political superiority for the "proletariat" as against the bourgeoisie. That the chief proponents of Existential Marxism (Jean-Paul Sartre, Emanuelle Mounier, Juan Axelos, Maurice Merleau-Ponty) are now either forgotten or are chiefly studied for their contributions to philosophy separate from their Marxist writings is testament to the verdict that Existential Marxism was a theoretical dead end and that it, like the dominant tradition of French Intellectual Marxism and French Communist Philosophy, contributed little of original and lasting value to Marxist philosophy or to the tradition of reading Marx.

Nonetheless, despite France's lack of original or influential contributions to Marxist philosophy, there are also some very good reasons to look at this tradition for tinder which might serve to re-ignite interest in him as a political philosopher and to suggest his work's contemporary relevance. If it is true, as Marx states in his reply to Proudhon in *The Poverty of Philosophy*, that history progresses by its bad side and if this maxim holds for the history of thought, then the history of French Marxism, never the most noble history, may be a particularly good place to seek answers to problems that have plagued Marxist thought. Certainly, in this tradition one finds examples of philosophers and tacticians attempting to deal with almost every theoretical problem and practical obstacle debated within or encountered by Marxism. These include problems of revisionism, orthodoxy, vanguardism, democracy, identification of the proletariat, the relationship between theory and practice, etc. That these issues were seldom or never resolved by French Marxism does not mean that the study of these attempts is worthless. On the contrary, each less than successful attempt should serve to indicate what is mistaken in a particular approach to understanding Marxism and may point towards the possibility of its correction or emendation such that it might be reconstructed to serve contemporary exigencies.

In addition to confronting all of the major issues in Marxist thought and practice, the history of French Marxism offers the philosopher who is looking to engage with the history of Marxist philosophy a relatively uninterrupted history of attempts to theorize and instantiate this philosophy. Unlike other Western European countries where Marxist philosophy and Marxist political practice were separate enterprises that often met two very different fates, the two have long been intertwined in French cultural and political life. Furthermore, while most other Western European countries abandoned or were forced to abandon Marxist philosophy and political practice for long periods, France has had a history of such efforts that runs unbroken from the 1920s until the present day. Thus while one can look to Germany, Hungary, Italy, and Switzerland for original and exciting contributions to Marxist theory and to communist practice, it is also a fact that these efforts were not sustained and that one can neither see them evolve over time nor view them in reaction to changing world historical conditions. Likewise, in comparison with the United States where Marxist philosophy and practice was successfully marginalized and in Russia where it became dominant, one can observe in France the play of theory and practice in a landscape that was for an extended period of time (1920-1978) ceded neither to the triumph of liberal democracy and capitalism nor to the victory of democratic centralism and Communism. In the history of French Marxism, one truly finds a unique vantage point from which to view the theoretical and practical debates that concerned Marxism as a whole during this past century.

By studying France's tradition of attempts to understand and practice Marxist philosophy and specifically by looking at the French Communist Party as it attempted to function in a Western democracy, one can observe the evolving history of a mass movement motivated in part by the theory that it was the vehicle of revolutionary political change. This evolution becomes increasingly interesting as it became apparent over the sixty-year period between 1920 and 1980 that it was not this vehicle. For, as the theoretical assumptions to which it anachronistically clung became less and less tenable, the PCF's defense of these became assumptions more and more outrageous. The very strangeness of this enterprise, an enterprise in which the PCF attempted to maintain that it was superior to bourgeois democracy even as it attempted to work its influence upon it, was summed up by its members' informal slogan: "*Un parti pas comme les autres*" [A party not like the others].[9] Indeed, the PCF was a political party and often found itself acting like one: running candidates, calling for referenda, demanding reforms, etc. However, the PCF also identified itself as Marx's "party of the working class" and therefore saw itself, unlike Socialists, Radicals, or Christian Democrats, as a revolutionary party, constituted not to participate in the existing order but established so as to overthrow it. Further, following the "science of history," the party was certain that only it constituted this revolutionary vehicle. This schizophrenic position makes the study of the PCF's theoretical underpinnings of particular interest. By looking at the PCF's attempt to simultaneously justify being a political party like the others (that is, like Léon Blum's Socialists, who are one variant of Marxist philosophy put into practice) and one unlike the others (that is, like Lenin's Bolsheviks, the other principal variant of Marxist philosophy put into practice) something close to the full complexity of Marxist political debate in the twentieth century may be addressed.

Given the history of the PCF's relation to the Soviet Union, one might plausibly argue that it never really functioned like a conventional political party and, consequently, that it cannot be said to have ever truly entertained or pursued revisionist Marxist options akin to those pursued by Socialists or other European CP's. Correspondingly, given that the PCF owed so much of its direction to the CPSU, it might also be argued that there is nothing of original interest in PCF theory or in its approach to political practice.[10] However, the fact remains that, even given the hegemony of the Soviet Union, the French Communist Party did not operate behind the "Iron Curtain." It could not therefore be subject to the same constraints as Eastern Bloc countries, nor were these restraints desirable given the political situation. Even at the height of Soviet influence in the late 1920s and during the early years of the Cold War, the PCF still found itself in a unique situation, trying to balance Moscow's demands for revolutionary discipline with its position as a political player in a "bourgeois" republic. This is not to say that the PCF was autonomous from the Soviet Union, but that, because of its unique situation, it often found itself justifying and thinking about its position in a way that the Soviet Union and its direct satellites—constituting their own political and ideological universe—never would until forced to in the late 1980s by economic and political circumstances. Consequently, though the theory produced by the PCF is marked by first Leninist and then Stalinist dogma, it is interesting because of the way in which it tries to carve out a role for Marxist revolutionary theory and practice in a national and international situation increasingly hostile to such action. Initiatives and treatises that now look crude, anachronistic, and depressingly quixotic were at the time serious attempts to interpret Marx's philosophy and to instantiate it. Likewise, attempts in the 1960s to find common cause with other groups such as the Christian Left and the oft-vilified Socialists were earnest efforts to understand Marx's philosophy and to make it work as the Eleventh Thesis seemed to demand. In the diversity and history of these attempts, much can be learned about the limits and possibilities of Marx's philosophy both insofar as it can be prescriptive of political practice and insofar as it is philosophically defensible.

Because the French Communist Party was sufficiently Leninist to think itself the vanguard of the proletariat and because this role demanded that it theorize the revolution, the PCF from its inauguration was concerned with the production and dissemination of Marxist theory. That its approach to reading Marx, Engels, and Lenin was—at least until the 1960s—neither sophisticated, nor erudite, nor innovative, hindered not its productive capacity in this area, nor did this lack retard its engagement with a diverse number of classical problems in Marxist theory. The PCF had much to say to its members and potential converts about the relationship between infrastructure and superstructure, the difference between idealism and materialism, the "cloud" of ideology, the scientific status of Marxism, and the theoretical justification of the revolutionary role to be played by the party and the proletariat. This engagement with Marxist philosophy was always made with an eye toward political strategy and to the justification of its political program. If this interpretation and the actions that resulted from it failed (and surely the judgment that it did can be made from almost any perspective, even especially the PCF's own as it failed to produce a revolution and mustered less than 5% of the vote in 2002 parliamentary elections),[11] then it would indicate either that Marx's philosophy is wrong or that it was misinterpreted and misapplied by the PCF. If the latter is the case, then we can learn much from studying PCF philosophy for insight into how *not* to understand Marxist philosophy and—by elimination—to discern what may still be of value.

Though the history of French Intellectual Marxism also provides many examples of how not to understand Marxist philosophy, it must also be granted that its engagements with Marx's texts and with Marxist philosophy were much more sophisticated and original than those undertaken by the PCF and that some of its insights still demand to be taken seriously. This is the case despite the relative neglect which this tradition currently suffers. Sophisticated intellectual engagement with Marxism and with Marx's texts began in France in the mid-1920s and continues there to this day. Much of this tradition of interpretation may be accused of idealism and moralism (as could much French philosophy), but it cannot be argued (as may be done with the majority of PCF theory) that readings of Marx by such philosophers as Cornu, Politzer, Maublanc, Lefebvre, Tran Duc Thao, Althusser, or D'Hondt are naive or simplistic or that they fail to provide plausible solutions to problems in Marx's philosophy. Rather, the relative prominence in France of Marxist intellectuals from the late 1920s until the 1980s combined with the quality of French academic philosophy assured that a relatively high level of debate and concern with the classic philosophical problems of Marxism was sustained and that these debates remain of more than historical interest.

Looking back on the history of French Intellectual Marxism, one does not find the theoretical wasteland that characterized much official Communist Party philosophy. What one does find are intelligent attempts to address such problems in Marxist thought as the meaning and import of the dialectic, the relationship between subject and object, and the development and status of Marxian epistemology. In addition, some of the same factors that make PCF theory of interest to the scholar who wishes to look at attempts to read and instantiate Marxist philosophy also animate French Intellectual Marxism. As David Caute shows very clearly in his *Communism and the French Intellectuals* (1964), the leftist French intelligentsia not only wrestled with abstract theoretical issues in Marx but also dealt with the way in which this theory should be applied. That the vehicle of this application was self-identified as the French Communist Party often made for strange and strained pairings between party and academic or party and artist, but it also made for some interesting philosophy as intellectuals attempted to balance and explain the claims of the PCF even as these claims troubled their "erstwhile philosophical consciences."

Even if it can be asserted and proven that good work was done by French Intellectual Marxism, the question might still be raised of the relevance to philosophy in general and political philosophy in particular of such work at a time when this philosophy and its concerns seem especially remote. Indeed, it is probably the case that one will not go back to Henri Lefebvre's *Le matérialisme dialectique* or to René Maublanc's *Hegel et Marx* and find definitive answers to questions about the role of dialectic in Marx's thought or about Marx's relation to Hegel. Such works were of and for their time. One does not look to them for definitive truths. Instead, one studies them to see the ways in which problems in Marxist philosophy have presented themselves and the ways in which they were or failed to be resolved. In sum, what these and other works constituting the tradition of French Intellectual Marxism provide the contemporary reader with is a well-documented history of sincere and diligent attempts to understand and instantiate Marxist philosophy, attempts that may provide resources for those who wish to reconsider Marxism as a political philosophy for today.

That both French Intellectual Marxism and French Political Marxism had by the early 1960s reached a crisis point is generally agreed. This crisis can roughly be attributed to the Soviet invasion of Hungary in 1956 and to the revelations of Khrushchev's "secret speech" given earlier that year at the Twentieth Congress of the Soviet Communist Party. Though the PCF and some French Intellectual Marxists were slow to respond to this crisis, it eventually became all too apparent that Marxist thought and Marxist practice had to change if it was to survive and retain any of its political or theoretical credibility. Though slow in coming, many attempts were eventually made to affect this change both in the French Communist Party and within French Intellectual Marxism. From the side of the PCF, these reforms occasioned a lessening in the rigid dogmatism that had theretofore characterized party theory and an opening up to or even a reconciliation with political enemies who were previously excluded from the party due to their class or ideological background. As these were more diverse, it is harder to generalize the responses of French Intellectual Marxism. However, this era was typified by projects in which Marxist philosophy either became more idealist, more literary and less political (witness Henri Lefebvre's and Lucien Goldmann's work during this period) or, in a few cases, more materialist and rigidly scientific (witness Lucien Sève's psychology or Louis Althusser's and Tran Duc Thao's analyses of the Hegelian dialectic).[12]

Though by the mid-1970s the Communist Party had abandoned its liberal and conciliatory positions and French Intellectual Marxism had decidedly fallen out of vogue, its theoretical projects abandoned, there did emerge from this period of rethinking Marxist philosophy one figure who may have succeeded in providing adequate solutions to the questions of how and whether—in the mid-1960s—Marx could be interpreted and read as a political philosopher with contemporary relevance. That this figure, Louis Althusser, emerged neither exclusively from the French academy nor from the cadres of PCF theorists may have something to do with the uniqueness of his solutions. As a serious academic philosopher who was also a committed and militant Communist, Althusser attempted to work out a reading of Marx that neither vitiated his political efficacy for the sake of theory nor subsumed theory to political tool. Further, his insights were of such probity and his solutions so original that it may be the case that his work provides resources for theorizing a Marxism that both takes into account its history and points to its future.

If this is a book which seeks to argue that the work of Louis Althusser provides interesting solutions to problems of Marxism such that these solutions might hold contemporary relevance, the question might be raised of why go to the trouble of showing how his philosophy emerged out of the concerns of French Intellectual Marxism and of the French Communist Party. Would it not be simpler (and indeed more in tune with contemporary philosophical methodology) to first directly show how Althusser interpreted Marx, then demonstrate how his reinterpretation is superior to contemporary Analytic and Continental approaches to Marxist thought, and then conclude by showing how Althusser's reinterpretation applies to and resolves certain contemporary problems in political philosophy? Though this would indeed be a simpler approach than the one here undertaken, there are several reasons, some practical, others philosophical, to choose another route.

On the practical side, this historical approach—considering first the history of French Marxist thought and then placing Althusser within it—fills a void in contemporary scholarship on the subject. While good histories of the French Communist Party and of French Intellectual Marxism exist, most are polemical in nature. Still involved in the rhetorical and ideological legacy of the Cold War, they argue for or against leftist philosophy and politics and desire to fix the memory of French

Communism either as tragedy or as an (admittedly failed) utopia. In addition, most tend to separate politics and philosophy into separate spheres and look exclusively at either the history of the French Communist Party in terms of political success or at the history of Marxist thought in terms of academic affiliation, debates, and influence. Thus while there exist interesting and informative intellectual histories of French Marxism, these works tend to focus on the history of ideas rather than on the relationship between ideas, politics, and history.[13] Likewise, though there exist comprehensive histories of French Communism and of the French Left, most of these choose to deal with the minutiae of historical detail and political decision making rather than with the ideas that justified these decisions and that were affected by the history.[14] In that this work provides an account which avoids both pro- and anti-leftist polemics and aims to supply a narrative detailing the relationship between Marxist thought and Marxist politics, *Louis Althusser and the Traditions of French Marxism* should prove useful to those who are interested more in the interplay of thoughts, actions, and events than in ancient ideological battles or speculative discourses.

On the practical but also theoretical side and in the attempt to fill yet another void, while very good studies of Louis Althusser exist, most tend to treat him in isolation, as a "philosopher" whose thinking is universal and therefore out of time.[15] Alternately, some studies of Althusser fix his thought as being too much "of its time" and see him as only one permutation of the general mid-century French trend known as "structuralism."[16] Thus, though one finds studies that provide convincing arguments for the relevance and coherence of Althusser's philosophy, they fall short of fully placing Althusser in the historical debates and situations which informed and called forth his philosophy.[17] As for the studies that group Althusser with the French Intellectual scene of the late 1950s and early 1960s, these succeed in emphasizing Althusser's affinities to other structuralists such as Claude Lévi-Strauss and Jacques Lacan at the expense of his original insights into Marxism specifically and political philosophy in general. Althusser thereby becomes just part of a trend and the seriousness and originality of his reinterpretation of Marx is lost. He is seen as just another structuralist, albeit one concerned with politics rather than with anthropology or with psychoanalysis.

Wishing neither to claim that Althusser was a philosopher whose insights were universal and timeless nor that he was to Structuralism what the Gang of Four was to punk rock—that is, the Marxist representative of a larger trend—this work will attempt to show how Althusser was both of his time and how the solutions he found to the problems of his time may suggest viable approaches to Marxist philosophy today. In addition, it will offer what no other study of Althusser sufficiently does; this is to demonstrate how Althusser's thought is the result of and a response to specific French intellectual and political traditions of reading Marx.

This historical approach to Althusser's philosophy allows his thought to be treated not in isolation but as a philosophy of practice with a history. If this history is to be meaningful, then this history must be acknowledged and its mistakes accounted for in order to correct or reconstruct Marxist theory for today. These then are the philosophical reasons for the historical approach of this book. It is only on this basis, one informed by the lessons of history, that one can evaluate what of Althusser's theory and—through him—Marxist thought, might retain philosophical and political value. Though it may be subject to debate whether or not Marx's early work attributed too much power to thought and to intellectual critique and his late work too little, it cannot be contested that he intended the results of his abstractions to be applied to the "real" world. From the 1842 editorial in the *Rheinische Zeitung* where he provides a philosophical argument for a repeal of the feudal law on the theft of wood,[18] to the 1875 "Critique of the Gotha Program," which directly links his philosophy to specific action, it is apparent that Marx's thought—even at its most speculative—was meant to proceed from an analysis or "abstraction" of the world undertaken with the aim of understanding it, to an application of this understanding that might, in fact, change it. His was not a strictly contemplative philosophy. Further, without the context provided by history and by the world, Marx's philosophy would not exist. History and the world as it actually functions provide the problems or "contradictions" which motivate and demand Marxist philosophy. It may be tempting as a philosopher who desires to rehabilitate Marxist philosophy to skip the embarrassment of the history of Marxism and Communism and to find in selective rereadings of his early or late works a "pure" philosophy complete with prescriptions which (had they been heeded) would have avoided the sordid mistakes perpetrated in Marx's name. However, this disregard for the history of the application of Marx's philosophy is antithetical to Marx's thought conceived of as a science of history and as a critique of socioeconomic formations which may result in theoretical and political practices designed to change these structures. Marxist philosophy does not exist in a vacuum. It draws its material from the events of history and it is in history that it seeks to act. To ignore the history of the application of Marx's philosophy is to remove his thought from its proper medium and to risk again the "theoreticism" of which so much Marxist philosophy has been guilty. If one is to avoid this error, then one must seriously undertake a study of the history of the application of Marxist theory. In this way, one can observe and critique Marxist philosophy not in an artificially created academic vacuum of texts, concepts, and arguments but through the study of actual events that occurred as this philosophy attempted to realize itself. One response to the failure of Marxist inspired practice may well be to jettison Marxist philosophy as a failed experiment. However, another and more intellectually honest response is to see what Marxist philosophy did, what problems it encountered, and what solutions it offered. Only then is it possible to decide whether some of these solutions may provide clues as to how Marxism can be reconstructed for today.

Notes

1. Marcus Roberts, *Analytic Marxism: A Critique* (London: Verso, 1996), 13.

2. Andrew Levine, "What Is a Marxist Today," in *Analyzing Marxism—New Essays on Analytical Marxism*, eds. Kai Nielsen and Robert Ware (Calgary: University of Calgary Press, 1989), 40.

3. Gedö, András. "The Irrevocable Presence of Marxist Philosophy in Contemporary Thought." *Nature, Society and Thought*. vol. 7, no. 2 (1987): 133–53. Gedo makes the argument that, despite this forgetting, Marx is a pervasive if unacknowledged influence on contemporary philosophy and theory.

4. This is the case only if one looks for direct influence. If one traces its indirect or unacknowledged influence on sociology, structuralism, poststructuralism, postmodernism, new historicism, philosophies of the self, literary criticism, French feminism, and historiography one would see that its effect has actually been overwhelming and, in many cases, determinative.

5. See Sudhir Hazareesingh, *Intellectuals and the French Communist Party: Disillusion and Decline* (Oxford: Clarendon Press, 1991), 312-14, and Tony Judt, *Marxism and the French Left: Studies in Labour and Politics in France, 1830-1981* (Oxford: Clarendon Press, 1986), 199.

6. See for instance Robert Garaudy, *Perspectives de l'homme* (Paris: PUF, 1960).

7. Gavin Bowd points out that this last tendency, that of reading French Communism as an anomaly whose eventual failure opened up the way for serious, ethical, neo-liberal thought and policy is a pronounced one in English-language scholarship on the topic. In this vein, he includes the work of Sudhir Hazareesingh, Tony Judt, and Sunil Khilnani. Bowd, *L'Interminable enterrement: le communisme et les intellectuels Français depuis 1956* (Paris: Digraphe, 1999), 9-11.

8. For examples of historians who see French Communism as a foreign cancer see Daniel Blume et al., *Histoire du réformisme en France depuis 1920* (Paris: Editions Sociales, 1976); Stéphane Courtois and Marc Lazar, *Histoire du parti communiste Français* (Paris: PUF, 1995); Annie Kriegel, *Les Communistes Français dans leur premier demi-siécle: 1920-1970* (Paris: Seuil, 1985); and Ronald Tiersky, *French Communism 1920-1972* (New York and London: Columbia University Press, 1974). For examples of historians who see French Communism as a continuation of native French socialist traditions see Claude Willard, *Socialisme et communisme Français* (Paris: Armand Collin, 1967); and David Lowe and Neill Nugent, *The Left in France* (New York: St. Martin's Press, 1982).

9. Lowe and Nugent, *The Left in France*, 34.

10. This argument is advanced by most historians who deal with the relationship betwen the PCF and the Soviet Union. However, there are a few, such as Maxwell Adereth in *The French Communist Party: A Critical History* (Manchester: Manchester University Press, 1984), who emphasize the PCF's relative autonomy.

11. This number is taken from the first round of voting on June 9, 2002. Due to the surprisingly strong polling of the Far-Right Front National party in this first round, some Communists apparently switched their votes to the Socialists and to the coalition Union pour la Majorité Presidentielle such that the PCF garnered merely 3.26% of the vote in the final round. See: "Assemblée Nationale de France, Elections Legislatives, 9 & 16 Juin" 2002, www.elections-legislatives.fr/elections/resultats.asp (accessed July 21, 2004).

12. For examples of the literary and idealist trend in French Marxism see Henri Lefebvre, *Le langage et la société* (Paris: Gallimard, 1966); and Lucien Goldmann, *The Hidden God: A Study of Tragic Vision in the* Pensées *of Pascal and the Tragedies of Racine*, trans. Phillip Thody (New York: Humanities Press, 1964). For examples of the "return to materialism" see Lucien Sève, *Marxisme et la théorie de la personnalité* (Paris: Éditions Sociales, 1969); and Tran Duc Thao, "Le 'noyau rationnel' dans la dialectique hégélienne," *La Pensée* (Jan-Feb 1965): 6-23. Althusser's critique of the Hegelian dialectic in such articles as "Contradiction et Overdetermination," (*La Pensée* 106 [1962]: 3-22) will be discussed in chapter 6.

13. Luc Ferry and Alain Renaut, *La pensée 68* (Gallimard: Paris, 1985); Judt, *Marxism and the French Left*; Michael Kelly, *Modern French Marxism*

(Oxford: Blackwell Publishers, 1982); and Sunil Khilnani, *Arguing Revolution* (New Haven, CT: Yale University Press, 1993).

14. Courtois and Lazar, *Histoire du Parti Communiste Français*; Jacques Fauvet, *Histoire du Parti Communiste Français* (Paris: Fayard, 1977); Annie Kriegel, *Les Communistes Français* (Paris: Seuil, 1985); and Yves Santamaria, *Histoire du Parti Communiste Français* (Paris: Éditions La Découverte, 1999).

15. See for instance Alex Callinicos, *Althusser's Marxism* (London: Pluto Press, 1976); and Michael Payne, *Reading Knowledge: An Introduction to Barthes, Foucault and Althusser* (Oxford and Malden, MA: Blackwell, 1997).

16. Miriam Glucksmann, *Structuralist Analysis in Contemporary Social Thought* (London: Routledge, 1974); and Edith Kurzweil, *The Age of Structuralism* (New Brunswick, NJ: Transaction Publications, 1996).

17. Gregory Elliot, *Althusser: The Detour of Theory* (New York: Verso, 1987); Warren Montag, *Althusser* (New York: Palgrave, 2002); and Robert Paul Resch, *Althusser and the Renewal of Marxist Social Theory* (Berkeley: University of California Press, 1992).

18. Karl Marx, "The Law on Thefts of Wood," in *Selected Writings,* ed. David McLellan (Oxford: Oxford University Press, 1977), 20.

Chapter 1

The PCF and French Intellectual Marxism: Paternity and Patterns

Historical and Methodological Background

While French Communism antedates by a few years the first mature texts of French Intellectual Marxism, the inauguration of both movements can be traced back to roughly the same time period and both owe their inception to the same confluence of events: the Bolshevik Revolution and the end of World War I. For young French political and intellectual leftists, the victory of the Entente forces and the triumph of Lenin politically (if not yet militarily) signaled that the time might at last be ripe for revolutionary change both in France and internationally.[1] This was a period of high hope for political reformers. It was widely believed that the Europe of old, that of states and parliaments and bourgeois democracies, had finally blown itself out and that new "rational" political orders must be formed to replace them.[2] Further, the Russian Revolution seemed to point to the future, to a time when such ancien régimes, replaced by a functioning Communism, would be considered as backward and barbaric as the feudal estate. It was not only young men radicalized by battlefield experiences or by wartime austerity who rushed to these conclusions. Older leftist intellectuals also greeted the end of the war with enthusiasm, aligning themselves with the newly formed Communist Party and hurrying to start journals and newspapers that were in the service of the "revolution."[3]

For the intellectuals initially attracted to the ideals of Communism and for the masses that had originally adhered to the new party after its split from the Socialists at the Congress of Tours in 1920, this initial optimism and outburst of enthusiasm was short-lived. The promise of imminent revolution and radical change, the optimism of reaching, educating, and mobilizing the working class, the hope of creating a genuine and French style of Communism, all of these projects initiated shortly after the end of the Great War were by 1929 in shambles. Global political changes, harassment from the Right, and its own poor strategic decisions had caused the Section Française de l'Internationale Communiste (as the Parti Communiste Français was originally known) to descend from an initial membership of 110,000 to an all-time low of approximately 30,000 in the span of only eight years.[4] As for the many intellectuals who had initially been attracted to the party, they had by the end of the decade either defected or had been thrown out when the party in 1924 began pursuing its process of Bolshevization at the behest of the Soviet-led Comintern. Identified as *petites bourgeoises*, sympathetic intellectuals once welcomed by the party were accused in party organs of being "Trotskyists" and class traitors.[5]

Despite this initial downturn in the fortunes of French Communism and of French Intellectual Marxism, a new cycle of enthusiasm, popular support, and theoretical and practical activity would occur for the radical French Left before the outbreak of World War II. By the mid-1930s, Communist Party membership and Marxist theoretical activity soared to levels that they had not seen even in the immediate postwar period.[6] Riding high on the PCF's alliance with the theretofore vilified Socialists and Radicals in the union known as the Front Populaire, it was again hoped and even for a time popularly expected that Marxist ideals of worker solidarity, international cooperation, and Socialist economic policies would be realized.[7] Further, given the mass support for this alliance of the Left, it was anticipated that this movement would check the tide of Fascism which threatened France internally from such groups as the Croix de Feu and Action Française and externally from its western and southern neighbors. Popular enthusiasm at the political level was mirrored by renewed intellectual activity and interest in the study of Marx and Marxism at the theoretical level. New publications and translations of Marx's work were complemented by books and articles from philosophers such as Auguste Cornu, Henri Lefebvre, Norbert Guterman, and Georges Politzer. Really for the first time, these works explored the intellectual roots and philosophical status of Marx's thought. In sharp contrast to the *classe contre classe* policies of the late 1920s, these texts and their authors were welcomed (if maybe still not read) by the French Communist Party and its leadership.

Even with this renewed political passion and the outburst of theoretical activity accompanying it, the alliance of the French Left and the political movement it engendered did not last long and would have little enduring political or intellectual impact.[8] By the time World War II finally broke out, the PCF—having flip-flopped positions in regards to Franco-German and Franco-Soviet nonaggression pacts and having soured its alliance with the broader Left—was again at a low point in terms of both popular appeal and in its ability to realize its political goals. In sync with this pattern, those Marxist Intellectuals who had aligned themselves with the party and who by the mid-1930s were doing original and interesting work in Marxist philosophy had either silenced themselves or were being silenced by a directorate that—at the insistence of the Comintern and coincident with the appearance of Stalin's *Short Course* in 1939—demanded theoretical consistency, rigidity, and obedience.

Seen for the first time in the 1920s and evidenced a second time in the years leading up to World War II, this pattern of optimism, action, failure, and retrenchment is one typical of the history of French Intellectual Marxism and of French Communism. Moreover, it is one that would repeat itself at least twice in the post-World War II period as the fortunes of the French Left and of French Communists rose and fell along with the Cold War's shifting ideological tide. Of course, many explanations for this pattern: economic, political, sociocultural, could be given. Correspondingly, as many histories could be written chronicling these cycles as there exist modes of explanation. Each would, no doubt, yield insights into the question of why French Communism and Marxism has been unable to consistently sustain itself in a century when it was at various and extended periods of time the dominant political and intellectual force in France, controlling more votes than any other party and exerting a hegemonic influence on sciences human and natural and even on the fine arts. Providing such explanations is not, however, the intent of this exercise. Instead, the next two chapters on the origin and development of French Marxist thought between 1920 and 1945 and the subsequent chapter dealing with the post-World War II period will focus upon the theory espoused by the PCF and that originated by French Intellectual Marxists. These chapters will show how this theory coincided with, allowed, and encouraged the periods of optimism as well as how it reacted to the manifest practical and theoretical failures that occasioned (or maybe should have occasioned) theoretical revisions. This task will be undertaken so as to examine the way in which French Communist and French Intellectual Marxist philosophy attempted to remain recognizably Marxist even as it changed and developed so as to better deal with the historical realities and possibilities which presented themselves as the century progressed.

This exercise is not undertaken to formulate a narrow or niggling critique of French Marxist philosophy. For instance, nowhere will it be suggested that, say, had the PCF not insisted on the theoretical validity of Lenin's epistemology, it would have enjoyed greater political success in the Cold War period. Though this may in fact be true, the historical significance of such a claim is minimal; the PCF never wanted for absurd positions and yet often managed quite well electorally and politically. Philosophically, the significance of such a critique may be even less meaningful for it says very little about the tenability and relevance of Marxist theory in general. This is, of course, the larger project of this book. Likewise, regarding Intellectual Marxism, disentangling the internecine quarrels between various French Marxist philosophers and between French Intellectuals and the PCF tends to occlude the larger issues surrounding Marxist philosophy's relationship to political practice. Foregoing these approaches, what this analysis of French Intellectual Marxism and French Communist theory aims to do instead is to examine the evolution of these linked theoretical traditions and to discern in their development the general patterns, problems, approaches, and solutions that characterize each interpretation of Marxist philosophy. From this initial examination, it should then be possible in later chapters to engage with questions regarding why these traditions could or should be judged as unsuccessful (politically or theoretically) and whether this lack of success is due to flawed appropriations and interpretations of Marx's philosophy such as might be amenable to correction or revision.

French Marxism: Import or Domestic Product?

Even if it is true that, properly speaking, French Communism and French Intellectual Marxism did not have their start until after World War I, it is also true that these movements did not appear ex nihilo. This is especially the case with French Intellectual Marxism, whose preoccupation with the idea of true self-realization through political change can be traced back at least to Rousseau and whose idiosyncratic concerns with the power of thought and culture arise more from the obscure pre-World War I tradition of French Hegelianism than they do from any texts of Marx, Engels, or Lenin. It is also the case with French Communism that its philosophy, though often retrospectively and even contemporaneously derided as doctrinaire "Diamatics" of the worst sort, also reflects its Gallic origins. Long after it was supposedly totally "Bolshevized," French Communism retained elements from its French Socialist antecedents; the ghosts of Proudhon and Fourier appear alongside Saint-Simon's in many of its policy positions, theoretical justifications, and pedagogical texts. Thus even if the majority of its theoretical and political program was dictated from the East (as most recent histories utilizing material from Soviet archives confirm to be the case),[9] French Communists derived many of their attitudes from the leftist groups: socialists, radicals, anarchists, revolutionary syndicalists, and even anti-clericalists who formed its original constituency and who continue to serve as inspiration and justification for its actions up until the present day. Even in the most "Stalinist" periods of the PCF, one can still identify traits and attitudes that are uniquely French and that color the way in which French Communists approach problems, be they domestic or international, theoretical or practical.

In the twentieth century, those contributions to Marxist philosophy that were uniquely French have been complimented by a French readiness to accept Marxist philosophy in the form presented by the Bolsheviks. Lenin's philosophy and the practical policies to which it lent support were mostly seen to reflect the French Left's own sympathies, predilections, and radical revolutionary traditions. Though some historians describe the Congress of Tours and the subsequent Bolshevization of the French Left as something like the rape of a pure-hearted *demoiselle socialiste*,[10] it is important to note that leftist French political movements and philosophical currents were especially amenable to Marxism as it was presented by the Soviet Union and by Lenin. Thus not only did French Intellectual Marxism and French Communism not emerge out of virgin earth, but the ideological ground could already be said to be prepared for their emergence and growth by pre-World War I French political and philosophical movements. In this respect, the France of 1918 was fertile soil for a radical revolutionary movement and was somewhat prepared for an intellectual re-evaluation of Marx. So far as politics went, both the old and the newly converted Communists at the Congress of Tours saw Marxism-Leninism not as a foreign import so much as an improved distillate of what were originally French ideas. For it was the case that almost every aspect of the platform of the Third International and the program suggested by the Twenty-One Articles of Confederation had their parallels (and possibly antecedent) in one or the other tradition of pre-World War I French Socialism. For instance, the idea of a "vanguard" and the downplaying of democracy was entirely consistent with the Blanquist tradition and can be traced back even further to Fourier's idea of the exemplary *phalanstère*.[11] Similarly, the idea of revolutionary struggle between workers and owners had been ingrained in the radical French Left's collective imagination at least since the Communes of 1848, if not since 1789.[12] Of course, the feelings of affinity with the Bolshevik program and the acceptance of its call for international implementation of and accession to its demands were not unanimous. After all, these fissures did cause the split which led to the formation of separate Socialist and Communist parties. However, they were prevalent enough to allow the acceptance of the Soviet plan and to convince three quarters of the congressional delegates at the Congress of Tours to align with the international Communist movement (and thereby with Lenin and the Bolsheviks).[13]

On the intellectual side, the Bolshevik Revolution and the Marxist-Leninist philosophy which provided its theoretical base were viewed by those few philosophers, scientists, and literary figures interested in Marxism as neither especially novel nor as corruptions of Marx (especially as their understanding of Marx was sketchy at best). Instead, these events and policies were seen to present a genuinely new way to approach philosophy, science, and life consistent with their own desires for a rational reordering of society in the wake of the horrors of World War I.[14] These feelings were also sufficient on the side of the intellectuals to inspire the new publication or the new consecration of various journals, articles, and books devoted to the understanding and dissemination of Marxist-Leninist philosophy, science, and literature.[15] Given that French Intellectual Marxism and French Communism cannot be reduced to a foreign imposition which French philosophy and the French political Left were forced to accommodate but must instead be seen as something much more complex, that is, as a blend of existent French attitudes and institutions with a new element (that of Leninist and then Stalinist Marxism) from which unique and new traditions would emerge, then in order to understand the two traditions of French Communism and French Intellectual Marxism it will be necessary examine the ways in which existing French political and academic institutions as well as individuals reacted to the Bolshevik revolution and attempted to integrate and involve themselves with this new future that in 1920 seemed so exciting and so full of promise.

Notes

1. Though I tend to use the terms "left" and "French Left" without qualifications, it is the case that the descriptive term "left," though useful for general classification, proves inadequate at the level of specific movements and their histories. This is particularly the case in France, where shifting parliamentary alliances often elude such easy classification and where political groups like the Radicals have gone from left to right over the course of a few short years. Nonetheless, Socialists and Communists for most of the twentieth century were safely ensconced on the left side of the political spectrum and could be distinguished at least by their Socialist rhetoric. For discussions of the complexity of the term "French Left" and of the groups which may be said to comprise it see Sunil Khilnani, *Arguing Revolution: The Intellectual Left in Postwar France* (New Haven, CT: Yale University Press, 1993), 7-13; Georges Lefranc, *Les Gauches en France* (Paris: Payot, 1973); Neill Nugent and David Lowe, *The Left in France* (New York: St. Martin's Press, 1982), 3-15.

2. Mark Mazower, *Dark Continent: Europe's Twentieth Century* (New York: Vintage Books, 2000), 6-7. Mazower makes this point particularly well. He also argues convincingly that this feeling of the need for radical change along rational lines was shared throughout the political spectrum. Leftist radicals wanted international Communism, centrists wanted sweeping democratic reforms, and even the Far Right foresaw the death of bourgeois institutions. The difference being that instead of looking towards Communism or expanded democracy and rational management, they saw fascism as the future.

3. These journals included Henri Barbusse's *Clarté,* Boris Souvarine's *Le Bulletin Communiste*, *L'Humanité* (an older Socialist journal taken over by Communists in 1920), and *La Révue Communiste.*

4. Stéphane Courtois and Marc Lazar, *Histoire du parti communiste Français* (Paris: PUF, 1995), 423.

5. David Caute, *Communism and the French Intellectuals: 1914-1960* (New York: Macmillan, 1964), 91.

6. The 1936 parliamentary elections saw the Communists nearly double their electoral base from 1932 to a total of more than a million and a half votes, representing 15% of the ballots cast. The Left as a whole (including Commu-

nists, Socialists, and Radicals) garnered 59% of the vote. See Ronald Tiersky, *French Communism 1920-1972* (New York and London: Columbia University Press, 1974), 58.

7. This was at least the view of the Communists who saw the Front Populaire movement as a potentially revolutionary force or at least as a force that would preserve the possibility for future revolutions. The Socialist Léon Blum, however, was careful to state that, despite the electoral victory of Front Populaire candidates, the government of France was still a bourgeois government. For the intricacies of the relationship between the Socialists and Communists, especially in terms of the decision by the Communists to participate at the parliamentary level see: Tiersky, *French Communism*, 69-95 and Maxwell Adereth, *The French Communist Party: A Critical History (1920-1984): From Comintern to the Colours of France* (Manchester: Manchester University Press, 1984), 74-76.

8. At least until after the war when its memory was evoked by members of the French Left for rhetorical purposes and when this same memory served as inspiration for liberalizations in the Communist Party during the 1960's.

9. For examples of recent histories that make use of archival sources see Roger Bourderon, *La Négociation: été 1940, crise au* PCF (Paris: Éditions Syllepse, 2001); Sophie Coeuré, *La Grande lueur á l'est: les français et l'union soviétique, 1917-1939* (Paris: Éditions du Seuil, 1999); Stéphane Courtois and Marc Lazar, *Histoire du parti communiste français dans las lutte pour la paix, 1914-1947* (Paris: S. Arslan, 2000); and Yves Santamaria, *Histoire du parti communiste français* (Paris: Éditions La Découverte, 1999).

10. For instance, the Socialist historian Daniel Blume argues that there was little change in the attitudes of the Socialists over the course of World War I, that the Socialists in no way supported Bolshevism, and that they were pressured into signing the Articles of Confederation in the name of international solidarity. See Blume et al., *Histoire du réformisme en France depuis 1920* (Paris: Editions Sociales, 1976), 14-28.

11. Claude Willard, *Socialisme et communisme Français* (Paris: Armand Colin, 1967), 16, 26.

12. For a thorough and compelling examination of the affinities between Lenin's program and the pre-World War I ideology of the radical French Left see George Lichtheim, *Marxism in Modern France* (New York: Columbia University Press, 1966), 1-30.

13. Nugent and Lowe, *The Left in France*, 26.

14. Bud Burkhard, *French Marxism between the Wars: Henri Lefebvre and the "Philosophies"* (New York: Humanity Books, 1999), 19-20.

15. These publications included the journals *Philosophies* (1924-26), *L'Esprit* (1926), *La revue Marxiste* (1928), *Europe* (1923), and *Monde* (1928).

Chapter 2

The PCF 1920-1923:
Origins, Events, and Foundations

World War I and *La Scission à Tours*

Prior to World War I and in the wake of the Dreyfus Affair and the Second (Socialist) International, the arguments over revolution and reform which had separated late-nineteenth-century French Socialists into divisive factions had largely been resolved. The two principal Socialist parties which existed in 1901—the Guesdiste Parti Socialiste de France and the Jaurèsian Parti Socialiste Français—had by 1905 acceded to the resolution passed at the Second International demanding unification of the French parties.[1] Though still subject to internal debate about its course of action, the newly consolidated and newly named party, the Section Française de l'International Ouvrière (SFIO) was unified both by its opposition to the second Dreyfus conviction and by its relative ideological homogeneity.[2] In the years leading up to the war, this organizational cohesion allowed the SFIO to participate in government to an extent and with an influence which previous factionalism and regionalism had denied the French Socialists. Mimicking developments in Germany with Bernstein and the Sozialdemokratische Partei Deutschlands (SPD), the Guesdiste revolutionary influence began to wane and the French party moved towards the use of Jaurèsian parliamentary and republican tactics in order to further its agenda.

Motivated by a concern for internationalism and a belief that modern wars benefited the bourgeoisie at the expense of workers' lives, part of the SFIO's agenda in the early 1910s was the prevention of war. However, in the event of war, the party was pledged along with other European Socialist parties to exploit the crisis and to foment international revolution.[3] When with the voting of war credits in 1914 it became obvious that the former goal was not met and that the latter pledge had been abandoned, the party's influence largely collapsed.[4] The anticipated international solidarity of workers against the war failed to materialize as did any revolutionary activity after the war began. French workers and French Socialists reacted to the conflagration just like other social classes and political groups: they desired to win the war for France. Thus the nationalistic and patriotic call to "the defense of beauty, life, and our threatened land"[5] led to the enlistment of workers at approximately the same levels as those of the general population.[6] For its part, the SFIO even welcomed the appointment of two of its members to a war government of national unity.[7]

The initial broad-based enthusiasm for the war and the nationalistic fervor that accompanied this enthusiasm were not long-lived. A conflict that was supposed to have lasted six weeks and that owed much of its initial popularity to this assumption stretched into years of literal entrenchment for the soldiers doing the fighting. For the general population who supported their efforts, this prolonged conflict meant season after season of domestic hardship. Under this stress, the Union Sacré formed between rival political parties during the nationalistic fervor at the start of the war began to break down. Slowly, what began as a much maligned and largely ignored antiwar movement gained support. Led by such writers as Henri Barbusse and Romain Rolland and augmented by the work of domestic trade unions such as the C.G.T. (Comité Général de Travail), this movement emphasized worker solidarity and internationalism as well as opposition to the continuation of the war.

By 1917 the antiwar movement had matured and grown such that the SFIO withdrew from the government in protest of the war's continuation. This decision led to a turnover in the party's membership. Those loyal to the war effort abandoned the party. However, some groups like the Revolutionary Syndicalists who were previously turned off by the party's social democratic tendencies joined the party en masse.[8] This radicalization and diversification of the party was further intensified by the events of 1918 in Russia which suggested for the first time since 1870 that revolution in France and Europe was again possible. Though finally unable to halt the prosecution of the war, it was this radicalization and diversification of the SFIO during the war that paved the way for its immediate popularity in the postwar years. It was also this radicalization and diversification that led to the Socialist party's split at the Congress of Tours into separate French Communist and Socialist parties.

Following the Treaty of Versailles in June 1919 and its loss of 30 parliamentary representatives in the French General Election of November that same year, the SFIO held its organizational meeting in December of 1920 at Tours. Despite the loss of seats, discussions of how to overcome this parliamentary setback were not nearly so important to the congressional delegates as debates about the import of the Russian revolution, the inauguration of the Third (communist) International, and the role French Socialists should or could play in a world revolution.

For the most part, the devastating effects of the Great War and the success of the Russian Revolution had inspired tremendous optimism on the part of the French and International Left. Many now believed that the war had shown the deep contradictions of capitalism and that the Russian revolutionaries had shown the way to solve them.[9] Adding to this excitement was the fact that, during the war, France had gone a long way to becoming an industrialized country. According to orthodox Marxist theory, it was therefore closer to fulfilling the conditions necessary for a communist revolution. Before the international conflict still mainly a country of artisans, the demands of the war economy had greatly augmented the number of factories and—concomitant with this buildup—the number of workers in France. What's more, these workers had also shown some evidence of "proletarian consciousness," organizing themselves during the last two years of the war and striking successfully for shortened hours.[10] Given these structural and ideological changes, by the time delegates convened at Tours, many were convinced that a revolution in France was both imminent and possible and that the time was right to throw in their lot with the Soviets.

This opinion was not, however, unanimous. On one side of the convention floor were delegates like the writer Raymond Lefebvre, who—representing the extreme left of Socialist and Revolutionary Syndicalist tendencies—were convinced of the Bolshevik program and in agreement with the policies of the Third International. Opposite these men were those like Léon Blum who were still loyal to the Second International and to its idea of accomplishing Socialist goals through parliamentary and educational reform measures.[11] Yet other groups resisted both courses of action or argued for some sort of compromise between the two extremes. For instance, the Syndicalists—long convinced that a general strike remained the best means of forcing change—held to their prewar convictions and resisted both the call to return to parliamentary participation and the call to give *"Tout le pouvoir aux soviets."*[12] Likewise the anarchists, fine with revolution, were hesitant to endorse any program that employed a centralized governing body (something the Leninist program certainly did). Surveying the whole landscape of opinion on the Left, France appeared much as other European countries did immediately after the war; it was divided between those who still adhered to the revisionist Marxism of the Second International, those who looked to the neo-orthodoxy represented by Lenin and the Third International, and those who still believed in trade unionist tactics but resisted participation in both bourgeois politics and Bolshevik revolution.

Whole books and numerous lengthy articles have been written on the subject of *"La Scission à Tours"* that attempt to take into account the full complexity of the debates between the various factions within the SFIO and the relationship between these debates and the domestic and international political situation—especially in their relation to Russia.[13] Without going into too much detail, however, it is safe to make a few generalizations about the conflict that led to the split insofar as this factioning relates to questions of Marxist theory. Though complicated by issues of trade union politics and the diversity of the delegates, there existed at Tours a fundamental ideological split between those who thought of Bolshevism as a perversion of Marxism and those who thought of it as a return to true Marxism.[14] Those wedded to the latter opinion believed that with the Russian Revolution and the Soviet system lay the best hope for the revolutionary future. For these delegates, to be Marxist was to be revolutionary. In contrast, those who concluded that the revolutionary moment had passed in 1870 thought the Bolshevik model misguided. Marxist politics, they believed, should now be understood as a process of democratic economic and political reform enacted at a national level[15] It should be inclusive and universal rather than divisive and particular.[16]

In retrospect it is ironic, however, looking back at the arguments made at Tours by representatives of both ideologies, it appears that those who thought of Bolshevism as a perversion of Marxism may actually have had a better understanding of Marx's texts and opinions than those who claimed to be its true representatives.[17] Such a discrepancy, though, is understandable given the personal histories of those who subscribed to each viewpoint. Largely, it was those Socialists who had been active in the labor movement and had been deeply influenced by the orthodox versus revisionist debates of the Second International that thought of Bolshevism as a perversion of Marxism. Léon Blum, a figure who would play a major role during the Front Populaire but who was already active during the Great War in French Socialist politics, is a good representative of the type of Socialist who came to an understanding of Marxism through theoretical and practical activity in behalf of the Socialist cause. Evidence of this understanding is seen in his 1919 arguments against Leninist policies where he challenged the idea that a vanguard can successfully lead the "inorganic" masses to social consciousness and revolution. Such "top-down" policies will fail, he argued, because the mass it attempts to lead will lack the necessary historical, educational, and conceptual development that would allow such a revolution to be successful.[18] Blum does not directly reference Marx, but his arguments show a familiarity with Marxist concepts not evidenced by his opponents who embraced the concept of vanguardism.

The reasons for this lack of acquaintance with Marxist concepts on the part of those who argued on behalf of adherence to Third International policies is also understandable given their backgrounds. For the most part, those who looked to the Bolsheviks as exemplars had come to this conclusion neither through theoretical study, through work in the labor movement, nor even necessarily by participation in Socialist politics. As such, they were rather poorly acquainted with Marxist philosophy in either its theoretical or practical guises. Instead of by direct acquaintance, they came to this opinion through their involvement—mainly as intellectuals—with the peace movement and by their judgment that internationalism provided a solution to the problem of how to make sure the Great War was truly the war to end all wars.[19] Radicalized by the experience of wartime resistance and inspired by the example of Russia and Lenin, their initial involvement with the SFIO was thus motivated by affinity rather than by deep philosophical agreement. Specifically, they felt that their utopian ideals of international peace, prosperity, and radical equality could be realized within a Bolshevik framework. More than any real understanding of a materialist dialectic of history, this was their motivation.[20] The writer Henri Barbusse provides perhaps the best example of such a type, for it was his popular antiwar novel *Le Feu*, published in 1918, that inspired many people to these opinions. Further, he is representative of those intellectuals like Jean-Richard Bloch, Romain Rolland, and Anatole France who followed him in joining the SFIO and, like him, became proponents of the view that the party should throw in its lot with the Soviets.[21]

Without the context of the war and the Soviet revolution, it is at first hard to understand the split at Tours and the fact that the overwhelming majority of delegates to the Congress voted for adhesion to the policies of the Third International. Though it seems fairly obvious from debates leading up to Tours that most Socialists had a good idea of the differences between Reformist and Bolshevist Marxisms, it is not so clear why so many delegates would choose to align themselves with a Soviet program that effectively did away with French sovereignty and that abandoned a moderately successful reform movement only to replace it with a revolutionary agenda whose policies were decided by a centralized international body. By no means would such a change have been accepted before the war when the SFIO was moving increasingly to social democratic policies and when French political and cultural nationalism was at a high point at the end of la belle époque. However, the prolonged war changed everything, including the stature and authority of the revisionist position. For, as Lenin took pains to point out, it was social democratic policies which had allowed the collapse of international solidarity among workers at the start of the war.[22] Further, it became apparent over the course of the war and in its immediate aftermath that, despite the great increase in numbers and strength of industrial workers occasioned by the military buildup, the actual power of workers to effect change by traditional means (strikes and votes) had failed to increase commensurably.[23] Consequently, revolution was again seen as an option by workers and their representatives who after 1915 had become increasingly militant. Worker radicalization was seconded and reinforced by those intellectuals involved in the antiwar movement for whom the internationalist and utopian aspects of the Third International held immediate appeal and who also recognized the revisionist Socialists' complicity in the prolonged war. What's more, the apparent success of the revolution in Russia provided compelling reasons for French leftists to throw their lot in with that of the Soviets in the hopes that this revolution could be expanded. Thus at the time when the decision was made to vote for adhesion to the Twenty-one Conditions demanded by the Comintern for admittance into its body, the idea that French Socialists break with reformist Marxists and organize themselves along democratic centralist lines seemed to many eminently reasonable.

While it is true that the war had made large parts of the French Left especially amenable to Bolshevik overtures, it is also true that this amenability was enhanced by the fact that the majority of delegates at the convention would not have found the theory and practice of Bolshevism especially strange or foreign. As David Caute points out in his consideration of the Congress, to the French Socialists at Tours, Bolshevism was "absolutely compatible with the sacred legacy inherited from the Jacobin Committee of Public Safety, [from] Babeuf's 'Conspiracy of the Equals,' from the June days of 1848, from the commune of 1871, from the Marxist wing of the Socialist Party, [and] from the anti-capitalist intransigence of the revolutionary syndicalists." Though there is no question that this is a diverse legacy which embodied at various times many contradictory tendencies, it is also true that it rarely shied away from citing revolution as a means of accomplishing its goals. Thus Bolshevist Communism, "with its promise to act where others had recently only talked, appeared to many as its [the legacy of French Socialism's] logical synthesis."[24]

The apparently revolutionary circumstances occasioned by the war combined with the traditional affinity of the French Left for the revolutionary methods of the Leninist program paved the way for the acceptance of the twenty-one conditions for joining the Third International by the overwhelming majority of delegates at Tours. As two of the twenty-one conditions imposed by the Comintern were that the new party adopt the name "Communist" and that the party break with reformist and centrist elements, this acceptance also occasioned the split within the Socialist movement.[25] Two parties were thus formed. The Communists took the name Section Française de l'International Communiste while the Socialists retained the moniker Section Française de l'International Ouvriére. Henceforth, the former would align itself with the directives of the Third International while the latter would continue to associate itself with the reformism of the Second International. Though the two parties would not infrequently cooperate during elections in order to assure that the most Left politicians possible were elected to parliament, the next sixty years would be characterized by acrimony between them, especially as one or the other attempted to position itself as the true heir to Marx's theoretical and practical legacy.

Origins of French Communist Philosophy: 1920-1923

At its founding in December 1920, the intellectuals, workers, and radicals who constituted the SFIC's initial membership were not as optimistic that a Europe-wide communist revolution would occur as they were the previous summer. Events like the assassination of Rosa Luxembourg and Karl Liebknecht eighteen months before the Tours Congress, the failure of the Hungarian Revolution, and the defeat of the Red Army at Warsaw in August 1920 seemed to indicate that bourgeois governments might be successful in their reconsolidation of power, at least for the short term. However, this did not mean that the newly formed French Communist Party or the Third International of which it was a member were about to give up on their revolutionary goals. In fact, the revolutionary policy was to be one of the most distinctive and longest-held positions of the French Communists.[26] What had become apparent at the time though was that Europe was not going to fall to the communists like so many dominoes (as would be feared forty years later in Southeast Asia).

The fact that the international triumph of communism would not be immediate hardly dampened the overall optimism of the new party; it still continued to form itself as an organization explicitly consecrated "in the service of the revolution." Despite persecution from the French Right and pronounced enmity from both the SFIO and the labor organizations it had split off from, during the years 1920-1923 the SFIC began to formulate and set in motion the policies that would typify its existence for the next fifty years. The majority of these policies were developed in conjunction with the directives of the Third International, which, in turn, took its leadership from Lenin and the Bolsheviks. However, it was also the case that these positions were seen as more a clarification of existing French Communist predilections than as impositions and that each was subject to its own uniquely Gallic interpretation. This "spin" was especially evident in the early 1920s when Lenin was really too busy prosecuting a war and solidifying his domestic position to be much involved in policing orthodoxy in a communist party a continent away.

Although they would trace the root and inspiration of many of their ideas to Karl Marx, the newly minted French Communists of 1921 were not very well acquainted with Marx's actual texts. Despite this deficiency, the party did not try very hard to correct this lack. For instance, the party's theoretical organ, *Cahiers de Bolchevisme*, dealt little with the philosophical justification for the positions it expounded. Though the party would frequently appeal to Marx as authority in its pamphlets, pedagogical texts, and speeches, the only actual volumes of Marx or Engels to be published by the party between 1920 and 1925 were re-editions of *The Communist Manifesto* and Engels's *Socialism: Utopian and Scientific*.[27] This less than ambitious publishing program is understandable at the practical level given the exigencies of a new political party struggling to hold on to and expand its base and persecuted by the wider political community. However, it is also makes sense at the theoretical and ideological level. These two texts, the one vulgar and revolutionary, the other slightly more sophisticated but scientistic and reductive, neatly reflected and justified party philosophy in a way that the more complex works by Marx himself did not. Indeed, when looking at party political and pedagogical propaganda, one can see the arguments of Lenin and Engels reflected in these texts in a more or less crude and unqualified manner.

In the formative years of the French Communist Party, there is a paucity of sources providing a theoretical justification for the party's positions. However, there exist a number of documents that, in articulating and publicizing party policy, reveal something about the theoretical background informing these policies. If such documents are read carefully, one can come to an understanding of the theoretical positions that the SFIC was willing to stake out and can venture an educated guess at these positions' antecedents (or lack thereof) in classical Marxist texts. One such representative document is a widely distributed PCF pamphlet titled *Thèses directrices sur la tactique de l'Internationale communiste dans la lutte pour la Dictature du Prolétariat*[28] [Guiding Theses on the Tactics of the Communist International in the Struggle for the Dictatorship of the Proletariat]. This document is meant as a compliment to the Twenty-one Articles of Confederation for adherence to the Third International. However, unlike the Twenty-one Articles, it is not merely a prescriptive demand that the Socialist Party remove reformists, agitate for revolution, organize on the basis of democratic centralism, and support the Soviet program. Instead, it outlines reasons for why these measures should be taken and attempts to describe the cogency and coherency of its positions especially as these are formulated in contradistinction to those of reformist Socialism.

Echoing the general sympathies of the battle-scarred French populace, the legacy of the war provides the immediate justification for many of the *Thèses directrices*' arguments. As the pamphlet describes the situation in 1921, the Great War has proven once and for all that the bourgeois political system is unable to control the forces of capitalism and that it is incapable of reassembling a world that the global contest has torn apart. By detailing the postwar scrambles of Entente powers to secure their colonies and their spheres of influence and by touching upon the failure to create a representative League of Nations, the pamphlet argues that the war has shown the existing political order to be fatally destabilized. Thus it states: "La guerre mondiale [a] prouvé que [le Capital de l'Entente] n'est pas capable de *reconstruire le monde tombé en ruines*, de lui donner même cette petite mesure de sécurité et d'ordre que l'organisation capitaliste a présentée jusqu'à ce jour."[29] [The world war has proven that (Entente Capital) is not capable of *reconstructing a world fallen into ruins*, it cannot even give it that minimal measure of security and of order that capitalist organization had theretofore presented.] Because this destabilization is worldwide and because it is a symptom of the shift to world markets, industrialized workers feel this crisis in terms of an increase in joblessness and in the burden of higher taxes. Thus the transformation of capital and the politics of the Entente: "fortifie les tendances révolutionnaires; elle pousse les masses ouvrières et paysannes des pays vaincus dans les bras de la révolution mondiale."[30] [fortify revolutionary tendencies; they have pushed the mass of workers and peasants in the vanquished countries into the arms of the worldwide revolution.] With class divisions so sharpened, the pamphlet argues, it is now manifestly and universally evident to workers that they alone are "appellées à mettre de l'ordre dans le chaos capitaliste, à construire le monde sur une base nouvelle."[31] [called to instill order into the chaos of capitalism, to construct the world on a new foundation.] Further, it is by grace of the transformation of capital that workers are now able to self-identify as that class which has the intelligence, the reason, and the power to reconstruct the world. It is thus the workers who can give the world a totally novel and stable foundation after they have succeeded in their task of the radical expropriation and re-appropriation of the means of production.

Though neither Marx nor Engels is explicitly mentioned in the text, it is fairly obvious that the *Thèses directrices* is an updating of *The Communist Manifesto* and that the pamphlet is meant to serve largely the same purpose as its model; both are designed to sway potential sympathizers to action in the Communist movement. As in the *Manifesto*, this persuasion takes two forms: first, a logical, historical argument is presented showing the necessity of worker revolution; second, a programmatic outline of the steps necessary to affect this revolution is given. Borrowed wholesale from Marx's and Engels's text, most of the document's logical and historical argument is familiar. The programmatic elements of it are less so. Though lacking the historical depth of the *Manifesto*'s genealogical section and concentrating mostly for illustrations of its points on the war years and not on the historical succession of social formations, capitalism is presented by the pamphlet as inherently unstable. This instability is shown to lead to crises. These crises are felt most acutely by the proletariat who, progressively impoverished, recognize their interests as different from those of the bourgeoisie. These workers then organize politically to fight on behalf of their own interests and, eventually. replace the chaotic capitalist order with a new rational and stable order.

The above account given by the PCF pamphlet differs little from the rather crude explanation of the materialist dialectic found in the *Manifesto*.[32] However, when the *Thèses directrices* shifts to discussion of programmatic concerns, its divergences are recognizable. In terms of the political program each describes, the principal differences between the pamphlets are three. First, the PCF's pamphlet places much more emphasis on the global character that capital has revealed in the wake of the war than does the *Manifesto*. This weight is seen in its discussion of "imperialism" or the global consolidation of finance and productive capital and would appear to be Lenin's distinct contribution. Second, the pamphlet dwells not only on the necessity of combating the bourgeoisie but focuses on a new threat, that of the *"illusion démocratique"* propounded by the Socialists.[33] Third, whereas the success of the Communist revolution was predicated in the *Manifesto* on the unification of the proletariat from each country, the success of the world revolution and the workers' movement is now shown to hinge upon the victory of the Soviets in their civil war.[34]

The influence of the Third International and of Lenin does not stop with these three divergences from classical and revisionist Marxism. The effect is also seen in the heightened emphasis that is placed by the pamphlet on certain aspects of Marx's original theory: specifically those of violent revolution, radical class division, the dictatorship of the proletariat, the concept of "democratic centralism," and the inherent rationality of the proletariat. Most of these emphases as well as reflections of the three major divergences noted above are seen in this passage where the reader is exhorted to believe that:

> Les Leçons de toutes les révolutions bourgeoises, ainsi que la
> révolution russe, ont démontré qu'un ordre social nouveau ne

peut être réalisé que par la guerre civile des masses populaires asservies, contre la classe dominante qui se meurt, et les porteurs victorieux de l'ordre nouveau ont à assurer par leur *dictature*, le passage de l'ancienne organisation sociale à la nouvelle. La révolution prolétaire russe a montré au prolétariat international, dans les "Conseils d'ouvriers," l'organe de cette dictature inévitable pour la réalisation de Socialisme.[35]

[The lessons of all bourgeois revolutions, as well as the Russian Revolution, have demonstrated that a new social order can only be realized by a civil war between the enslaved masses and the class which dominated them, and the victorious deliverers of the new order assure by their *dictatorship* the transition from the old social order to the new one. The Russian proletarian revolution has, with its Workers' Councils, shown the inevitable organization of that dictatorship for the realization of Socialism.]

One can see explicitly in this passage that what was barely touched upon in the *Manifesto* (and then only as one possibility among many, including democratic transition) has by 1921 become central.[36] It was now assumed as a necessity for revolutionary success that the proletariat be organized and governed by a central decision making body, the Workers' Council. As the pamphlet explains this necessity, all of history has revealed the truth that a new social order can only be won when, in a civil war, a dictatorship of the proletariat assures the passage from the old to new social order. As the text unequivocally states: "La conquête de pouvoir politique de la dictature du prolétariat est la condition nécessaire de l'expropriation des expropriateurs."[37] [The conquest of political power by the dictatorship of the proletariat is the necessary precondition for the expropriation of the expropriators.] All the questions of orthodoxy and revisionism that bothered the Second International have here been settled negatively. Changes in the economy will not inevitably lead to a successful revolution, nor will progressive democratic reforms. The sole route to successful revolution is the organization of a central governing body that oversees the struggle and administers the transition to a new order.[38] Though it is not explicitly spelled out, with its emphasis on "*l'organe de cette dictature inévitable pour la réalisation de socialisme*," the thrust of the text's argument here points both toward the justification of "democratic centralism" and toward "vanguardism."[39]

Just as the PCF's pamphlet reduces the multiple possibilities that Marx and Engels articulate for the transition to communism to a singularity, the pamphlet also reduces the subtle analysis of class relations found in the *Manifesto* to a simple binary opposition between workers and bourgeoisie. Though at this point in the early 1920s the Comintern and the SFIC included sympathetic intellectuals among the ranks of the workers and invited them to participate in the revolution,[40] it would not be long before this identification would change from one based upon ideological sympathy to one based upon an "empirical" distinction that would exclude such petty bourgeois types from participation in the Communist Party. The reasons for this distinction and the excommunication of intellectuals have to do with the development of a distinctively Marxist-Leninist epistemology—an epistemology that will become an issue for the party with its adoption of Front Uni policies in 1924 and that is particularly evident in those texts that take their theoretical cues from Lenin's readings of Engels's *Socialism: Utopian and Scientific* (1880) and *The Dialectics of Nature* (1883).

Perhaps the most startling difference between *The Communist Manifesto* and the *Thèses directrices* is neither the latter pamphlet's voluntarism nor its reductivism but the emphasis that it places on the link between world revolution and the success of the Soviets in Russia. Like the concept of imperialism that theoretically justifies Lenin's contention that a successful revolution must be international and that also explains the expansion of capital before and during the war, the emphasis on Russia has its own theoretical and empirical justification. This justification is the concept of the "Weakest Link" or the belief that revolution is possible only where the "chain of imperialism is weakest."[41] It is not necessary to understand this concept, however, in order to recognize the persuasive force that the appeal for solidarity and identification with the Soviet cause had at the time. The Hungarian, Bavarian and Slovakian revolutions—all short lived—had already by 1920 petered out. This left the Russian Revolution as the only one that looked like it had a good chance for success and for eventually aiding revolutionary movements in other countries. Thus when the pamphlet argued that "la défense active de la russie des soviets par les masses prolétariennes de tous les pays représente un devoir qui doit être rempli sans égards aux sacrifices que la lutte exigera"[42] [the active defense of the Russian Soviets by the proletarian masses of every country represents a task that must be fulfilled without regard to the sacrifices that the battle will demand], it was the case that the need for this defense was pretty much accepted as a given by the radical left and was extended by the Section Française de l'International Communiste and other sections of the Communist International as best they could.

At this early juncture, the French Communist Party's support for Soviet Russia did not mean that it was in full ideological agreement with Moscow and with the Comintern. In fact, the fledgling party was often at odds with the central governing body on issues of political leadership, freedom of speech, and party constitution. Nonetheless, a precedent was set in these early years in which Moscow—location of the Comintern and "the base of world revolutions"—came to have an authority which was expanded and exploited by both Lenin and Stalin such that the will of the PCF to go its own way was increasingly limited. The hegemony of Moscow should not, however, be seen as an imposition on a formerly independent Communist Party. Really, even into the 1980s,[43] the PCF was quite content to follow the directives of the Soviets because they believed that Russia was "*le point de départ de la politique mondiale du proletariat*"[44] [the point of departure for proletarian world politics]. Ironically, this belief was strengthened and not weakened by the failure of world revolution in the post-World War I period. The complementary theories of "Socialism in one country" and the subsequent "two worlds" hypothesis nicely painted a picture of a noble Soviet Union, the only revolutionary hope, besieged by the forces of capitalism.[45]

Even in the early and rather brief *Thèses directrices* from 1921, it is easy to discern many of the policies and concepts that would dominate PCF philosophy and politics for the next sixty years. These include its perceived revolutionary mandate and its emphasis on class struggle. By 1923, however, it was becoming fairly obvious to both the PCF and to the Comintern that the revolutionary situation that had existed at the end of World War I was over and that its short- and long-term strategies needed reconsideration. This was especially the case if the party was to substantiate its claim to be the party of the working class and the party of revolution. In addition to strategic problems, the PCF also had troubles with its membership. Its claim to be the party of the working class was belied by the plurality of its constitution, which then consisted only of a minority of genuine workers.[46] In 1924, the party sought to address both of these issues. It did so first through the clarification of its strategies and, second, through a purification of its ranks. Known as "Bolshevization," these processes resulted in an intensification of the antidemocratic, class partisan, pro-Soviet, and anti-imperialist policies that had previously been little enforced. More importantly for this study, unlike the years 1920-1923 when it was merely trying to incite a revolution and could not be bothered with such considerations, the party now took the time to do theoretical and pedagogical work, outlining to its membership the philosophy of Karl Marx—at least as far as it understood it.

Notes

1. Neill Nugent and David Lowe, *The Left in France* (New York: St. Martin's Press, 1982), 25.

2. David Caute, *Communism and the French Intellectuals: 1914-1960* (New York: Macmillan, 1964), 64.

3. Adherents to the Second International signed agreements at the 1912 Basel Congress stating that, should a war break out, they would: "exploit the crisis . . . to hasten the downfall of capitalist domination." See Maxwell Adereth, *The French Communist Party: A Critical History (1920-1984): From Comintern to the Colours of France* (Manchester, Manchester University Press, 1984), 16.

4. Jean-Jacques Becker, *The Great War and the French People*, trans. Jay Winter (Dover, NH: Berg Publishers, 1985), 76.

5. André Suarez, editorialist for *L'Opinion* from 1914-16, quoted in Becker, *The Great War*, 165.

6. For an account of the paucity of antiwar opposition in 1914 see Becker, *The Great War*, 77-93.

7. Adereth, *The French Communist Party,* 16.

8. Nugent and Lowe, *The Left in France,* 26.

9. Caute, *Communism and the French Intellectuals*, 67.

10. Adereth, *The French Communist Party,* 22.

11. Nicole Racine and Louis Bodin, *Le parti communiste Français pendant l'entre-deux-guerres* (Paris: Presses de la Fondation Nationale des Sciences Politiques, 1982), 16.

12. Annie Kriegel, *Aux origines du communisme Français, 1914-1920: Contributions à l'histoire du mouvement ouvrier Français*, vol. 2 (Paris: Mouton, 1964), 731.

13. See especially Yves Santamaria, *L'Enfant du malheur: le parti communiste Français dans la lutte pour la paix, 1914-1947* (Paris: S. Arslan, 2002); Daniel Blume et al., *Histoire du réformisme en France depuis 1920* (Paris: Editions Sociales, 1976); Kriegel, *Aux origines du communisme Français*; Ronald Tiersky, *French Communism 1920-1972* (New York and London: Columbia

University Press, 1974); and Sophie Coeuré, *La Grande lueur á l'Est: les Français et l'Union soviétique, 1917-1939* (Paris: Seuil, 1999).

14. Blume et al., *Histoire du réformisme*, 6.

15. Kriegel, *Aux origines du communisme Français*, 871.

16. Stéphane Courtois and Marc Lazar, *Histoire du parti communiste Français* (Paris: PUF, 1995), 66.

17. This is even doubly ironic given that the reformists who knew Marx best at the time of the *Scission* would all but abandon the Marxist influence on their politics after World War II. Correspondingly, that faction which knew Marx the least would evolve into a Communist party that treated his words (or at least Stalin's formulations of his words) as scripture.

18. As quoted in Blume et al., *Histoire du réformisme*, 21-23, Léon Blum wrote: "Nous croyons que dans l'état actuel de la société capitaliste, ce serait folie de compter sur les masses inorganiques. Nous savons derrière qui elles vont un jour et derrière qui elles vont le lendemain. Nous savons quelles masses inorganiques étaient un jour derrière Boulanger et marchaient un autre jour derrière Clemenceau." [Given the present state of capitalist society, we believe that it would be crazy to count on the inorganic masses. We know who they go for one day and who they go for the next. We know that the inorganic masses were once behind Boulanger and then marched another day right behind Clemenceau.] Blum goes on in this work to argue that, because of their caprice, the masses are unsuitable for making and sustaining a revolution until they are properly educated such that they can understand what revolution means and what it entails.

19. Yves Santamaria shows that this popular desire for peace and to avoid future wars was something that the PCF continued to exploit throughout the first half of the twentieth century. Whenever it needed to rally its membership or desired to recruit new supporters, it issued a call for peace and internationalism. See *L'Enfant du malheur*, 291-99.

20. Caute, *Communism and the French Intellectuals*, 77.

21. Michael Kelly, *Modern French Marxism* (Oxford: Blackwell Publishers, 1982), 20.

22. See for instance Lenin's essays: "Opportunism and the Collapse of the Second International (January, 1916)," *Collected Works,* vol. 22 (New York: International Publishers), 108-120; and "A Basic Question Used by Socialists Who Have Gone Over to the Bourgeoisie (20 April, 1917)," www.marxists.org/archive/lenin/works/1917/apr/20g.htm (accessed July 21, 2004).

23. Adereth, *The French Communist Party,* 22.

24. Caute, *Communism and the French Intellectuals*, 13.

25. The Twenty-one Conditions were made public in August 1920 and published in *L'Humanité*, the party newspaper, on October 8, 1920.

26. The PCF has consistently held that it is a revolutionary party constituted to overthrow the existing bourgeois regime and to replace it with a transitional government until a truly communist state could come into existence. At different times, the PCF thought that it was closer to realizing this goal than at others. For instance, during the Front Populaire it believed that it might not only be able to roll back fascism but also to take the opportunity this rollback provided to replace the bourgeois government. Likewise, the end of World War II and May 1968 were seen as presenting such opportunities, however briefly. Even in 1984, the PCF Politburo member Pierre Juquin would state in an interview that the PCF was a revolutionary party and that a "revolutionary solution [is] the only way out of the capitalist crisis." See Adereth, *The French Communist Party,* appendix 7: interview with Pierre Juquin, April 1984. See also Nugent and Lowe, *The Left in France,* 98-100.

27. Kelly, *Modern French Marxism,* 21.

28. *Thèses directrices sur la tactique de l'Internationale communiste dans la lutte pour la Dictature du Prolétariat* (Geneva: La Nouvelle Internationale, 1920/21).

29. *Thèses directrices,* 1. Emphasis in original. All translations are my own unless noted.

30. *Thèses directrices,* 3.

31. *Thèses directrices,* 3.

32. Karl Marx and Friedrich Engels, *The Communist Manifesto* (New York: International Publishers, 1948), 13-21.

33. *Thèses directrices,* 2.

34. *Thèses directrices,* 16.

35. *Thèses directrices,* 4. Emphasis in original.

36. The relevant passage from the *Manifesto* is: "If the proletariat during its contest with the bourgeoisie is compelled, by the force of circumstances, to organize itself as a class; if by means of a revolution it makes itself the ruling class, and, as such sweeps away by force the old conditions of production, then it will, along with these conditions, have swept away the conditions for the existence of class antagonisms." Marx and Engels, *The Communist Manifesto,* 31.

37. *Thèses directrices,* 11.

38. *Thèses directrices,* 10.

39. "Democratic Centralism" is the organizational principle wherein a party's members participate in the decision making process—the democratic part—and the centralized leadership sees to it that these decisions are followed by all. In Marxist-Leninist practice, the "centralism" part always dominated the "democratic" component. Vanguardism is the theory wherein the leadership and will of an elite group can lead a mass toward proletarian revolution that might otherwise be spontaneously sidetracked into counterrevolutionary practices such as sabotage and general strikes.

40. *Thèses directrices,* 4.

41. Joseph Stalin, "The Foundations of Leninism," in *Problems of Leninism* (Moscow: Foreign Language Publishing House, 1947), 31-32.

42. *Thèses directrices,* 16.

43. Sudhir Hazareesingh, *Intellectuals and the French Communist Party: Delusion and Decline* (Oxford: Oxford University Press, 1991), 306.

44. *Thèses directrices,* 16.

45. First used rhetorically by Stalin in 1919 to differentiate between "Imperialist" and "Socialist" nations, the strategic decision to consolidate support for the struggling Soviets in 1923 gave momentum to the idea of "two camps" or "Socialism in one country." This concept was explicitly posited against Trotsky's position that the revolution should continue to be international in character. Stalin later developed this position into the "two worlds" hypothesis in which the simultaneous development of capitalism in the west and communism in the east would show the superiority of the latter. See Joseph Stalin, "Two Camps," in *The Essential Stalin: Major Theoretical Writings, 1905-52* (New York: Anchor Books, 1972), 85-88, and *Deux Mondes (Rapport au XVIIème congrès de Partie Communiste de l'U.R.S.S.* (Paris: PCF Bureau d'Editions, 1933).

46. Adereth, *The French Communist Party,* 37.

Chapter 3

The PCF 1923-1945: Theoretical and Pedagogical Positions on Marx

Bolshevization and the Formalization of Marxist-Leninist Philosophy, 1923-1934

Party Practice

In a *Cahiers du bolchevisme* editorial from November 1924 titled "Idéologie, direction et organisations homogènes," the directorate of the French Communist Party argues for an *"épuration idéologique rigoreuse"* [rigorous ideological purification] of the party. This purification is needed, the directorate argues, because even though it is apparent that young party members have understood the teachings of Lenin and the need for ideological purity within party ranks, the *anciens cadres* have yet to purge themselves of anachronistic and contradictory ideas. With a party philosophy consisting of *"20% de jauréssisme, 10% de marxisme, 20% de léninisme, 20% de trotskysme et 30% de confusionnisme,"* the directorate wonders whether such a diverse group will be capable of enacting a revolution and of leading the proletarian and peasant masses. It asks itself this because—as the success of the Russian revolution and the failure of other revolutions have shown—it is only an ideologically pure organization, a 100% Leninist party, that will have the rigidity and strength to win the decisive battles necessary to overthrow bourgeois governments.[1]

Appearing in 1924, the editorial position of "Idéologie, direction et organisations homogènes," was representative of the party's viewpoint and direction for the next ten years. Between 1923 and 1934 and with only minor inconsistencies, the party's activities largely consisted of the ideological purification on behalf of which this editorial argues. During this time, this mission's achievement was perhaps the best met of its policy goals.[2] Known as "Bolshevization" but enacted under the umbrella of programs variously known as the Front Uni or Front Unique,[3] this process took many forms, some mild and some severe. On the milder side, there were mass education efforts and the dissemination of propaganda designed to inculcate Stalin's version of Leninist philosophy and to deride other variants of Marxism as "bourgeois," "opportunistic, "social-fascistic," and "pseudo-leftist." On the severe side, there was the accusation, prosecution, and expulsion of party members and sympathetic individuals for actually being "bourgeois," "opportunistic, "social-fascistic," and "pseudo-leftist."

In this concerted attempt to separate the *ouvrière leniniste* from the *opportuniste bourgeois*, the PCF progressively soured its relationship with the broader French Left and ended up alienating its own membership and voting bloc as well. What was done with the goal of creating a stronger and more revolutionary party ended up weakening it significantly. It did, however, succeed somewhat in its goal of creating ideological purity and cohesion. The Stalinist version of Marxist-Leninist philosophy as it was defined and schematized by the party in these years had a permanent impact on future positions and policies such that, even in the 1980s, the speeches of PCF bureaucrats were still peppered with Marxist-Leninist rhetoric and concepts.[4]

The Stalinist interpretation of Marxist philosophy to which the PCF and the Comintern demanded ideological adherence during the years of the Front Uni was, for the most part, already implicit in the organizational demands made in the Twenty-one Conditions for Adherence to the Communist International. From periodic purges, to anti-reformism, to the neutralization of the peasantry, to the support of liberation movements in the colonies and of the Soviets in Russia, all of these were part of the original program determined by the Third International. The same was true of the ideas and justifications for democratic centralism, of the revolution to come, and of the dictatorship of the proletariat as the necessary vehicle for directing capitalism's transition to communism. All of this was implicit or even explicit in the Twenty-one Articles of Confederation. However, as should be clear from the discussion of the competing ideological elements at play during the Congress of Tours, these demands and their theoretical justifications were not only misunderstood by the French party but were often altogether ignored by those caught up in the revolutionary and organizational excitement of the early twenties. Pragmatic considerations further retarded their implementation until late 1923. After the situation in Russia and in France had somewhat stabilized, though, the PCF at the behest of the Comintern began a process of making this philosophy explicit and of implementing Comintern policies. It achieved these goals through a process of ideological education and by more active measures such as the elimination of those whose views were at variance with official party policy and through the alienation of potential sympathizers, *faux camarades* who lacked the proper class background or who harbored "anachronist" perspectives on Marxist philosophy.

As ordered by the Comintern after its Fifth Congress in July of 1924, the process of "Bolshevization" in the French Communist Party found its first targets in the intellectuals who a few years earlier had been instrumental in the party's founding and critical for its prestige. The case of Boris Souvarine is representative of this targeting. One of the chief proponents of the alignment of the French Socialists with the Third International at the Congress of Tours, he continued his dedicated involvement with the party after the Congress as editor of *Le Bulletin Communiste* and of *l'Humanité*. For three years, he positioned himself as one of the party's most eloquent advocates and passionate supporters. Beginning in 1924, though, he began to use his column inches to argue against what he saw as "excessive centralism" and "mechanical discipline" in the party.[5] Souvarine also had the gall to publish Trotsky's *New Course* just a few months after Trotsky himself had been condemned by the CPSU for arguing on behalf of the active continuation of the world revolution and against the idea of "socialism in one country." For these "errors," Souvarine was relieved from his editorships and was expelled from the party.

The reasons for Souvarine's expulsion are fairly obvious and are consistent with those views expressed in the PCF directorate's editorial on ideological, directional, and organizational homogeneity. Following the directives of the Fifth Congress, the Comintern and the PCF were (as Souvarine correctly identified) precisely involved in trying to eliminate ideological fringes and to impose mechanical discipline on the party. Championing Trotsky, Souvarine represented one of these fringes and, as such, was a threat to party discipline. He therefore needed to be eliminated. As the party leadership took pains to point out at the time, Souvarine also committed what is sometimes referred to as the "original sin" of intellectuals, that of being petty bourgeois.[6] Though a radical change in party policy from the time when "manual workers as well as intellectual workers" were invited to join the party,[7] this diagnosis was consistent with Leninist theory as Stalin interpreted it. Other intellectuals similarly afflicted with the epistemological and genetic handicap that rendered them incapable of ever really understanding Communist philosophy followed Souvarine en masse away from the party. Some were expelled, some voluntarily defected, but all left after the party made it clear that, as revisionists, mystics, and idealists, they were no longer wanted in the ranks.[8]

Sympathetic intellectuals were easy targets for Bolshevization. Their pedigree was suspect and they often did hold fast to outrageous beliefs—such as in free speech and democracy—that were seen by the PCF as iconoclastic, anachronistic, and counterrevolutionary when compared to Stalinist orthodoxy. Sitting ducks, most intellectuals had departed or had been expelled from the party by 1927. So far as Bolshevization included the elimination of inherently suspect classes from party ranks, it was by this time mostly accomplished. Significant exceptions to this rule were the philosophers associated with the journal *Esprit* and the members of the Surrealist Group under the leadership of André Breton. However, these intellectuals joined the party in the mid-1920s for almost entirely different reasons than those who had joined the party at its founding in 1920. These intellectuals' affiliation and their motivations will be discussed in the next chapter.

More difficult than free-thinking intellectuals for the party in its mission of consolidation and ideological purification were its associations with the broader Left and with its own internal ideological makeup. As far as the former went, the Communist Party's relations with the broader Left (which then included the Socialist Party, the Radicals and the unions) went from a sort of schizophrenia in the mid-1920s to an attitude of consistent hostility when the party officially adopted its *"classe contre classe"* policy in 1927. Obviously and from the beginning, great tensions existed between the French Socialist and French Communist Parties. These tensions were exacerbated by the Communists' pronounced tendency to refer to the Socialists—even in conciliatory documents—as "traitors of Marxism" and "bourgeois apologists."[9] Despite this acrimony, the PCF did at least make overtures to the broader Left during the elections of 1924, inviting the SFIO to join in an alliance and to work toward the establishment of the "dictatorship of the proletariat." Not surprisingly, given the Communist Party's inconsistent rhetoric and the fact that it was clear that the self-identified "party of the proletariat" would be the power that would establish the terms of this dictatorship, the SFIO chose to align itself with the Radicals.[10]

With the adoption in August 1927 of the *"classe contre classe"* strategy, the PCF at least became consistent in its attitude and politics vis-à-vis the French Left. Defined by the Comintern at its Sixth Congress, this strategy was based on the Stalinist assertion that capitalism had entered a new stage, that of "stabilization," which had rendered its contradictions increasingly evident. Internationally, these contradictions were supposedly shown by the spread and intensification of imperialism. Domestically, they were revealed by an intensification of "class antagonism" and the "radicalization of the masses." While there was empirical evidence for the former claim, at least in France there was little indication of the latter. Nevertheless, the PCF stuck by this analysis until 1934, when it saw the need to unite with the broader Left in an effort to combat fascism.

Characterized by the rigid "line of demarcation" that it wished to draw in every instance between that which was bourgeois and that which was proletarian, the upshot of *classe contre classe* policy was the increasing isolation and marginalization of the PCF both from the broader Left and from those whom it identified as its natural constituency, the French workers. This isolation was evidenced both in its relationship with the Socialists whom it now refused to collaborate with even during electoral cycles and with the unions who did not recognize and in fact resented the party's self-proclaimed authority as organizer of the working class. Where before the party had entertained the idea that a broader alliance of the Left might help to accomplish political goals such as the adoption of an eight-hour day, the party leadership now decided that the Socialists were irredeemably bourgeois and that the purity of the revolutionary movement would be compromised by any affiliation with them.[11] Similarly, though relationships with unions like the C.G.T. were always strained due to the unions' anarcho-syndicalist heritage, all potential alliances between unions and party were compromised by a theory and policy which held that the leaders of these unions were "labor aristocracy" prone to involvement in social-democratic politics.[12] Unwilling to deal with the "class traitors" and "labor parasites" who ran the unions, the

PCF was increasingly estranged from the bulk of the *ouvrières* whose party it was supposed to be.

So much then for the PCF's external relations with the broader Left between 1923-1934. As far as the internal politics of the party went, the leadership during this period began to see all ideological deviation as detrimental to the realization of its policies. Increasingly intolerant of ideological diversity, the party sought to purge its left and right wings so as to present a Front Uni. To this end, it agitated in print and made moves to expel from its ranks those who subscribed to either *"l'opportunisme à droite"* or the *"purisme révolutionnaire gauchiste."*[13] The fight against opportunism was not a new one, it was just the battle against revisionist or reformist socialists under a different, explicitly Leninist name.[14] However, where before this fight was largely rhetorical and inconsistent, the battle against social democratic elements within its ranks now had the effect of driving away large chunks of the party's core membership base as well as its voting bloc.

An even older battle in that its roots can be traced to the struggles between Marx and "ultra-Leftists" like Bakunin at the First International, the struggle against left-wing Communism took on new forms during the late 1920s. Now, its scope expanded to include arguments against Trotskyism and neo-Syndicalism. This rhetorical line had much the same effect as the battle against "opportunists" in terms of driving away the party's members and supporters. Though persecution by the existing French government may have had some influence in its decline,[15] it is certain that internal struggles against left- and right-wing "factions" led directly to a decrease in party membership. Between 1924 and 1933, the PCF's rolls decreased from 60,000 to 28,000, its nadir.[16] It is also sure that this decline was abetted by the party's insistence—consistent with its *classe contre classe* policies—that its composition be formed by a majority of workers and by the active efforts it took to assure this composition by way of encouraging non-workers to leave the party.[17] After this mass exodus, the party was undoubtedly more ideologically pure than before Bolshevization. Theoretically, it should also have been better able to successfully enact a revolution because it now constituted a disciplined revolutionary vanguard and its leadership consisted of members of the working class, not intellectuals. However, it cannot be denied that its actual influence on French politics had become negligible. By conforming rigidly to the Marxist-Leninist theoretical model for a revolutionary party of the working class, the French Communist Party had with its *classe contre classe* program effectively forfeited the possibility of practical revolutionary agency.

Party Theory

It is apparent that between 1923-1934 a Stalinist model of Marxist-Leninist theory drove the policies of the Comintern and of the French Communist Party. But what were these policies and what was their theoretical justification such that the PCF was willing to run itself into the ground in behalf of their defense and application? As noted above, these policies were felt in terms of their deleterious effects on the party's less orthodox members and could be inferred from the nature of their persecutions. These policies were also, however, explored and detailed in the mass education efforts and propaganda pieces designed to justify Front Uni policies. Unlike the documents related to the expulsion of suspect party members, which mostly consist of epithets and sloganeering, these texts are fairly explicit with regard to the theory that drove such policies. It is through an examination of such material that one may come to an understanding of how these policies were justified at the theoretical level.

Really until the mid-1930s and the era of the Front Populaire, the French Communist Party was not concerned with the philosophical basis of its political positions. What it was concerned with was that its political positions be made explicit and that it distinguish itself ideologically from other socialist variants.[18] In order to communicate these ideas, to assert their distinctiveness, and to establish ideological heterogeneity within the party, the PCF established schools designed to give an *"introduction systématique à la doctrine."*[19] For these schools, it published pamphlets and "philosophical" texts that could best be described as Marxist-Leninist "catechisms." These came complete with comprehension questions at the end of each explanatory section and were designed to methodically lay out the rudiments of Marxist-Leninist philosophy in a way that workers (and possibly even atavist intellectuals) could understand and memorize.

Though the PCF's educational materials actually include quite a bit of Marxist philosophy and though these materials will be used extensively in this book to illustrate the party's Marxism, it must be noted that, in them, "Marx's philosophy" is usually given without qualification and the works are frustratingly un-self-critical. Further, these pedagogical texts are marked by the poverty of their source materials. Short of the *Communist Manifesto*, they reference almost none of Marx's or Engels's texts directly (though Engels's late work seems to be one of their primary theoretical sources). Even the works of Lenin, which would seem necessary to providing an understanding of Bolshevist Marxism such as *The State and Revolution*, are hardly or rarely acknowledged. What does form the basis for their explanation of Marxism-Leninism is really only three books, themselves vulgarizations. These are: Plekhanov's *Les Questions fondamentales du marxisme* (1908, 1927 in France) and Stalin's *Léninisme théorique et pratique* (1924) and *Bases de Leninisme* (1926). While Plekhanov's introduction to Marxism retains some value for the clarity with which it exposits Marx's ideas, it is, like Stalin's work, notable for its reductionism and for its insistence that the dialectic is the "algebra of revolution."[20]

Consistent with their source materials, if there is one dominant theme expressed in the educational literature published during the Front Uni, it is that there is a formula for revolution and that the Communists have found it. Further, it is suggested in these materials that this formula is justified both philosophically and scientifically by the work of Marx and Engels and that this work is then clarified and made practicable by the work of Lenin for the age of imperialism. Thus, though Marx and Engels are hardly mentioned and Lenin is only recognized by grace of Stalin's vulgarization of his work, it is assumed that the philosophical and scientific groundwork justifying the educational materials' propositions have already been established in works like Marx's *Capital*, Engels's *Anti-Dühring* and *Dialectics of Nature*, as well as in Lenin's *Materialism and Empiriocriticism* and *Imperialism: The Highest Stage of Capitalism*.

But what is this formula for revolution and what is its implicit justification? Manifestly, it is the prescription that though capitalism will necessary transform into communism by dint of its own internal logic and dynamism, it is also necessary to affect this change with the centrally directed action of a political organization dedicated to this specific purpose. Betraying a queer mixture of determinism and voluntarism, PCF educational pamphlets such as *Six cours élémentaires d'éducation communiste* (1928) that explain this recipe contend that the proletariat is historically destined to overthrow the existing capitalist order and to establish socialism.[21] Though this is depicted as a necessary development, it is strenuously argued that the proletariat can only achieve this victory

if it is organized by a select group which directs all of its diverse movements. Thus a paragraph from *Six cours élémentaires* explaining the concentration of capital into the hands of the few and headed with the statement: "*Le développement du capitalisme prépare le socialisme*" is
followed by one in which it is asserted that the "*mission historique du
prolétariat*" can only be assured by the direction of this mission by the
Communist Party.[22]

The justification for the acceptance of this formula for revolution is
based on an understanding of dialectic, science, and epistemology that is
Leninist in inspiration but that owes its direct source to Stalin's formalization of Lenin's interpretation of Marx in *Foundations of Leninism*
(1924) and *The Problems of Leninism* (1926). Though not explicit in
PCF propaganda and educational texts, the rudiments of this understanding can be teased out of the arguments they present in support of
their position that the Communist Party is the true and only organizational vehicle for the revolution.

Certainly, the economic deterministic component of the revolutionary formula is recognizably based upon the Leninist interpretation of
Marx's materialist dialectic. This interpretation holds that Marx's main
contribution to philosophy and science was the reversal of the Hegelian
dialectic and the application of this reversed dialectic to the social sciences and, especially, to history. In this reversal, "Spirit" is replaced by
"class struggle," the "Ideal" is replaced with the "material," and the
process of history is described as the necessary development of the economy in which one mode of production, in reproducing itself, produces its
opposite.[23] After Marx, classes and structures, not people or ideas, are
understood as the makers of history. History itself then becomes the detailing of progressive "modifications of the economy" that, in turn, mod-
ify men and their ideas.[24] What's more, history must be understood as
proceeding according to dialectical laws; just as certain as feudalism
produced the bourgeoisie, which was its undoing, capitalism will produce the worker, which will be its undoing. This is the materialist dialectic of history or "Historical Materialism."

At least in this explanation, the Leninist interpretation of the Marxist
dialectic does not seem to differ significantly from the "orthodox"
Marxist position that the Communist Party wished to differentiate itself
from both philosophically and from its political consequences. Sometimes derisively described as "mechanism" or "vulgar Marxism" in party
literature, this is the position that—given the dialectical logic of his-

tory—a proletarian revolution is inevitable.[25] Despite this inevitability, to realize the revolution one must wait until the economy produces the necessary and sufficient conditions for a revolution to occur. These conditions include an impoverished working class majority, the concentration of capital in a few hands, the existence of modern economic infrastructure and communication technologies, and the development of a proletarian class consciousness. According to the orthodox theorist, unless such conditions have been realized, any attempted revolution will be premature and unsuccessful. Because such a theory allows no agency on the part of persons to control their own destiny but instead has their destiny dictated by the economic position in which they find themselves, in addition to being called "mechanistic," it is also sometimes described in party literature as a "fatalistic" theory.

Eager to enact a revolution in Russia, a land that, lacking any significant "working class," in no way met the mechanistic criteria for a successful transition to communism, Lenin did not subscribe to the "fatalist" or "orthodox" version of Marxism. However, because he understood the materialist dialectic as simply a reversal of the Hegelian dialectic, he had the task of explaining how, given economic determinism, it was possible to enact a successful revolution when prevalent socioeconomic conditions would seem to structurally disallow such an event. Lenin's solution to this problem, and that which the Comintern and the CP's under its direction subsequently adopted after this position was codified by Stalin, involved the assertion of a rather curious epistemology which was itself based upon what now seems a rather strange philosophy of science.

Though in Marx's texts it is often difficult to discern the exact relationship between his philosophy and science[26] and though in Lenin's own work it is apparent that he held philosophy in high esteem, in PCF texts from the late 1920s based on Stalin's vulgarization of Lenin, this relationship has been clearly delineated: Marx the social scientist has clearly come out ahead of Marx the social philosopher. As a scientist, Marx's great contribution is presented as the discovery of the law of the dialectic of nature, a law that governs and therefore can potentially explain all natural processes, be they cosmological, natural, biological, mental, social, or historical. Given the import of this epochal discovery, the work of the natural or social scientist should properly become the explanation of natural phenomena as they are manifestations of this general law. Science for the PCF becomes the empirical study of phenomena in the process of their transformation from one state to the next. As one

French Communist educator wrote in 1927 in reference to Marx's method in *Capital*:

> Il [Marx] emprunte donc aux sciences naturelles leur *méthodes descriptives*, l'étude minutieuese du *fait*, dont aucun aspect n'est négligeable. Mais, ayant affaire à des phénomènes d'ordre humain, essentiellement changeants, presque insaississables au cours de leurs processus, il applique encore à leur étude la *méthode dialectique* qui les suit dans ce processus et tient compte, dans leurs formes présentes de leurs formes antérieures et de leurs formes futures.[27]

> [He (Marx) borrows from the natural sciences their *descriptive methods*, the minute study of *facts* of which not one aspect is negligible. But, concerning himself with human phenomena, with those things that are always in the process of change, he then applies to their study the *dialectic method* which follows them in the course of the processes, through their present, past, and future forms.]

Those who thought about such matters in the Communist Party believed that by combining the observation of empirical "facts" with a logic capable of describing them in their transformation Marx was able to arrive at a very powerful method of scientific research and explanation. What's more, because this theory held that it was a basic ontological feature that all phenomena behaved according to a dialectical logic, the method had claims to universal application. Given sufficient research and attention to physical and social phenomena in their historical development, it was believed by Communist theorists that valid dialectical explanations could be given for all phenomena, physical as well as social. Adding to the appeal provided by the tremendous scope of this method was the terrific power ascribed to it. Not only could the "materialist conception of history" explain phenomena as they are objectively but, given that all phenomena follow a dialectical logic, it could also describe them in their transition from what they were to what they will be. Potentially then, an account could be given for the future transformation of any physical or social phenomenon into its opposite. This would hold true for objects studied by sciences as diverse as mathematics, astronomy, biology, physics, economics, psychology, politics, and linguistics (though the last would prove to be somewhat of a special case).[28]

According to the party, Marx's discovery made it possible for the laws and conditions which dictate the transformation of any phenomena to be understood. In theory, this understanding could also allow one to direct any transformation providing that one could supply the necessary material. In the realm of the physical sciences, this new method of science was expected to yield results in the understanding and control of the natural world. For instance, the dialectical physicist might encourage quantitative changes in matter that would lead to their qualitative transformation into another state, a type of dialectical alchemy. In the realm of the social sciences, social and political change would also be expected to proceed and to be manipulable by those who understood the laws that underlay such transformations. Thus, if it be the case that the social scientist through research into history knows that a quantitative change in the number of factories yields an ideological change in the population, then it should also be the case that, through the building of steel works, a new proletarian class might be created or sustained. To effect such transformations was, in party lingo, to "prove the theory in practice."

This account of the relationship between Marx's philosophy and science does not seem like the one an attentive reader would take away from studying the *Grundrisse*, *Capital*, or even and perhaps especially early works like *The Poverty of Philosophy* and *The German Ideology*. Though the tendency is more pronounced in these early works, Marx consistently maintains that the empirical sciences provide "alienated" and not objective knowledge and that this knowledge is quite distinct from that provided by his "Human Science" or "critical science." This master knowledge he understands as the comprehension of the historical movement as a whole. The human and natural sciences are only components of it. Though this critical science might prove useful for correcting the "mistakes" caused by the ideological nature of the sciences (and this is what Marx did in *Capital* with regard to economics), he does not maintain that his dialectical method is universally applicable to all natural and social phenomena, only that we cannot fully understand natural and social phenomena unless we do it from a critical position that is informed by history.[29]

That the *Grundrisse* and *The German Ideology* were not available to PCF and Comintern philosophers to "correct" the party's assumptions about the relationship between Marx and science does not really matter. Both the first volume of *Capital* and the *Poverty of Philosophy* were available but were not read for their insights into this relationship.

Really, the authority on these matters was Stalin, who took his cues from Lenin, who in turn arrived at his position through a consideration of Engels's works, *The Dialectics of Nature* (1883), *Ludwig Feuerbach and the End of Classical German Philosophy* (1886), and *Anti-Dühring* (1877). As with Stalin's accounts, each of these books is hostile to the notion of philosophy as "Science of the sciences" and sympathetic to the view that the materialism of the sciences is complementary to and complemented by Dialectical Materialism. Thus Stalin's vulgarization of Marxist philosophy of science agrees with Lenin, who argues with Engels that philosophy has no privilege over science and that, instead of absolute truths, one should now pursue "attainable relative truths along the path of the positive sciences, and the summation of their results by means of dialectical thinking."[30] Though it is apparent that Engels took the claim more seriously than Lenin that science had largely replaced philosophy (Lenin subscribed to the view that there is interaction between the two and that philosophy is important to the revolutionary movement), it is also the case that, in Stalin's reading of Lenin, the relationship between science and Marxist philosophy was such that the former established the general laws or formula (dialectics) by which the latter could understand and make use of its results, be they in physics or politics, chemistry or sociology.[31] Marxist philosophy in this sense was downgraded in its Marxist-Leninist incarnation to a "scientific-philosophical theory of materialism" with science being the dominant term.[32]

Though undoubtedly compelling for the wide scope and power of its explanation, the adoption of the idea that dialectical logic is the key to the scientific understanding of the natural and social world posed problems for the party not only at the level of scientific practice but also at the level of epistemology and political practice. For, while the Comintern and the PCF wished to maintain a quasi-positivist approach to science that held that empirical facts could be understood by the discovery of the dialectical logic which explained their appearances, it was also the case that this was a privileged access. Thus unlike "true" positivists who maintain that a world of facts exists independently of our minds that, if studied scientifically, can be known by anybody as the objective manifestations of tendencies or laws, the Communists wished to argue that (1) all laws would be found to be dialectical and (2) that these tendencies could only be understood as such by those whose social and historical backgrounds granted them this privileged access. In the 1940s and 1950s this position would have dire and absurd consequences for the physical sciences. However, it also had immediate and deleterious effects on party constitution, direction, and political success in the mid-1920s to mid-1930s for it is the case that Front Unique and *classe contre classe* policies represented the practical implementation of these hypotheses.

The idea that members of the working class have an epistemic advantage over the bourgeoisie and the middle class is one that Marx and Engels first posit explicitly in *The German Ideology* (1845-1846). As they describe the historical progression of the capitalist mode of production, one of its effects is the creation of a class—the proletariat—who because of its relation to the production of material goods is unable to see itself as composed of free, creative individuals. Those who benefit from the workers' toil and have the leisure to "choose" their lifestyle are, however, able to maintain the illusion that they are self-directing agents as they acquire property, vote, marry, run for office, and write philosophy.[33] Though the bourgeoisie and its representative politicians, intellectuals, and teachers believe and proclaim that every man is free and autonomous, the practical experience of the worker belies this claim. Because of the nature of their work, because of their class situation, the worker is able to see beyond the self-supporting and illusory claims of bourgeois ideology. The workers may, for instance, be able to recognize and describe the fundamental structure of exploitation upon which the economic system that enchains and impoverishes them is based. Seeing this pattern, they may also be able to picture the conditions for a world in which they are no longer alienated from that which they produce. In this scenario, the position of the workers would allowed them to understand the world as it is and to change it to what it can be. Though this theory of the epistemic privilege of the working class undergoes modifications (chief among them being the substitution of the concept of "fetishism" for those of "alienation" and "ideology"), it is a consistent feature of Marx's philosophy and is a prominent theme in Engels's major works *Anti-Dühring* and *Ludwig Feuerbach and the End of Classical German Philosophy.*[34]

Despite the attention that Marx and Engels devote in *The German Ideology* to documenting how workers are that class which can best understand the necessity of a revolution, this epistemic advantage is not shown to be the exclusive province of the working class. Instead, the German philosopher and the English factory owner maintain that it is possible for classes other than the proletariat to come to the "consciousness of the necessity of a fundamental revolution" given sufficient "contemplation of this [working] class."[35] This epistemological loophole is stated even more strongly in the *Manifesto*, where Marx and Engels write that, in times of crisis, sympathetic bourgeois ideologists may "have raised themselves to the level of comprehending theoretically the historical movement as a whole."[36] In later works, Marx does not state this position so explicitly nor so strongly but, given the fact that *Capital* was conceived as a project designed to provide such an understanding of the whole historical movement of capitalism and that it was written by a man who cared about finding proper marriages for his daughters and retaining his servants despite penury, it can be assumed that the position is a consistent one.[37]

Though Marx was consistent in maintaining that ideology does not constitute an epistemological prison, Engels in later works like *Anti-Dühring* and *Ludwig Feuerbach* does indicate that true knowledge is dependent upon class position. For example, in the chapter on Dialectical Materialism from *Anti-Dühring*, Engels gestures to the fact that the hope for the implementation of "scientific socialism" lies exclusively and substantially with the proletariat and its organic knowledge when he states that:

> the conflict between productive forces and modes of production is not a conflict engendered in the mind of man. . . . It exists, in fact, objectively, outside us, independently of the will and actions of the men that have brought it on. Modern Socialism is nothing but the reflex, in thought, of this conflict in fact; its ideal reflection in the minds, *first, of the class directly suffering under it, the working class.*[38]

Although Engels at other times and in other writings is less insistent on the exclusive epistemological privilege of the working class and the corresponding epistemological barriers faced by the bourgeoisie, he was read by most Marxist-Leninists as the last word on these theoretical matters. Certainly it is Engels' "scientific socialism" that informed Lenin's own understanding of the relation between class and knowledge.

Following Engels then, Lenin was not nearly so charitable as Marx in his estimation of the members of the dominant class and their ability to understand the historical totality or to aid and direct the revolution. As his epistemology is developed in works like *Materialism and Empiriocriticism* (1908) and as this theory of knowledge is formalized by Stalin in works like *Problems of Leninism* and *Foundations of Leninism*, a rigid distinction is made between those who can see the world as it is and those who see the world through a cloud of ideology. This epistemological distinction is the result of a class division; unlike the working class, the bourgeoisie is condemned to see the world only from its own perspective and to take this perspective as representing universal truth. To them their particular morality is universal morality and their science is universal science.

Attacking this position as it is represented in 1906 by neo-Kantian positivists like Ernst Mach, Lenin takes pains (1,300 pages in *Materialism and Empiriocriticism*) to argue that, in every instance, that which is said to constitute knowledge for the bourgeois philosopher is merely subjective ideology that mistakes itself for universal truth. Fitting this pattern, Mach (following Kant) argues that the world as it is cannot be known and that only sensations organized by the mind constitute knowledge. Just like all idealists, Lenin argues that Mach and other neo-Kantians privilege the structure of thought over the abundant evidence of the primacy of the material, even going so far as to deny the knowability of the material world apart from the mind.[39]

In contradistinction to the idealist position represented, however cryptically, by Mach's philosophy of science, Lenin states that the consistent materialist recognizes the primacy of the material in all aspects of cognition. In this sense, thought is understood to be a natural phenomenon, the result of the evolutionary and material development of the mind.[40] As a material sublimate, thought "reflects" the real, material world-as-it-is because this is what it has evolved to do.[41] The fact that Mach argues the contrary position (that thought organizes the world) shows that the Austrian thinker is part of the long tradition of idealist philosophers who mistake their thought about the world for the world itself. The "universal knowledge" of idealist philosophers is, according to Lenin, illusory. Further, it is symptomatic of the thinking of a certain class: the bourgeoisie or those that have the leisure to entertain the dream that the world is only their conception of it and that its structures mirror the structures of their own mind.[42]

Victims of this conception, the working class and the social revolutionary do not have the luxury of illusion. Lenin argues that they "see" the world objectively because their subject positions have produced them as persons capable of recognizing the materialist basis of knowledge. This does not mean that every person who punches a time clock is a materialist scientist but that, like the materialist scientist, the worker recognizes the power of the external world that is arrayed against him and doubts neither its efficacy nor his representation of it. After all, its effects are felt by him every day. What's more, because the worker is aware that he himself is in the process of a historical transformation, the worker does not see this material world like the mechanist scientist, as inert, nor like the idealist philosopher, as the product of thought. Instead, he sees the material world as undergoing a process of transformation. Though this process is most apparent to the worker at the political and ideological level, the logic of his thought is conceptually identical to and reflects the movement found at the level of the material.

Undoubtedly, the above discussion of Lenin's theory of knowledge misses many of its subtleties. However, it does not miss this epistemology's most important distinction, the one that Lenin says he got from Engels, and that Stalin then formalized and simplified. This is the assertion that the world is increasingly divided into two groups of people. On the one side are the workers; they are the people who are able to see that the world develops dialectically and that they and it are the result of material processes. On the other side are the bourgeoisie; they are the people who cling to the illusion that history and the world are the result of ideas.

Applying the overarching theory of Marxism-Leninism that all is governed by the logic of the dialectic to this distinction, one arrives at the conclusion that the world must be understood as a battle between those who know this truth and assert it in their practice and those who resist this truth because its acceptance would mean the dissolution of their illusions and of the institutions that perpetuate them. To the consistent Marxist-Leninist, the world is thus cast as a battle between those who have knowledge (the Communist Party and the workers who compose it) and those who do not (the bourgeoisie or those who labor under bourgeois illusions). The victory of history and of truth, then, would be a revolution in which those who understand the world better are those who direct it politically and economically. In other words, a successful revolution could only mean the installation of a dictatorship of the proletariat.

For the Comintern and for the PCF carrying out the Comintern's directives in France, Marxist-Leninist epistemology, philosophy of science, and its understanding of the dialectic provided sufficient justification during the late 1920s and early 1930s for the pursuit of its *classe contre classe* policy and for its embrace of the "two worlds" distinction.[43] Simply put, the Comintern and the PCF leadership believed that the historical development of capitalism had produced a class that understood the world better than did the bourgeoisie. Having discovered the "formula for revolution," these natural cultural critics believed that they could and would prove the worth of this theory through revolutionary practice.

The philosophical justification for *classe contre classe* policy does not sound that different from classical Marxist theory or even from orthodox or mechanist versions of Marxism. However, whereas classical Marxist theory would leave room for non-workers to understand Marxist theory and to participate in the revolutionary movement, the rigid epistemological distinction that Stalinist Marxism makes between workers and bourgeoisie demands the exclusion of non-workers from the party because it is impossible for them to truly understand revolutionary theory. Even if they profess sympathy for the worker's plight, the bourgeoisie must always be suspected of working in the interests of their own class. As for the problem of actual workers who should but, in fact, do not share the same perspective as the party on the correct path to revolution, they must either be educated to understand their own best interests or, as "labor parasites" and "socialist opportunists," must be excluded from the party. That they deviate from party orthodoxy is proof enough that they harbor bourgeois illusions.

As Stalinism resembles classical Marxism in terms of its epistemological privileging of the working class, it likewise resembles orthodox Marxism in its claim that workers—pushed by economic circumstance—will eventually realize their oppression and will strive to end it through a revolutionary movement. However, it differs in that—unlike the orthodox position—Leninist theorists believe that, though this realization may be "spontaneous," the workers themselves will never be in a position to effectively battle against the arrayed and entrenched forces of capital without the political organization provided by a central body dictating their actions. It is the combination of these two dogmas that differentiates this theory from classical and orthodox Marxisms and that yields the strange mixture of voluntarism and determinism that characterizes Leninist philosophy. For the Leninist, history inevitably produces a class of people that understands the necessity of the revolution: the workers. Despite this inevitability, the workers themselves are easily swayed by such counterrevolutionary tendencies as socialism and syndicalism. Without the help of a central organizing body managing and directing them, they are unable to sufficiently articulate this theoretical necessity themselves or to enact a revolution.

According to Marxist-Leninist theory, the communist party is the only party that fulfills this need for a directing agent. It is the only party that can do so because it corresponds to the actual (as opposed to illusory) interest of the working classes. It is, *sans pareil,* the party of the working class because it is the only political party that is composed exclusively of members of the working class and comprehends the working class' true interests. Given this conclusion, even if most actual members of the working class continue to labor under the spontaneous illusion that socialism or syndicalism present the best option for the improvement of their lot (and in France in the mid-1920s to early 1930s this was indeed the case), the PCF could still claim to be the only legitimate party of the working class and to assert that only it knew how to prepare the path for revolution. The party could claim this because—unlike every other Left party—it embodied no contradictory tendencies. Unlike the Socialists, for instance, it did not ask that revolutionary goals be met through the reform of state institutions. The party strove to be a pure instantiation of one side of the class struggle. This purity was supposed to assure revolutionary potency, unity of direction, and, finally, infallibility. As one PCF educational pamphlet of the era put it, "on ne peut pas dire qu'à chaque classe correspond exactement un parti. Exception: *le parti communiste, lui, est l'avant-garde revolutionnaire du proletariat,*"[44] [one cannot say that for each class there exactly corresponds a political party. The exception: *the Communist Party which is the revolutionary avant-garde of the proletariat.*]

From the Front Populaire to the *Précis*: 1934-1945

By 1933, the theory-driven policies of the PCF had relegated the party almost to the status of a queer and ineffectual cult. If it were not for the rise of another political cult in the early 1930s, there was a good chance that the PCF would have remained a marginal player in French politics or that it might have disappeared altogether. However, the rise of fascism combined with the economic crisis that precipitated this ascent allowed the PCF to once again come to public prominence, to effect national policy, and to be optimistic that a revolution was imminent.

While a curse to both the French working and middle classes, the world economic slump that hit France in the early 1930s was a boon to the French Communist Party. Accompanied by rampant inflation, drastic wage reductions, massive unemployment, and the near collapse of the *Bourse*, but also by an increase in the profits of monopoly industries,[45] the depression seemed to be exactly the "world crisis of capital" that the Communists had been predicting in their literature since the Congress of Tours. After the long and self-imposed isolation resulting from its *classe contre classe* policy, the PCF was both eager and prepared to take advantage of this coincidence. Though its relations with the mass of workers and with the unions like the C.G.T. and the C.G.T.U. that represented them were still characterized by acrimony, it began to reach out to the broader French population radicalized by economic hardship.

At first, the PCF engaged in this outreach not by moderating its positions but with a propaganda program designed to make the populace see that its positions were the only ones that made sense of the crisis. Thus it took pains to publicize the fact that not only was it the sole party that had foreseen the economic crisis but that it was the only organization offering a real solution to it. The Socialists, it made clear, were caught in a trap. Desiring only to restabilize capitalism in the hopes that socialism could then be peacefully implemented, the SFIO was attempting to restabilize the very institutions which had and always would precipitate such crises. By way of contrast, the PCF pointed out that, just as it knew that the economic crisis would occur, so also did it know that the only solution to this crisis and to the cycle of recurrent crises was a revolutionary one: the expropriation of the expropriators and the foundation of a communist state. As proof of this contention it offered the Soviet Union, a state where there existed no crisis because the economy was directed not by the greed of the monopoly capitalists but by the needs of the masses.[46]

No doubt, the PCF's overtures to the broader French political community in the early 1930s were quite crude (basically, the PCF made a small effort to connect its program to the domestic French political situation). However, for a party whose policies had previously been so divisive, this was at least a first step and it had the effect of attracting people to a French Communist Party that in 1932 was in danger of disappearing. The chief factor though in the renaissance of the PCF was the rise of fascism and the leadership role that the party took in French politics in response to this domestic and international threat.

In the late 1920s and early 1930s, the PCF was cognizant of the up-surge of fascism both in France and abroad. However, still pursuing its Front Uni policy, which held that only it was truly revolutionary and that everybody else was a representative of the capitalist status quo, the party was quick to lump together genuine fascist movements such as the Ligue d'Action Française and the Croix de Feu with mainstream conservative and even leftist political groups. Often in this regard it singled out for its most caustic treatment the socialists, whom it labeled "social fascists" for their social democratic positions.[47]

Even with the events that took place in Germany and Italy in 1933 and 1934 and despite the domestic violence associated with native fascist groups (both of which demonstrated that fascism had distinctly differen-tiated itself from other political philosophies), the PCF maintained its position throughout 1933 that fascism was merely a facet of the capitalist system and that all political groups which supported the capitalist system were, in some sense, fascistic.[48] Analyzed according to this dichotomy, anybody who was not a communist was de facto fascistic: the difference between the Socialist minister casting votes in parliament and the street thug casting stones at windows was just a matter of degree and of habit.

By February 1934, however, events both domestic and international conspired to change the PCF's position on this matter. These were the recognition on the part of the Soviets of the German threat[49] and the coming to prominence of domestic fascist leagues in France. From this time, the PCF liberalized its policies such that it was willing to entertain and to pursue alliances with the broader Left. In turn, this opening up provided for a renaissance of the PCF that resulted in an increase in its membership and support. For the first time, it also allowed the party to play a major role in French politics. In addition, the PCF again had rea-son to think that—if it played its cards right—a potentially revolutionary situation could be created.[50]

Though the real threat that domestic fascist groups represented to the French government is subject to debate, the effect on the French Left of the attempted coup on the Chamber of Deputies by various fascist leagues on February 6, 1934 is not so controversial.[51] While the coup failed, it succeeded in mobilizing the broad French Left against this threat and in inspiring them to work together against it.[52] Originally, this unity took the form of mass anti-fascist demonstrations called for by the PCF but attended by a wide cross-section of the French Left.

When a short time after these mass demonstrations the PCF's "spontaneous" movement toward joint action was seconded by the Comintern, the PCF began to aggressively pursue a policy of *"unité d'action"* with "socialist workers" and other political groups such as the Radicals. Concomitant with this change, the slippery term "Front Uni," which had previously been used by the party to indicate the concepts and policies of democratic centralism and *classe contre classe* tactics, now was changed to signify the "united front" of various leftist political groups against fascism.[53]

As with almost every policy shift by the PCF, there has been much debate in relevant literature about the role that the Comintern and the Soviets played in this policy change. Recent research making use of Soviet archives has shown that the Soviets indeed played a large role in dictating this change even if the PCF and Comintern were not always on the same page.[54] However, there is no doubt that—at this particular juncture—the interests of the PCF and those of the Comintern were complementary and that little coercion was needed to compel policy changes. Further, there is abundant evidence that by early 1934 the Comintern had come to see fascism as a movement and German fascism in particular as a threat to the Soviets in a way it had not recognized at the time of the signing of the German/Soviet nonaggression pact in 1933. It would therefore make sense that the Comintern would desire the coalition of Left parties in Europe against fascism and would support the signing of the Franco-Soviet pact in 1935. It also seems to be the case that the motivation for coalition had abundant domestic justification and would interest the French Communist Party for a number of reasons. Chief among these justifications is certainly the perceived threat that fascism represented. But also, and perhaps more importantly, there is the dire economic situation encouraging such unified activity. Providing yet more motivation was the opportunity on the part of the PCF to reintegrate and involve itself politically at a time when, due to the economic crisis, it might have some effect and when it could dust off its old "antiwar" tropes. These actions would have been particularly appealing to a PCF that after years of *classe contre classe* policies had grown tired of its self-imposed isolation.[55]

Upon its signing of the *Unité d'action* pact with the Socialists in 1934 and with the expansion of this coalition under the banner of the Front Populaire to include the Radicals and other sympathetic antifascists, the Communist Party understandably needed to affect some liberalizations if it wanted to maintain this alliance. Despite this need, the Bolshevist habit of dividing the world into two competing spheres was not abandoned. However, the complexion of these two spheres was revised. No longer did the PCF split the world into the Communist Party versus everybody else. Now the world was understood to be animated by the conflict between fascist monopolists and all those resisting this oppressive minority and fighting for the good of humanity. In conjunction with this revision, the PCF put on the back burner some of its conclusions about the inherent correctness of its theoretical positions and the historical mandate of its organization to lead the workers' revolution.

Of course, if the PCF was to participate with unions in the organization of strikes and if unionists were to reciprocally support it in elections, it was also the case that these reforms were practical necessities. And support it did find. Capitalizing on the leadership position that the party had taken in initiating the alliance against fascism, the PCF was able to attract members to its ranks and voters to its side in a way that it had not done since the end of the Great War. While in 1932 its membership stood at 30,000 and it could only muster 800,000 votes, by 1936 party membership had risen almost tenfold and it was able to command 1.5 million votes in the parliamentary elections of that year. This strong showing increased the PCF's seats in parliament from 12 to 72 and gave the Left a majority in the Chamber with the Communists controlling a large percentage of the Left vote.[56]

Despite this newfound strength, the PCF declined the postelection offer by Prime Minister Léon Blum to join the government in any ministerial capacity. Instead, the party created for itself the informal position of the *"ministère des masses."* Basically, this post was that of policy advisor to the government. The nonparticipatory stance allowed the PCF to suggest reforms such as the Matignon agreements while not implicating it in a bourgeois government.[57] Though this refusal to actively participate in the government was later regretted by the party, it had the advantages of being consistent with its position as a "revolutionary party" and of protecting the Communists from the political fallout associated with unpopular decisions or those inconsistent with their core philosophy.[58]

As part of its new ecumenicalism and liberalization, the party welcomed affiliation and joint action not only with Radicals and Socialists but also with those with whom its previous class puritanism had precluded any possibility of solidarity. These groups included the Left-Catholic community whose opium addiction was previously a problem as

well as that class whose genetic handicap had earlier gotten them expelled from the party, namely, sympathetic intellectuals. To both of these
groups, the party offered "*La Main Tendue*," [The Outstretched Hand.]
With this gesture, it asked for these groups' political support and, in the
case of intellectuals, for their theoretical support as well.[59] In return and
to allow for the success of this extension, the party made a point of re-
laxing some of its own theoretical conclusions.

Perhaps as a direct nod to the Catholics, the party also toned down its
rhetoric with regard to the class struggle. No longer did it present its goal
as the revolutionary overthrow of capitalism by the working class (a
revolution in which it was clearly stated that the masses, not men, made
history). Now, the Communists identified their struggle as a humanist
campaign, one that focused on the liberation and happiness of the individual through the overcoming of his alienation. As party leader Maurice
Thorez wrote in his auto-hagiography *Le Fils du peuple* (1937):

> Le communisme, c'est la lutte pour l'homme libre et heureux.
> Loin de vouloir détruire la grandeur humaine, le communisme
> lié à la vie veut l'asseoir sur des bases vraies, réelles, il veut
> créer les conditions nécessaires à l'épanouissement de toutes
> les facultés humaines, le communisme est un véritable hu-
> manisme.[60]

> [Communism is the struggle for man's freedom and happiness.
> Far from wanting to destroy the greatness of humanity, com-
> munism, bound to life, wants to establish humanity on its real
> and true foundations, it wants to create the necessary condi-
> tions for the blossoming of every human faculty, communism
> is a veritable humanism.]

Though this sentiment was probably genuine on the semi-intellectual and
semi-idealist Thorez's part,[61] humanism does not really gibe with a
Marxist-Leninist philosophy that, following Marx's rejection of Feuerbach, is hostile to the sort of philosophical anthropology that sees the
process of history ending with the restoration of human beings to a non-
alienated state.[62] However, this revision of the Marxist-Leninist line was
consistent with the values of the Front Populaire and probably did much
to win over Catholics and intellectuals, types sympathetic to the notion of
ending man's alienation from worlds both immanent and absolute.

As for those intellectuals and specifically those philosophers that the
newly liberalized party attracted, they themselves can be divided into

two groups. On the one hand, there are those who joined the party and who supported its political positions but whose research was not drastically affected by their associations with the party. Included among this group would be the Marxist philosophers Henri Lefebvre and Norbert Guterman, philosophers who thought of themselves as communists but who were more concerned with Marxism than with Marxism-Leninism. These philosophers will be discussed in the next chapter on Intellectual Marxism.

On the other hand, the party also attracted some philosophers who embraced the Marxist-Leninist philosophy of the PCF. These folks were, in turn, embraced by a party that published their books and encouraged them to teach in party schools. Unlike the crude pedagogic texts produced during the Front Uni, philosophers like René Maublanc and Georges Politzer produced works for the party that evidenced a detailed understanding of the history of philosophy and a sophisticated take on the role and meaning of the dialectic. Though they often came to exactly the same conclusions as Stalin did in his *Foundations of Leninism* about the universal application of the dialectic, the fundamental nature of the class struggle, and the role of the Communist Party in the revolution, they at least were able to justify these conclusions with an argument that made explicit the link between theory and practice and which showed both the differences and the similarities between Marxist and pre-Marxist philosophies. For instance, a text of Maublanc's written for the party's École de Contre-Enseignement does a particularly good job of describing the difference between Dialectical Materialism and classical mechanical materialism, taking the time to show how mechanist causal explanations are incapable of dealing with supervenience.[63] Though less nuanced and dogmatically Leninist, the writings of Politzer also show a greater understanding of the philosophical position which a Marxist orientation entailed than did previous party efforts in this direction.[64]

Despite the publication of works like those by Lefebvre and Guterman that really expanded the theoretical possibilities of French Marxism and those by Maublanc and Politzer which deepened and substantiated Leninist philosophy, the long-term effects of the PCF's welcoming gesture toward intellectuals were not profound. When with the August 1939 signing of the Molotov-Ribbentrop pact the Comintern and the French Communist Party decisively shifted away from Front Populaire policies, those philosophers and the wider public attracted to the party again fled it in droves. In general, they did so because—not being die-hard democratic centralists—they could not stomach the abrupt about face of a party that in the span of a few short months had gone from vilifying the German fascists to applauding the signing of nonaggression treaties with them. That this treaty seemed to sacrifice France to the Germans made the reversal all the worse.

These reasons alone were sufficient for philosophers attracted to the Communist Party during the Front Populaire to flee it. However, if they needed another one, they got it with the party's 1939 publication of Stalin's *History of the Bolshevik Communist Party of the Soviet Union (Short Course)*. Known in France as the *Précis*, this book contained a chapter titled "Dialectical and Historical Materialism" that contained Stalin's formulation of the essentials of Marxist philosophy. With a celebratory conference dedicated to the publication of the *Précis*, the French party made it clear to wayward intellectuals that they especially would profit from reading the text.[65] In addition, the PCF took great pains to broadcast the fact that this essay constituted not only the final word on Marxist philosophy but also on the social and physical sciences. Though the party made it clear that it would welcome the prestige that the support of prominent intellectuals afforded it, the party also made explicit that intellectuals would not be needed for theoretical work as this had already been accomplished by Stalin.

As the party signaled a return to the dogmatism of the *classe contre classe* era, intellectuals who could no longer see themselves in the party and who failed to appreciate Stalin's contribution to Marxist philosophy severed their alliances with it. However, the core of the party, its leadership, and its permanent membership embraced the text. After all, educated in party schools and acquainted with the philosophical principles articulated in Front Uni pamphlets, the ideas contained in "Dialectical and Historical Materialism" were really not that foreign. For its part and to such minds, Stalin's prose seemed to offer a marvelous distillation of Leninist philosophy. As party philosopher Georges Cogniot wrote about the text, the reader of "Dialectical and Historical Materialism" will find:

> exemples qui illustrent à merveille la façon d'appliquer la théorie génerale, la méthode du matérialisme marxiste, aux phénomènes de la vie sociale. Loin de la rendre plus difficile, tout ces paragraphes théorique rend donc plus facile l'assimilation de *l'Histoire du parti bolchévik*.[66]

[examples which marvelously illustrate the application of the general theory, the method of Marxist materialism, to the phenomena of social life. Far from making it more difficult, all the theoretical paragraphs make it easier to assimilate *The History of the Bolshevik Party*.]

Cogniot is partially correct in his assessment of Stalin's text. In fact, despite the text's notorious reputation, Stalin does a remarkable job of conveying the essential features of Marxist-Leninist philosophy in a few short pages. However, his formulation of the dialectical method and his application of this philosophy, especially to the "science of history," leave much to be desired. As Michael Kelly notes of the work, "the dialectical method, developed to grasp a shifting and complex reality, comes to resemble a blunt instrument in Stalin's hands. That which in Marx and Engels was a supple and responsive guide to inquiry becomes a rigid and imperious set of rules."[67]

To be sure, the rules formalized in the *Précis* were already well established in Stalin's earlier writings of the 1920s and it was these rules that had found their expression in Front Uni policies. The *Short Course*, however, made clear Stalin's understanding of the relationship between dialectical method and materialist philosophy in a way that progressively closed off many avenues for the interpretation of Marx and, consequently, for communist political practice. This clarification also solidified and reinforced thinking about the political and epistemological status of the party. Basically, what the *Short Course* did was to make explicit a split that was latent in Stalin's earlier work. This distinction is the one between Dialectical Materialism (or Marx's philosophy) and the science of Historical Materialism.

The separation between Dialectical Materialism and Historical Materialism is not total. Stalin does maintain in his chapter on Marxist philosophy from the *Précis* that the science of Historical Materialism is allowed by an "extension of the principles of dialectical materialism to the study of social life."[68] However, there is abundant textual evidence that what Stalin thinks the philosophy of Marxism to be is not the subtle critical tool which Marx and Engels developed but an explanatory method that can be applied to any phenomena, social or natural. He therefore offers a very schematic and truncated version of Marxist philosophy in the form of a simple formula. What this formula or "dialectical method" boils down to is this: both natural and cultural history consists of the inevitable development through "contradiction" or "struggle" of new and progressively more complex structures that are qualitatively different than their predecessors.[69] This is Stalin's "Law of development" and it is that principle which he identifies as the essential aspect of Dialectical Materialism.[70]

The epistemological problems that bothered Lenin about how the Communist Party could be sure that the course of action it chose was the correct one are in the *Précis* totally resolved. As Stalin writes: "Marxist philosophical materialism holds that the world and its laws are fully knowable, that our knowledge of the laws of nature, tested by experiment and practice, is authentic knowledge having the validity of objective truth."[71] Given this fact, once the party understands the world as the manifestation of dialectical laws, then it can be certain that its knowledge—once tested in practice—is authentic.

Of course, there is the problem with this theory of those who would deny the fact that the world is knowable as the manifestation of dialectical laws. One might, for instance, believe that the rise of Nazism was due to deep tendencies in the German character and not to the growth of the "most reactionary, most chauvinist, most imperialist elements of finance capital."[72] However, the Stalinist formulation of Marxism-Leninism would maintain that one's belief in this instance was erroneous and is due to the fact the one who holds such an idea is: "the representative of moribund forces of society."[73] Of course, given Stalin's theory of infrastructure and superstructure in which the former is identified as solely determinative of the latter, those who hold the opposite idea are likewise representatives of a specific economic determination.[74] As representatives of "new and advanced" ideas, however, these people can critique the mistaken beliefs of the moribund because they themselves are the products of a dialectical development. As representatives of the working class engaged in the struggle against the ossified ideas and institutions of capitalism, members of the proletariat (and its representative, the party) are able to recognize and understand parallel transitions in the world.[75]

This ability to correctly interpret the world on the part of the proletariat and its party holds for phenomena both natural and cultural. Stalin takes pains in the *Short Course* to demonstrate this fact by repeating examples given by Engels in the *Dialectics of Nature* about the way in which natural processes like the freezing of water and the process of biological evolution can only be understood as the result of slow quantitative changes which have resulted in rapid and total qualitative changes.[76] By an argument that a less than charitable reader might characterize as unwarranted analogy, Stalin then extends this insight to maintain that the processes of nature are logically identical to those of culture. As he writes:

> If the connection between the phenomena of nature and their interdependence are laws of development of nature, it follows, too, that the connection and interdependence of the phenomena of social life are laws of the development of society.[77]

With this transition between natural and sociohistorical phenomena made, Stalin is then able to claim that, just as the philosophy of Dialectical Materialism allows us to understand and direct the processes of nature, it also allows those who recognize those laws to direct the processes of society. This is not described as intuitive knowledge but as a sort of practical wisdom: given sufficient observation of phenomena, the party should be able to arrive at "an advanced theory which *correctly reflects* the needs of development of the material life of society." The party that does this can thus "elevate theory to a proper level" and "utilize every ounce of the mobilizing, organizing, and transforming power of this theory."[78]

With the *Short Course*, the French Communist Party found its primer to teach the algebra of revolution. By separating the philosophy of Dialectical Materialism from the science of Historical Materialism and, most importantly, by reducing the former to an easy prescription or method with universal application, the Comintern and the PCF had firmly cemented, at least for the next 15 years, some of its worst tendencies. These included the crude distinction between true communist knowledge and faulty bourgeois knowledge, the flawed philosophy of science and of history that went along with this distinction, and the economism associated with crude infrastructure/superstructure relationships. They had also solidified their self-identified status as the only legitimate party of the working class and Leninist revolution as the only method for achieving communist goals. For different reasons, World War II and its aftermath would allow the party to maintain these theoretical positions and to pursue the policies that this position entailed. However, with Krushchev's revelations at the CPSU's Twentieth Congress and after the 1956 Hungarian uprising, the PCF would again be in a position where its theory had effectively compromised the success of its political practice.

Notes

1. "Idéologie, direction et organisations homogènes (à l'occasion du pro-chain Congrès national de Paris)," *Cahiers du bolchevisme* (Nov. 28, 1924): 65-67. Anthologized in Louis Bodin and Nicole Racine, *Le parti communiste Français pendant l'entre-deux-guerres* (Paris: Presses de la Fondation Nationale des Sciences Politiques, 1982), 144-146.

2. The party's anti-imperialist actions in regards to the Rif Conflict in 1925 might be held as an exception to this generalization. However, even in this protest, the party's efforts to promote international strikes had little substantive results.

3. The Front Uni or Front Unique was the PCF's official guiding policy from 1923 until the Front Populaire. Inconsistently applied, it is hard to define but basically consisted of three positions that alternated in prominence according to exigencies and direction. The first, consistent with Bolshevization, emphasized ideological and organizational purity: a "united front." The second was a policy of interaction with the broader Left in order to win elections and enact reforms. In this sense, overtures and compromises with the Socialists (sometimes) and radicals (rarely) were presented as a "united front" of the Left. The third position was one of "exclusive leadership." In this guise of the "unique front," the PCF promoted its policies as the only correct ones for the French Left and derided those of the Socialists. For an extended discussion of the meaning and import of the terms Front Uni and Front Unique see Maxwell Adereth, *The French Communist Party: A Critical History (1920-1984): From Comintern to the Colours of France* (Manchester: Manchester University Press, 1984), 43.

4. Annie Kriegel, *Les Communistes Français dans leur premier demi-siécle: 1920-1970* (Paris: Seuil, 1985), 258.

5. David Caute, *Communism and the French Intellectuals: 1914-1960* (New York: Macmillan, 1964), 89.

6. Caute in *Communism and the French Intellectuals* (page 90) cites this epithet toward Souvarine from *L'Humanité*, July 15, 1924.

7. *Thèses directrices sur la tactique de l'internationale communiste dans la lutte pour la dictature du prolétariat* (Geneva: La Nouvelle Internationale, 1920/1921), 4.

8. These intellectuals included Henri Barbusse and Paul Vaillant-Couturier along with many others who were instrumental in the founding of the French Communist Party. See Caute, *Communism and the French Intellectuals*, 88-91.

9. *Six cours élémentaires d'éducation communiste* (Paris: Section d'Agitation-Propagande du P.C.F., 1928), 16-19.

10. Adereth, *The French Communist Party*, 48.

11. Adereth, *The French Communist Party*, 47.

12. Bodin and Racine, *Le parti communiste Français*, 99.

13. "La Lutte sur les deux fronts," *Cahiers de bolchevisme* (September 1930): 850. Anthologized in Racine and Bodin, *Le parti communiste Français*, 90.

14. As defined by Lenin in *State and Revolution*, opportunism is the belief that a communist revolution can be effected by the proletariat's taking over of the existing state apparatus by parliamentary or other means, thereby replacing "bourgeois democracy" with "proletarian democracy." Lenin argues that such a transition is impossible because proletarian democracy must be understood as something fundamentally different from bourgeois democracy and that the installation of the former requires the existence of new types of institutions, specifically revolutionary ones. See V. I. Lenin, "Chapter VI: The Vulgarization of Marxism by Opportunists," *The State and Revolution* (September 1917), 1993, 1999, www.marxists.org/archive/lenin/works/1917/sep/staterev/index.htm (accessed 31 July 2004).

15. For example, in May 1929, 4,000 communist militants were peremptorily arrested to prevent street demonstrations and in August most of the PCF leadership was arrested and charged with a plot against the security of the state. See Bodin and Racine, *Le parti communiste Français*, 97.

16. Ronald Tiersky, *French Communism 1920-1972* (New York and London: Columbia University Press, 1974), 36, and Bodin and Racine, *Le parti communiste Français*, 97.

17. This insistence also resulted in false pedigrees by party leaders to substantiate their class background. One was Maurice Thorez's claim in his autobiography *Fils du peuple* that he was a miner.

18. Kivisaari, Marja. "The Decline of the French Communist Party: The Party Education System as a Brake to Change, 1945-90," (Ph.d. diss., University of Portsmouth, 2000). Abstract in *Communist History Network Newslettter On-Line*, Issue 12 (Spring 2002), http://les1.man.ac.uk/chnn/CHNN12PCF.html (accessed August 1, 2004).

19. *Cahiers de bolchevisme*, no. 13 (February 15, 1925). Cited in: Kriegel, *Les Communistes français dans leur premier demi-siécle*, 249.

20. Michael Kelly, *Modern French Marxism* (Oxford: Blackwell Publishers, 1982), 21. See also George V. Plekhanov, *Fundamental Problems of Marxism* (New York: International Publishers, 1969).

21. For examples of other pedagogical materials that take the same position but address a variety of topics see *Les 21 conditions d'admission à l'international communiste* (Paris: PCF Bureau d'Editions, 1928); *La Position de l'I.C. devant la crise, la guerre et le fascisme* (Paris: PCF Bureau d'Editions, 1928); *and Le Chemin de l'internationale communiste: guide pour l'histoire de l'I. C.* (Paris: PCF Bureau d'Editions, 1928).

22. *Six cours élémentaires*, 13-15.

23. For instance, in this quotation from "The Three Sources and the Three Component Parts of Marxism" Lenin argues that: "The chaos and arbitrariness

that had previously reigned in the views on history and politics gave way [with Marx] to a strikingly integral and harmonious scientific theory, which shows how, in consequence of the growth of productive forces, out of one system of social life another and higher system develops—how capitalism for instance grows out of feudalism." See V. I. Lenin, "The Three Sources and Three Component Parts of Marxism," in *Collected Works*, Vol. 19 (Moscow: Progress Publishers, 1970), 25.

24. *Six cours élémentaires,* 13.

25. René Maublanc, "La Philosophie du marxisme et l'enseignement officiel," *Les Cahiers de Contre-Enseignement Prolétarien* No. 19 (July 1935): 32.

26. Indeed, his position on this seems to change over time and between different works. In some writings it is apparent that Marx believes that his philosophy is a type of comprehensive science or Hegelian *wissenschaft* that encompasses and explains all other sciences. In other works it seems like Marx is making claims only for Historical Materialism as a science among other sciences. Philosophy in certain passages seems to have been superseded or is no longer necessary.

27. Lucien Monod, *Éléments de philosophie marxiste* (Cannes: E. Cruvés, 1927), 37. This text consists of a series of 3 colloquia given at the École de Rayon de Cannes for "quelques camarades." It deals with Marxist philosophy and the method that it inaugurates. It is not explicitly published by the PCF but is aimed at workers and was probably written by a party member. It seems to be written by a committed communist academic who has a knowledge of the history of science and of logic but whose understanding of Marx, though philosophically richer than most party members', is consistent with Leninism both in its attempt to ground Marxism as a science and to cast materialism and the dialectical method as just a way to describe objects in their historical movement and development.

28. For examples of the Marxist dialectic's application to diverse sciences see Henri Wallon, *A la lumiére du Marxisme, essays,* 2 vols. (Paris: Éditions Sociales Internationales, 1935-1937). For Stalin's argument that language is not necessarily part of the superstructure nor beholden to the infrastructure but enjoys a sort of independent existence see Joseph Stalin, "Marxism and Linguisitics," in *The Essential Stalin: Major Theoretical Writings, 1905-52* (New York: Anchor Books, 1972), 407-39.

29. Karl Marx, *Capital: A New Abridgment,* ed. David McLellan (Oxford: Oxford University Press, 1995), 4, 10-11, 314; *The German Ideology* (London: International Publishers Company, 1989), 47, 58; and "Economic and Philosophical Manuscripts of 1844," as excerpted in *Karl Marx: Selected Writings,* ed. David McLellan (Oxford: Oxford University Press, 1977), 93.

30. Margaret Majumdar, *Althusser and the End of Leninism?* (London and East Haven, CT: Pluto Press, 1995), 74.

31. I am indebted here to Majumdar's discussion of Lenin's reading of Engels on science in *Althusser and the End of Leninism?*, 74-76.

32. Joseph Stalin, "Dialectical and Historical Materialism," in *The Essential Stalin: Major Theoretical Writings, 1905-52* (New York: Anchor Books, 1972), 301.

33. Karl Marx and Friedrich Engels, *The German Ideology* (New York: International Publishers, 1989), 53.

34. For a discussion of this difference and transition between the concepts of alienation, ideology, and fetishism see Étienne Balibar, *Philosophy of Marx* (New York and London: Verso, 1995), 74-76.

35. Marx and Engels, *The German Ideology*, p. 94. The complete quote is: "connected with [the historical development of the productive forces] . . . a class is called forth, which has to bear all the burdens of society without enjoying its advantages, which, ousted from society, is forced into the most decided antagonism to all other classes, . . . and from which emanates the consciousness of the necessity of a fundamental revolution, the communist consciousness, which may, of course, arise among other classes too through the contemplation of the situation of this class."

36. Karl Marx and Friedrich Engels, *The Communist Manifesto* (New York: International Publishers, 1948), 19.

37. Francis Wheen, *Karl Marx: A Life* (New York: Norton, 2000), 220-22.

38. Friedrich Engels, *Socialism: Utopian and Scientific* [2002] (Marx/Engels Internet Archive, 1993), www.marxists.org/archive/marx/works/1880/soc-utop/index.htm (accessed July 21, 2004). My emphasis.

39. Vladimir Lenin, *Materialism and Empiriocriticism* [1908] (Lenin Internet Archive, 1993), www.Marxists.org/archive/lenin/works/1908/mec/01.htm (accessed July 21, 2004).

40. Lenin, *Materialism and Empiriocriticism*. "Organic matter is a phenomenon, the fruit of a long evolution. Matter is primary, and thought, consciousness, sensation are products of a very high development. Such is the materialist theory of knowledge to which natural science instinctively subscribes."

41. Lenin, *Materialism and Empiriocriticism*. "Natural science leaves no room for doubt that its assertion that the earth existed prior to man is a truth. This is entirely compatible with the materialist theory of knowledge: the existence of the thing reflected independent of the reflector (the independence of the external world from the mind) is a fundamental tenet of materialism. This proposition of natural science is incompatible with the philosophy of the Machians and with their doctrine of truth: if the truth is an organizing form of human experience, then the assertion that the earth exists *outside* human experience cannot be true."

42. Thus in *Materialism and Empiriocriticism* Lenin takes pains to differentiate between bourgeois philosophers like Kant, Berkeley, and Hegel and

revolutionary, materialist philosophers like Spinoza, the French *Encyclopédistes,* and, of course, Marx.

43. Sophie Coeuré, *La Grande Lueur á l'Est: les Français et l'Union sovié-tique, 1917-1939* (Paris: Éditions du Seuil, 1999), 247-251.

44. *Six cours élémentaires,* 12. Emphasis in original.

45. Adereth, *The French Communist Party,* 58-59.

46. This argument is a paraphrase of the one given in *La Crise économique et les partis politiques,* #2 in the series published by the PCF Central Committee Agit-Prop: "Les Dossiers de l'Agitateur" (Paris: Éditions du PCF, April, 1932).

47. D. S. Bell and Byron Criddle, *The French Communist Party in the Fifth Republic* (Oxford: Clarendon Press, 1994), 69.

48. Yves Santamaria, *L'Enfant du malheur: le parti communiste Français dans la lutte pour la paix, 1914-1947* (Paris: S. Arslan, 2002), 198-201.

49. Stéphane Courtois and Marc Lazar, *Histoire du parti communiste Fran-çais* (Paris: PUF, 1995), 120-124.

50. Tiersky, *French Communism,* 72.

51. For a discussion of different historians' opinions about whether French fascist groups such as Action Française and Croix de Feu ever posed the same threat that similar groups did in Italy and Germany such that they would be ca-pable of a government takeover see Adereth, *The French Communist Party,* 70.

52. In this contention, both pro- and anti-communist historians are in agreement. See Tiersky, *French Communism,* 55; Adereth, *The French Commu-nist Party,* 68; and Bell and Criddle, *The French Communist Party in the Fifth Republic,* 60.

53. Bodin and Racine, *Le parti communiste Français,* 207.

54. Santamaria, *L'Enfant du malheur,* 190-222.

55. Maurice Thorez described this isolation as a *"vide,"* as an "emptiness" or "void." See Bodin and Racine, *Le parti communiste Français,* 209.

56. Adereth, *The French Communist Party,* 74-75. See also David Lowe and Neill Nugent, *The Left in France* (New York: St. Martin's Press, 1982), 32.

57. The Matignon agreements were the greatest legacy of the Front Popu-laire. They provided for a forty-hour week, paid vacations, the provisions for collective bargaining, and salary increases. Their effect is felt each time a French family takes to the road in August and each time an American tourist is stymied in her attempt to get into the Louvre or ride the Metro due to a strike.

58. It also allowed the PCF to fence sit. For instance, when the Spanish war broke out the PCF was able to urge intervention at the same time as it was aware that the government would not allow this aid. Thus it could appear to support the liberal cause against Fascism without committing French troops and without really upsetting the balance of power that the Comintern wanted to maintain in Spain. See Bodin and Racine, *Le parti communiste Français,* 211.

59. Caute, *Communism and the French Intellectuals,* 26.

60. Maurice Thorez, *Fils du Peuple, Oeuvres, Tome 14* (Paris: Éditions Sociales, 1937), 168.

61. Thorez fashioned himself as an autodidact and a man of culture. He read widely in literature and philosophy and it seems that his predilections were rather humanistic. This did not, however, stop him from enforcing Stalinist policy during the Cold War, policy which explicitly denied the concept of humanism. For pertinent information with regard to Thorez's personality see Kriegel, *Les Communistes français dans leur premier demi-siécle*, 211-21.

62. Stalin, "Dialectical and Historical Materialism," 301.

63. Maublanc, *La Philosophie du marxisme*, 28-35.

64. See for instance Georges Politzer, *Principes élémentaires de la philosophie* (Paris: Éditions Sociales, 1945). Based on a lecture course of 1935-1936, after Politzer's martyrdom by the Nazis in 1941, this volume became one of the party's standard introductory texts to Marxist-Leninist philosophy. One letter by Althusser from 1966 complains to a friend that he has repeatedly been asked the question why he persists in studying Marx's work when it has already been explained satisfactorily by Politzer.

65. Georges Cogniot, "'L'Histoire du parti bolchévik,' conférence faite par Georges Cogniot sur le *Précis* de 'l'Histoire du parti bolchevik de l'U.R.S.S.','" *Ce Que Nous Enseigne* (April 12, 1939), 27.

66. Cogniot, 'L'Histoire du parti bolchévik,' conférence, 26.

67. Kelly, *Modern French Marxism*, 40.

68. Stalin, "Dialectical and Historical Materialism," 300.

69. Stalin, "Dialectical and Historical Materialism," 305.

70. Stalin, "Dialectical and Historical Materialism," 307.

71. Stalin, "Dialectical and Historical Materialism," 311.

72. This is how Maurice Thorez defined fascism in an address to the eighth PCF Congress. See Tiersky, *French Communism,* 70.

73. Stalin, "Dialectical and Historical Materialism," 314.

74. Stalin, "Dialectical and Historical Materialism," 309.

75. In a postwar document covering this same epistemological terrain, party theorist Jean Desanti selectively quotes Lenin's *Materialism and Empiriocriticism* in support of this point, noting that: "'*la conscience humaine est en voie de développement*' et parce que la science réalise '*la concordance entre la conscience, reflétant la nature, et la nature reflétée par la conscience*,'" (emphasis is Desanti's and marks Lenin's words.) See Jean Desanti, "La science idéologie historiquement relative," in Laurent Casanova, Francis Cohen, Jean Desanti, Raymond Guyot, and Gerard Vassails, *Science bourgeoise et science prolétarienne* (Paris: Les Éditions de La Nouvelle Critique, 1950), 11.

76. Stalin, "Dialectical and Historical Materialism," 303-305.

77. Stalin, "Dialectical and Historical Materialism," 311.

78. Stalin, "Dialectical and Historical Materialism," 315. My emphasis

Chapter 4

French Intellectual Marxism, 1920-1945

French Intellectuals, Marxism, and the War

Though many prominent French intellectuals were associated with the founding of the French Communist Party, the majority of them were not concerned with the exploration of Marxism as a philosophical system. There are many reasons for this disinterest, some of which were explored in the last chapter and which include both the unavailability of Marx's texts and the general consensus that Marx was more political organizer and economist than philosopher.[1] Perhaps more responsible than these causes for the lack of Marxist scholarship is the fact that most of the intellectuals originally attracted to communism and to the party were drawn to the organization because they saw it as complementary to their moral positions on internationalism and pacifism. They were not drawn to it because they were intellectually persuaded by Marxist philosophy and believed the Communist party to be an instantiation of it. Thus while intellectuals at the Congress of Tours would rhetorically acknowledge certain tenets of Marxist philosophy, there is scant evidence of an understanding of Marx's thought beyond that provided by party theoretical statements or that which they had absorbed through osmosis from their association with French Socialist culture. For most of the intellectuals who joined or were active in the party during its early years, it is not even apparent that they wished to go beyond this crude understanding.[2] However, the way in which Bolshevism at first seemed to echo their internationalist and pacifist goals combined with its resemblance to traditional French revolutionary politics made it easy for many intellectuals to identify with the movement on an emotional if not conceptual basis.

Given that the first wave of French intellectuals associated with

Marxism in the postwar period owed this affinity more to political sympathy with Marxist goals than to intellectual engagement with Marx's thought and given that, for the most part, the prior sympathy did not lead to the latter engagement, it was left to the next generation of French intellectuals to take up a philosophical consideration of Marx based upon a reading of his original texts. This consideration of Marx as philosopher had the same original motivation (that of the aftermath of World War I) as that which animated the Tours intellectuals' affiliation with the Communist Party. However, this impetus manifested itself belatedly and in a different fashion, being more theoretical than political, more academic than activist, and beginning only in the late 1920s.

The aftermath of the Great War left the French people with the feeling that the claims to legitimacy enjoyed by prewar institutions were now not so tenable. The state, religion, family, economic, political, and philosophical systems were all put into question by the carnage and hardship that the war had exacted and for which these institutions seemed culpable. The French response to this loss of faith in the rational defensibility of prewar institutions was varied. Some groups like the SFIC and the syndicalists immediately and optimistically jumped into the revolutionary task of creating new institutions on new foundations. Yet others pursued drastic democratic reforms in political and cultural institutions. For their part, conservative elements sought to re-establish the legitimacy of that which the war had torn apart or even argued for a return to premodern institutions.[3] Having the leisure and inclination to do this type of thing, many postwar French intellectuals simply wallowed in what Paul Valéry labeled "*la crise de l'Esprit*,"[4] a depression precipitated by the feeling that those ideas that they had previously regarded as most stable had now been revealed as false. Rather than attempting to change the situation, for nearly two decades many intellectuals simply bemoaned and diagnosed it, authoring extended exegeses lamenting the fragmented character of postwar culture.[5]

At least as Valéry pictured the situation and as many intellectuals agreed with him on this point, the state of the postwar intellectual and cultural spirit was abysmal.[6] Having the traditional rational foundations of their culture eroded, intellectuals after the war sought solace and firm ground in "innumerable schools of thought: dogmas, heterogeneous idealist philosophies, three hundred ways of explaining the world, one thousand and one nuances of Christianity, two dozen from positivism."[7] According to Valéry, these individual quests would offer no solace for the intellectual infected by this *inquiétude*. For him and for many others, the possibility for certainty provided by common beliefs had been eroded by the war and would not be restored by quixotic explorations. The individual found himself unable to reconcile with culture. War had replaced certainty with uncertainty. A unified world had disappeared and a fragmented one had taken its place.

The Philosophies Group

Despite Valéry's general pessimism about the possibility of finding resolutions to the crisis of spirit that he diagnosed as a lingering symptom of the war, some of the quests undertaken by young thinkers and artists to explore new intellectual foundations did meet with some success. In art, the postwar work of Le Corbusier and the Surrealists comes to mind as two very different ways to unify fragmented experience, the former by recourse to "fundamental laws," the latter by an "aesthetic practice of reconstruction."[8] More important, though, for this study were those investigations begun in the mid-1920s by a group of young intellectuals associated with the series of journals *Philosophies*, *Esprit*, *La Revue Marxiste*, and *Avant-poste* who attempted to find philosophical solutions to the postwar mal du siècle. At first consisting of a rather loose aggregation of radical literary figures and students from the Sorbonne and the École Normale Supérieure, this group coalesced around the figures of the poet and editor Pierre Morhange, the writer Paul Nizan, the activist Georges Friedmann, and the philosophers Norbert Guterman, Georges Politzer, and Henri Lefebvre.[9] Though each made his own distinct contributions, the members of the Philosophies group were, like their contemporaries in the Institute for Social Research in Germany and that group centered around Lukács in Hungary, a Marxist philosophical school. The members considered their work collaborative and they believed that they were working on projects designed to first understand and then fundamentally to change the world.

Between the years 1924 and 1939 the Philosophies group worked on the modest project of discovering an Absolute foundation for moral philosophy, theology, and science and on the construction of a new conceptual and cultural order upon this bedrock.[10] Like their fellow Parisian intellectuals and sometime collaborators the Surrealists, this novel base was at first looked for in that which transcended the everyday and therefore could not be suspected of supporting the discredited cultural order. However, while the Surrealists searched for that which would destabilize all conventional order and found this agent in the unconscious and the irrational, the Philosophies group—being good philosophers—were more interested in re-establishing order on a stronger yet more rational foundation than the *raison éternelle* and *raison d'état* the war had discredited.

When the group first embarked on its project, they were convinced that they would locate this new, more fundamental base for the reconstruction of the world in individual mystical experience. Philosophers of presence, the group looked for that which transcended human reason and revealed an identity with the Absolute. As the group evolved, it began to realize that, while mysticism was perhaps capable of providing individuals with solace, it was incapable of establishing conceptual and moral foundations for the larger culture. After this recognition, the Philosophies group began to look for other philosophical resources to fulfill the needs of its project. Rejecting traditional French thought's emphasis on eternal reason as theoretically bankrupt, it turned in 1926 to the German Rationalists. The hope of the group was that this tradition would provide the tools to reconcile the individual, the community, and the Absolute in a way that a recourse to presence had not. A few years later, when the Philosophies' discovery that action was necessary for the realization of their project led them to political participation, these investigations into German Idealism steered them to the philosophy of Karl Marx. With Marx, most of the group believed that they had at last found a philosophy that could reconstruct the world.

Good self-publicists, each of these three phases in the Philosophies' development was accompanied by forums, manifestos, and the publication of a journal that signaled the change and advertised the group's new position to the wider intellectual community.[11] The first of these journals, the eponymous *Philosophies*, corresponds to the time between 1924 and 1926 when this cadre of *normaliens* and *sorbonnards* was heavily involved in the pursuit of revelatory solutions to the postwar spiritual crisis. *Esprit,* the second journal published by the Philosophies, appeared in the period between 1926 and 1928 when the group turned to Schelling and Hegel for inspiration and to provide a theoretical framework for their investigations. Finally, *La Revue Marxiste* and *Avant-poste* are associated with the period after 1929 when an intellectual exploration of the resources that Marxism offered for their individual and collaborative projects led to the consideration of Marx's, Lenin's, and Hegel's original philosophical texts and to the affiliation by many of the group's members with the PCF.

Though a consideration of the last two journals and the works that accompanied them is most important to providing an understanding of French Intellectual Marxism as it was formulated by the Philosophies group, it is also the case that this consideration will benefit by an analysis of those tendencies apparent in the earlier publications that subsequently inform and color the group's interpretation of Marx. This analysis will likewise profit from the situating of these texts in relation to those developments in French intellectual and political life that encouraged the group's progression from mysticism to Marxism. For these reasons, this chapter will first turn to a brief analysis of the projects initiated in the pages of *Philosophies* and *Esprit* before concentrating on the readings of Marx and Lenin undertaken during the period of publication of *La Revue Marxiste* and *Avant-poste* and up until World War II.

Mysticism and Revolution: The Journal *Philosophies*

Dominated by their editor Pierre Morhange, the first few issues of *Philosophies* were characterized by a messianic tone. In editorials written under the appropriate pseudonym of "John Brown," Morhange combined revolutionary exhortations with grand claims to the effect that the contributors to the journal were in the process of renewing French cultural and intellectual life.[12] Though slightly more outrageous in his expression of this spirit than other members of the group, it is apparent in their essays and reviews that fellow contributors Lefebvre, Politzer, and Guterman were, like Morhange, caught up in a type of postwar apocalyptic and revolutionary optimism.

Being mostly students and this not being 1968, the form this revolution took was not rioting in the streets but instead consisted of rather juvenile denunciations of the group members' philosophical masters in the academy. As represented by the neo-Kantian Brunschvicg and the anti-scientific intuitionist Bergson, these "philosophers of the established order" were taken to task by the journal and its contributors for the bankruptcy of their ideas and for the conservative conclusions to which these ideas led.[13] The review also made it clear that philosophical systems like Brunschvicg's and Bergson's were symptomatic of and responsible for the rotten and dying Europe which was their generation's postwar inheritance.[14] In contrast to these dead or dying ideas, notions that could no longer explain the world and that had led to its abasement, *Philosophies* emphasized the search for ultimate truth in solitary contemplation and mystical experience.[15] The experience of presence, of the Absolute, of that which was beyond the everyday held for them the promise of renewal and of a solution to their *inquiétude*.

Though at first more of a literary magazine with an abstruse bent than a philosophical journal, *Philosophies* over the span of its two-year run became increasingly involved in the pursuit of a theoretical solution to the crisis of spirit that its contributors were experiencing. Thus while after its first few issues the journal continued to publish poetry, reviews, and critiques of older philosophers, it also began to publish original essays by Lefebvre and Politzer, both of whom were attempting to develop their own alternatives to the "putrid systems" of their philosophical masters. Characteristic of these essays is Lefebvre's *"Critique de la qualité et de l'être,"* which appeared serially in the third and fourth issues of the journal in 1925. Representing a type of proto-existentialism and influenced by Nietzsche and also by those neo-Kantians whom Lefebvre wished to critique, this study argued that there exists an ontological separation in the individual between universal and finite elements and that this separation can only be reconciled by individual, self-conscious action.[16] In line with the mysticism of the group and the tenor of the times, he specified that this divorce between infinite and particular was the cause of the *inquiétude* that he and others of his generation were experiencing. Further, he argued that its solution could be found in "those certain privileged moments" when personal revelation disclosed "a reality knowable, definable, perceptible even to the heart or the mind."[17] Though Lefebvre would later offer a self-critique of this early work and existentialism in general as a *"métaphysique de la merde"* (metaphysics of shit),[18] these proto-existentialist essays pointed to the twin themes of action and the end of alienation that would figure prominently in his later work and in that of other group members.

Abandoning some but not all of the outrageous pretenses and mystical leanings characteristic of their student days and of their first journal, between 1926 and 1928 members of the Philosophies group sought to develop a consistent analytical framework within which they could anchor their search for ultimate meanings and universal values.[19] They did not, however, develop this framework from scratch. Instead, they found it already mostly articulated in the philosophical tradition of German rationalism whose synthetic vision appealed to their desire to reconcile the individual and the absolute.

The "final unity of mind and soul": *L'Esprit* and the Embrace of German Rationalism

Like their subsequent move to Marxist thought, the Philosophies' embrace of German philosophy in 1926 can be seen as both reactionary and inspired. There is little doubt that the German Idealist tradition appealed to the group because it was so derided by their masters at the Sorbonne and at the École Normale Supérieure. Under the influence of the neo-Kantians in general and Lefebvre's teacher Brunschvicg in particular, the French academy in the 1920s had made a point of explicitly abandoning post-Kantian German philosophy for its tendency to erase the gap between reason, reality, and history.[20] Heirs to the revolution and to the Enlightenment, this older generation of French philosophers believed that reason stood outside human culture and history and that it could serve as a guide for a culture's moral development. To the Philosophies, this hypostasis of reason was exactly the type of thinking that they believed had led to the Great War and whose tenability the war had shown to be tragically risible. An argument by demonstration, to these young philosophers the war had proven that morality and ideals were not timeless but cultural and historical. It was this thesis that they wanted to defend against the tradition of French Moral Idealism. However, they also wanted to go beyond critique and to posit an alternative conception of reason that acknowledged its timely origins but that still provided a firm moral foundation.

For almost the same reasons then that their philosophical masters had rejected German rationalism, the Philosophies group embraced it. They were interested in German Rationalism precisely for the emphasis it put on the relation between (or even identity of) culture and thought, between reason and reality, and, finally, between individual and social action. Inaugurated by the 1926 publication of Politzer's translation of Schelling's *Recherches philosophiques sur l'essence de la liberté humaine* to which Lefebvre provided the introduction, this turn to German Rationalism was characterized by the group's new emphasis on the dialectical production of thought through its interaction with the material and cultural world.[21] Fittingly, the journal consecrated to the announcement of this orientation toward German Rationalism was named *L'Esprit*.

Though not uncritical of the work, Lefebvre's introduction to *Recherches sur l'essence de la liberté humaine* indicates the promise

that he believes Schelling's philosophy in particular and German Rationalism in general seem to hold for providing a conceptual foundation for the Philosophies' revolutionary project. In particular, Lefebvre was thrilled by Schelling's rejection of the Kantian thesis that
identified thought exclusively with subjective consciousness. By locating thought not just in the subject but in the reciprocal interaction
between subject and object, Lefebvre argued that Schelling had gone a
long way toward indicating the way in which a new philosophy could
be anchored in the desiring subject's need to understand more and
more of the world (and, reciprocally, about himself).[22] Further,
though Schelling seemed to isolate and privilege individual consciousness, Lefebvre contended that the work was nonetheless valuable for
its preservation of contradiction and its emphasis on action as a necessary component in the production of thought.

    Though it is not obvious that he grasped the full sweep or inten-
tion of Schelling's argument, Morhange was even more enthusiastic in
his reception of Schelling's idiosyncratic work than was Lefebvre. Instead of merely seeing *La Liberté humaine* as a treatise on the relationship between thought and freedom, he saw in it an outline of a
formula for the "final unity of mind and soul through a total revolution that stripped away the variable, the individual and the false while
leaving the true and essential."[23]

    If not as fervent in his rhetoric as Morhange or as careful as Le-
febvre, Politzer was likewise inspired by Schelling's work on freedom.
This inspiration is evidenced in his introduction to the first volume of
L'Esprit from 1926. In this introduction, he argues that Schelling's
Idealism provides the philosophical framework to overcome the isolation—imposed since Descartes—of thought and existence. For Politzer, then, German Rationalism held out the possibility of restoring
man to himself and to his proper essence. In that this conclusion echoes Lefebvre's and Morhange's sentiments, such a claim would not be
remarkable but for the fact that Politzer went on in this introduction
to suggest that this isolation could be overcome not just theoretically
(as in Schelling's work) but practically by the elimination of the material constraints that denied man his true liberty. With these constraints gone, Politzer hypothesized, man could fully realize himself
in a realm that reflected back to him his essential freedom.[24] This acknowledgment of material constraints and the need for their elimination includes the first reference made by any member of the Philosophies group to Marxism. Though Politzer's formulation of the
relation between the material and thought is crude and is intended

only to buttress a Schellingian project focusing on the liberation of the human essence as the proper object of thought, it does signal the group's increasing openness to Marxist ideas.[25]

Despite Politzer's nods to Marxism and materialism and Lefebvre's lip service to action, the two were still in 1926 very much in the thrall of idealism and under the spell of reason and universal consciousness. In this, they shared the general conviction of the Philosophies group that "the essence of human existence lay in the realm of the mind and spirit" and that what was required to end their malaise, anchor philosophy, and enable revolution was the "direct, immediate comprehension of absolute knowledge."[26] Never an unlikely position for a group of young philosophers obsessed with ideas and culture, this conviction that humanity's problem was caused by a spiritual division between thought and reality which prevented man from realizing his true essence was reinforced and deepened when the group turned for inspiration from Schelling to his colleague G. W. F. Hegel.

Prior to the mid-1920s, French philosophers who dealt at all with Hegel had mostly utilized his logic to construct an anti-positivist philosophy of science. Most though had rejected his theory of history for its pan-logicism and for its perceived endorsement of Prussian cultural superiority.[27] Consistent, however, with a small movement in French philosophy that was trying to rehabilitate Hegel as a progressive philosopher, the Philosophies group eventually came to see Hegel as a philosopher of history involved with the problem of human freedom and action.[28] In this vein, the work of Hegel that truly resonated with the Philosophies was *The Phenomenology of Spirit*. Out of this work and particularly from the section on "unhappy consciousness" (a section translated by Jean Wahl and that appeared in the first issue of *L'Esprit*) they took the idea that not only was man on a spiritual quest to end his alienation, but that this quest was historical. Further, it was one which must be realized in and through the movement of culture. In many ways, this discovery of Hegel and, really, also of history was pivotal for the group. As Burkhard puts it, not only did "the absorption of Hegel . . . mark the end of their search for a rigorous theoretical guide . . . [but] . . . Hegel and Schelling became bridges by which the Philosophies approached Marx."[29]

From Hegel to Marx: *La Revue Marxiste* and *Avant-poste*

In one of his memoirs, Lefebvre writes that he came to Marx
through a reading of Hegel's *Science of Logic.*[30] Though this path of
affiliation with Marx through a deep reading of Hegel is reflected in
his writings, it is also certainly the case that both his and the Philosophies' motivation to explore Marxist philosophy was given added impetus by their involvement with Marxist intellectuals and with the
Communist Party which began in the mid-1920s. As self-declared
revolutionaries and avant-gardists, the group was always essentially
progressive in their sentiments. While still in their mystical phase,
this progressive tendency did not lead to much in the way of political
involvement. However, this posture changed with Lefebvre's and the
group as a whole's emphasis on action rather than contemplation as a
means to realize the union of mind and spirit. Thus, even before any
Marxist proclivities had manifested themselves in the group's theoretical writing, the Philosophies group found themselves involved
with Communist politics when, in 1925, they heeded the call of the
Marxist cultural journal *Clarté* for radical intellectual groups to unite
in protesting the French government's violent suppression of a Mo-
roccan nationalist movement.[31] Being intellectuals and idealists, this
protest of the Rif Conflict by the Philosophies and other avant-garde
groups such as the Surrealists took the form not of direct action but of
the issuance of manifestos calling for revolution, liberty, and spiritual
satisfaction.[32]

Despite the manifestos' manifestly bourgeois concerns, these pro-
tests put the Philosophies group in at least tangential contact with the
French Communist Party. More directly, it put them in touch with
the Sorelian Marxists who ran the journal *Clarté*. In this respect, the
Philosophies' political activity in the mid-1920s both encouraged
their exploration of Marxist ideas and precipitated their eventual
alignment with the French Communist Party in late 1928. However,
it also seems to be the case that, like the intellectuals who had preceded them into the party in 1920 and who by 1927 had already left,
the Philosophies group was at first attracted to the party not because
they understood or had even read Marxist philosophy but because
they thought of themselves as revolutionaries and saw the Communists as one of their few potential allies in their quest to overthrow
the dominant order and to replace it with something richer.[33]

Even if the Philosophies group was motivated to align itself with
the PCF in 1928 because of perceived affinities between its mission

and their own, unlike the intellectuals who had preceded them into the party, this alignment motivated the group to embark upon a serious investigation into the philosophy of Karl Marx and to examine the resources that his philosophy offered them in their revolutionary quest. However, unlike such intellectuals as René Maublanc who took their academic training and used it to articulate the philosophy of Marx in a way that was consistent with the tenets of Marxism-Leninism, the Philosophies group at first approached Marx with the same body of concerns and tendencies that had led them first to mysticism and then to German Idealism.

Intellectual Marxism in the 1930s: Three Approaches

Though still definitely a minority tendency in French intellectual life, by the late 1920s there existed basically three schools of Marx interpretation.[34] One of these schools was that inaugurated by the Philosophies group and emphasizing the affinities between Marxism and German Rationalism. Because of the centrality of this group to the present study, their interpretation of Marxist philosophy will be discussed at length below. The other two schools, however, bear mention as they represent trends that, though marginalized or variously assimilated, were never entirely absent from the field of French Intellectual Marxist interpretation and thus could be said to constitute its limits.

Clarté and the Residue of Utopian Socialism

The first of these schools of Marx interpretation is that represented by those intellectuals like Henri Barbusse and Paul Vaillant-Couturier who contributed to the journal *Clarté* and with whom the Philosophies group collaborated in actions protesting the Rif Conflict. More militant than theoretical and possibly acting as a party front, this group can be seen as heirs to the older traditions of French Utopian Socialism and to the Sorelian school of Marx interpretation.[35] Explicitly sympathetic with party goals, the theoretical writings contained in the journal attempted to demonstrate the continuity between the French revolutionary tradition and the Bolshevist vision. They thus emphasized those aspects of Sorelian Marxism and French Utopian Socialism that reinforced or at least did not explicitly contradict party positions. These aspects included the need for ideological manipulation of the masses, for consistent revolutionary policy, as well as the goal of founding a new, reasonable, and moral state.[36] Consistency of interpretation not being their strong point, there is little use in attempting to explicate the thought of the *Clarté* writers except to acknowledge that they best represented the tendency of French Utopian Socialist philosophy and pre-Leninist French Marxism to impose themselves upon French readings of Marx throughout the first half of the twentieth century.

Marxist Philosophy of Science: *La Cercle de la Russie Neuve*

The second of the three schools of French Intellectual Marxist interpretation has already been mentioned. It is that which is best represented by René Maublanc and by the study group he joined in 1929, *La Cercle de la Russie Neuve*.[37] Begun in 1927 at the behest of the Comintern and dedicated to fostering amicable relations and intellectual ties with the U.S.S.R., over its nine-year existence the group became increasingly focused on scientific research into Marxism and less and less an outlet for pro-Soviet propaganda.[38] Though attracting intellectuals from diverse academic disciplines, the other philosophers and "scientists of stature" who joined Maublanc in the *Cercle* resembled him in viewing Marx as a process philosopher whose work suggested the possibility of a new materialist method of science. This new philosophy of science, they believed, might solve problems endemic to both empiricist and rationalist approaches to the justification of scientific knowledge. Because the group followed Kant in specifying that no analysis of constitutive parts was capable of fully accounting for the structure and logic of a whole, they were critical of empirical science's ability to know and understand the world. The *Cercle* was also, however, critical of the Kantian or Cartesian Rationalist solution to the problem of empirical knowledge that explained the whole and its relation to its parts by recourse to the hypothesis of a unifying consciousness. As it was static rather than developmental and synchronic rather than diachronic, the group believed that the Classical Rationalist solution could not account for newly recognized phenomena such as the evidence for biological and social evolution. Empiricism, with its logic of cause and effect, was even more impoverished in this regard.

Though a minority sentiment, by the early 1920s some French

philosophers frustrated with the dominant neo-Kantian philosophy of science had identified Hegel and particularly his dialectical logic as a possible solution to the problems of empiricism and rationalism. Because the Hegelian dialectic dealt with the complexity of relations between parts and wholes in the historical continuum, it seemed to allow for the description of systems and their development in a way that empiricism and rationalism could not.[39] For reasons similar to the ones that led philosophers like Émile Boutroux and René Berthelot to Hegel, Maublanc and the members of *La Cercle de la Russie Neuve* also turned to dialectics. However, the *Cercle* followed Marx in specifying that the dialectic in Hegel was "mystified" by Hegel's privileging of the Idea over the material, a privileging that resulted in the absurd position that the world was perpetually in transition and yet was completely understood.[40] In that the Marxist method avoided this contradiction by holding that the world consisted of *"realités concrètes et pratiques,"* they judged it applicable to the post-Darwinian world they observed, one that was in the process of becoming something else and that was analyzable but was not, however, totally known.[41] They thus saw materialist dialectics as a powerful analytic tool, one that could advantageously be applied to the study of both natural and social phenomena.

This description of *La Cercle de la Russie Neuve* makes the group sound both better and worse than they actually were. As is apparent from the two-volume collection *À la lumière du Marxisme* (1935/1937) that anthologizes their research on the relationship between Marxism and science, the group and especially Maublanc were quite adept at articulating the difference between Marx's materialist dialectic and Hegel's idealist dialectic and at explaining why the former might provide a better analytic framework for the contemporary natural and human sciences than classical models.[42] However, heavily influenced by Engels's *Dialectics of Nature* and by Lenin's *Materialism and Empiriocriticism*, the group's explanations were also characterized by the excessive attribution of dialectical processes to phenomena such as mathematical objects that did not benefit from this description.[43] Similarly, the group was sometimes guilty of the type of Stalinist positivism that held that all empirical facts could be understood by the discovery of the dialectical logic that explained their appearances. They were also culpable (though to a lesser degree than some Soviet scientists) of equating proletarian knowledge with scientific knowledge. Of course, in the early 1930s, these tendencies were not something frowned upon by the party. Consequently, the work of

the group and of Maublanc in particular received the PCF's approval.
Though Maublanc himself did not become a party member until the
Occupation, his work was published by party presses and taught in
party schools.[44]

Hegelian Marxisms: "Philosophies" in the 1930s

If the interpretation of Marx given by *La Cercle de la Russie
Neuve* was indebted to the scientific materialism of Lenin and Engels
and the interpretation of Marx given by the *Clarté* group particularly
indebted to French Utopian Socialism, then the Philosophies' interpretation was indebted to a particularly academic reading of Marx that
sought to understand Marx through the tradition of German Rationalism. Unlike Lukács' attempt to connect Hegel to Marx, a link which
seems to come almost out of nowhere,[45] the attempt to understand
Marx through Hegel was allowed and encouraged in France both by the
new availability of Marx's early works that made this connection obvious and also by an academic tradition in France of understanding
Marx through Hegel that went back to the nineteenth century.[46]
Though this interest in discovering the affiliation between Marx and
Hegel had somewhat abated in the years before World War I, by the
time that the Philosophies group showed interest in Marx in the late
1920s, it had again become a prominent topic of discussion among
progressive members of the academy.[47] The pioneering work of
Auguste Cornu on the German Romantic roots of Marx's thought represents the early fruition of this debate.[48]

As products of an academic tradition that tended to emphasize the
continuities rather than the discontinuities between Hegel and Marx,
some of the first projects undertaken by the Philosophies after their
"conversion" to Marxism were attempts to assess this relationship
and to discover what resources it offered their revolutionary project.
Because most of the texts authored by Hegel and Marx that the Philosophies group needed to make this assessment were no longer or had
never been available in France, they took it upon themselves to
translate or to analyze such early writings as the recently discovered
1844 Manuscripts and *The German Ideology*.[49] Not coincidentally,
these writings reinforced the group's conviction—born from readings
of Fichte, Schelling, and Hegel—that Marx was a philosopher working
within the tradition of German Rationalism.

Along with the works published serially in its new journal *La Revue Marxiste* consecrated to the dissemination of Marxist philosophy, the group in the 1930s also translated and anthologized texts by Engels, Hegel, and Lenin that they felt added to their (and the French Communist movement's) comprehension of Marxist philosophy.[50] By 1938, this endeavor had resulted in the publication of a tome containing selections from Hegel's *Logic, History,* and *Phenomenology,* another of excerpts from Lenin's *Philosophical Notebooks,* and two volumes concentrating on Marx's philosophical and economic writings respectively.[51]

Many of the texts that appeared in *La Revue Marxiste,* its successor *Avant-poste,* and in the separate volumes anthologizing Marx's, Hegel's, and Lenin's philosophical writings were translated by Norbert Guterman and were accompanied by introductions authored by him and by Lefebvre. Though not representative of the development of the Philosophies group as a whole, it is really in these introductions, in their collaborative work *La Conscience mystifiée* (1936), and in Lefebvre's *Le Matérialisme dialectique* (1940) that one can see the way in which a Hegelian reading of Marx based on his early writings came to dominate one approach to French Intellectual Marxism.[52]

Of the introductions Lefebvre and Guterman authored, the one that is probably most illuminative of their take on the relationship between Marx and Hegel is the one-hundred-and-twenty-eight-page introduction to Lenin's *Cahiers sur la dialectique de Hegel.* As Kevin Anderson points out in his survey of Lenin's relationship to Western Marxism, this introduction is mostly useless as an analysis designed to provide insights into Lenin's reading of Hegel's *Greater* and *Lesser Logics.* What the text does do, however, is provide Lefebvre and Guterman a platform for articulating their own Hegelian Marxism.[53]

Though largely concerned with the import and meaning of the dialectic for Hegel and Marx, in the first seven pages of the introduction Lefebvre and Guterman do manage to bring Lenin into this consideration. Specifically, the collaborators concern themselves with the insights they believe Lenin provides into the relationship between the Marxian and Hegelian dialectics. The argument they make is that, through his reading of the *Science of Logic* in 1914 and especially of the last chapter on the Absolute Knowing, Lenin came to a deeper understanding of Marxist philosophy and the dialectic than he had had when he wrote *Materialism and Empiriocriticism* in 1908.[54] As an alternative to the radical break Lenin insisted upon in that work between materialism and all other bourgeois philosophies (including idealist dialectics), Lefebvre and Guterman maintain that in 1914 Lenin came to see Marxist materialism as not simply a correction that rendered all of Hegel's idealistic categories obsolete, but as itself the result of a larger dialectical process.[55]

For Lefebvre and Guterman, Lenin's correct recognition of the fundamental truth of dialectical logic led to two conclusions. First, in that Marx's advance from Hegel was itself a dialectical development, this proved the necessity of the dialectic as a tool for explaining any type of change. Second, because according to dialectical logic any synthesis is both a preservation and an overcoming of the opposites that comprise it, Lefebvre and Guterman posited that Dialectical Materialism as the synthesis of materialism and idealism does not totally do away with Hegelian categories. Rather, as a dialectical advance, it transforms them and deepens them. From these conclusions, the argument followed that, because the contents of the stages that preceded it are preserved in every dialectical synthesis, there is no need to jettison the categories and insights Hegel established. Rather, what is needed is a reworking of these categories according to the materialist insight.[56]

After Lefebvre and Guterman abandon their discussion of Lenin's work, the remainder and majority of the introduction to Lenin's *Cahiers* is taken up with "materialist" analyses of the stock of concepts that they perceive to be common to both Marx and Hegel. It being the case that most of the analyses undertaken in the remainder of the introduction are informed by Lefebvre and Guterman's suspicion that Hegel holds the key to understanding Marx, the "materialist" aspect or "correction" of the elucidation of concepts such as consciousness, contradiction, and alienation is often hard to ferret out. In their consideration of consciousness, for example, though the duo recognizes the ontological priority of matter over thought, they are also quick to specify that *"Hegel . . . ouvre la conscience et la réintegré dans l'interaction universelle"* [Hegel opens up consciousness and reintegrates it into universal interaction.][57] This rhetorical nod to idealism and to the power of thought is given further support in their discussion of contradiction. Making a distinction between the contradiction in Being from the consciousness of contradiction that reflects reality,[58] Lefebvre and Guterman attribute great power to consciousness insofar as it is increasingly capable of understanding and directing dialectical historical movement. In this attribution, the materialist contention that the movement of consciousness lags behind economic advances in production is implicitly denied. Instead, the two domains are depicted as developing in tandem. As Michael Kelly notes in regard to this attribution, in Lefebvre's and Guterman's work, "the process of reflection is conceived as taking place entirely within thought, and the existence of practical sanctions and determinants is but barely hinted at."[59]

While Guterman and Lefebvre in the late 1920s were immersing themselves in Marx's early works and in Lenin's reading of Hegel's *Logic*, another member of the group, Georges Politzer, was immersing himself in Lenin's *Materialism and Empiriocriticism*. As we have seen in his consideration of Schelling, prior to this reading Politzer had been greatly attracted to German Rationalism and to the promise it seemed to hold for the liberation of consciousness. Influenced by this promise, Politzer turned in 1927 to psychology and began seeking solutions to the problem of alienated consciousness. He did so in what he called "*la Psychologie concrète*," in the complex interactions between individual and society. The results of this investigation were published in his own journal *Revue de la Psychologie Concrète* and in the book *Critique des fondements de psychologie* (1928). In these writings, he proposes an alternative to both Freudian and traditional French psychological schools that parallels Erich Fromm's in that it recognizes the connections between individual consciousness, experience, the unconscious, and social structures.[60]

After reading *Materialism and Empiriocriticism* in 1938, Politzer abruptly abandoned this project. In Lenin's blanket critique of "idealist" philosophies, Politzer recognized a condemnation of his own work and especially of that part of it that depended on the articulation of "categories of thought." Convinced of Lenin's contention that there is a radical break between idealist and materialist philosophies and that only materialist philosophies are revolutionary, Politzer forsook both his studies in psychology and the more heterodox positions on Marxist philosophy evidenced in his introduction to the first issue of *L'Esprit*. From the time of this epiphany until his assassination by the Nazis in World War II, Politzer committed himself to defending Dialectical Materialism as it was articulated by the party. Though this break resulted in his estrangement from Lefebvre and Guterman and in a condemnation of their Hegelian Marxism, Politzer never totally abandoned his idealist roots.[61] Most of his subsequent theoretical and pedagogical work, including that which became the PCF's canonical statement of Marxist philosophy, *Principes élémentaires de la philosophie* (1945), evidenced an appreciation for Hegel's rational dialectic and the contribution that it made to Marxist philosophy.[62]

Though it is convenient to cite Lenin's book as the reason for Politzer's embrace of party philosophy, it is also probably the case that the tenor of the times had much to do with Politzer's choice. From his student days and the first issues of *Philosophies*, Politzer was an intellectual committed to the need for revolutionary change. At first, he looked for this in mysticism. However, he quickly abandoned this personal quest in favor of its *concrète* realization in the social body. This change of direction led him to idealism and psychology but it also led him to Marxism. In 1929, an era still dominated by *classe contre classe* policy, it was probably the case that Politzer felt he needed to make a decision: either commit wholly to the party and its goals or be a counterrevolutionary, idealist intellectual. Choosing the latter option, he involved himself wholeheartedly as a partisan.

Less involved politically and more interested by the philosophical problems posed by Marxism than by their practical solutions, Lefebvre and Guterman did not make the same choice as Politzer. Fortunately, with the ascenscion of the intellectual Maurice Thorez to party leadership and with the success of the Front Populaire, they did not have to make such a choice. Between 1934 and 1938, the *main tendue* that the party extended to classes and groups it had previously vilified was also offered to various heterodox theoretical positions that it had previously tolerated badly. This freedom and the optimism of the time contributed greatly to the spirit of Lefebvre's and Guterman's reformulation of Marxism and to this reformulation's content. During this time and in works like *La Conscience Mystifiée* and especially in Lefebvre's 1938 book *Le Matérialisme dialectique*,[63] the tendency of French Intellectual Marxism to understand Marx through Hegel reached its highest and most subtle expression.

Intended as a general introduction to the philosophy of Marxism, the first part of *Le Matérialisme dialectique*, titled "The Dialectical Contradiction" consists of a long exegesis pursued with the intention of demonstrating that the philosophy of Dialectical Materialism is itself the result of a dialectical process. In this endeavor, it is consistent with Lefebvre and Guterman's introduction to Lenin's *Cahiers* but takes much more care to show the specific steps involved in the dialectic's development. Starting with a critique of "formal logic" (which Lefebvre maintains is based on a denial of the content that it is intended to express), he proceeds in the first section of the book to demonstrate how the dialectical logic of Hegel, starting from content, is able to account for the determination of form.[64] Sparing his reader a close reading of the *Science of Logic,* the critique of formal logic's doctrine of identity leads to a discussion of the distinctions between Being and Nothingness, between quantity and quality, between Idea and Nature, and between Thought and Matter. From this discussion in which he shows how, in each case, the former concept entails recognition of the latter, he attempts to convince his reader of the necessity of positing a "Third Term" able to describe the relation between each of these opposites.[65]

The Third Term, which accounts for the relation between opposites, is generalized by Lefebvre as the concept of "Becoming." He specifies repeatedly that this is the most important part of the dialectic. Following Hegel, Lefebvre explains that Becoming is the process by which opposites, the First and Second Terms, come into contradiction with one another and generate a Third Term which contains and transcends the elements of its constituents. The result of this transcendence is a new unity that is itself "the start of a new determination." As part of an endless cycle, this new determination must, in turn, come into contradiction with its own opposite.[66]

From this description of dialectical logic, Lefebvre proceeds in *Le Matérialisme dialectique* to show how Hegel constructs a system that explains the world as the progressive and multiform self-negation or "alienation" of Mind in Matter and its reunification in Absolute Consciousness. Though applauding the ambition of Hegel's endeavor "to abandon and transcend every one-sided position" as "the only road a spiritual optimism or dynamism can take if it is to be formulated,"[67] Lefebvre is critical of Hegel's project in the *Science of Logic* on four counts. First, he points out that it is inconceivable that the "limited" mind of an individual philosopher could be able to grasp and understand a world that is infinitely rich. If this is to be done, Lefebvre writes, "this content will only be attained by the joint efforts of many thinking individuals in a progressive expansion of consciousness."[68] Second, he argues that to say with Hegel that one has understood *all* is to admit no possibility of further progress or differentiation, this despite the fact that history and the world have continued to offer up new contents and concepts. Using the surprising example of the new perspective that Nietzsche's *Birth of Tragedy* gave on Greek art, Lefebvre argues that the world and our understanding of it have developed since Hegel and therefore concludes that Absolute Knowledge is insufficient to deal with real historical development.[69] Third, and commensurate with his existentialist proclivities, Lefebvre notes that Hegel in his narrative of the development of Mind missed the concept of action. For Hegel, Lefebvre notes, the concept of action is super-fluous. Being only mental phenomena, contradictions dissolve them-selves into syntheses without struggle. However, echoing the *Theses on Feuerbach*, Lefebvre maintains that "since Hegel's time, the problem of action and practice has imposed itself on philosophy."[70]

The fourth issue that Lefebvre critiques Hegel's *Logic* for is the quietism to which it leads. As he writes, one tendency of Hegel is to sometimes posit "absolute, motionless Being, eternal self-knowledge, an objective identity which abolishes all contradiction forever."[71] This, he maintains, is Hegel's conservative side, that which justifies the status quo. In addition to this conservative tendency, however, Lefebvre recognizes that there is also a revolutionary disposition in Hegel. Though this does not much appear in either *Logic*, Lefebvre believes that it does manifest itself in *The Phenomenology of Spirit* in those places where Hegel describes not the "cosmic adventures of Mind" but "the torment of unrealized being."[72]

Given his preference for its narrative of struggle and becoming over the circular rhythms found in the *Logic*, it is no coincidence that it is in those sections of *The Phenomenology of Spirit* where Hegel describes the attempt by alienated self-consciousness to restore itself to its proper being that Lefebvre locates both the decisive correspon-dence and the decisive distinction between Hegel and Marx. In Marx's study of the *Phenomenology* presented in the *1844 Manuscripts*, Le-febvre argues that Marx discovered "the key to the Hegelian system," the place where "we recover the actual content of human life, that upward movement from earth to heaven."[73]

The "key discovery" that Lefebvre argues Marx appropriates from Hegel is *The Phenomenology*'s account of man's self-alienation and eventual reunification through his activity. However, because this re-unification is accomplished in this narrative only in consciousness, Lefebvre argues with Marx that Hegel's account was a "'disguised' and mystified critical analysis."[74] What Hegel's tale missed—and Lefebvre argues that this is the central distinction between idealist and materi-alist dialectics—is that man is not alienated by his possession of ob-jects, but that he is

> alienated by being temporarily dominated by a world that is "other" even though he himself gave birth to it, and so equally real. In this alienation man remains an actual, living being who must overcome his alienation through "objective action." The critique of the *Phenomenology* therefore, and of Hegel's

> theory of alienation, opens the way for a positive humanism, which has to transcend and unite idealism and naturalism (or materialism).[75]

It is precisely this attempt to "transcend and unite idealism and materialism" that Lefebvre argues is the impetus for the formulation of Historical Materialism. Though in the *1844 Manuscripts* this project is still somewhat cloaked in Hegelian idealist notions, Lefebvre argues that—after Marx's confrontation with Feuerbach—Historical Materialism found its proper object in the investigation of the progressive historical alienation of man from himself through his material life processes. After this insight, Marx realized that, even though it had led him to the position of Historical Materialism, as one of the forms of man's alienation, philosophy had to be abandoned in every speculative form, including that of the Hegelian dialectic.[76]

In the place of philosophical speculation that only ever succeeded in "reifying" particular as opposed to universal interests, Lefebvre argues that between 1845 and 1857 Marx abandoned any formal analytic structure and involved himself exclusively with the investigation of the economic processes that determine human relations.[77] Though Lefebvre admits that these investigations focused on conflict and its overcoming, he contends that this methodology was not truly dialectical because it was not "linked to a structure of the Becoming which can be expressed conceptually."[78]

Starting in 1857, with Marx's rereading of Hegel's *Logic*, Lefebvre believes that Marx began to reintegrate the dialectic into his analyses. Citing Marx's critique of Lasalle where he wrote that "[Lasalle] will learn to his cost that it is not the same thing to bring a science to the point where it can be stated dialectically, and to apply an abstract ready made system of Logic,"[79] Lefebvre argues that Marx himself—through years of empirical study—had come to the conclusion that economic processes behaved according to a dialectical logic and that they followed dialectical laws of development. From this point on, Lefebvre contends that Marx combined the research methods of Historical Materialism with the philosophical assumption that a dialectical logic governs material and conceptual processes. As evidence of the reintegration of dialectical logic into Marx's thought, Lefebvre offers the examples of the *Critique of Political Economy* (1859) and *Capital* (1867), where Marx's study "went beyond empiricism and attained the level of a rigorous science—then took on the form of a dialectic."[80]

It is not coincidental that the intellectual development of Marx between the years 1845 and 1857 is itself described in dialectical terms. For Lefebvre, Marx's journey from first discovering the dialectic in an idealist form in the *Phenomenology*, to rejecting this logic for the empirical study of the economic processes, to the eventual recognition that these processes themselves function dialectically, was a process by which "idealism and materialism [were] not only reunited but transformed and transcended" in Marx's own thought.[81] The result of this transformation and transcendence was the philosophy of Dialectical Materialism, a philosophy that was "formed and developed dialectically."

With the dialectic and its motor of Becoming restored to its proper place and its proper function in Marx's philosophy, Lefebvre argues that the two essential aspects of Marx's critical worldview had come into place. The first of these was the insight traced back to Marx's reading of *The Phenomenology of Spirit* that man is alienated. The second of these is the recognition, traceable to Marx's rereading of *The Science of Logic* in 1857, that this alienation is in the process of Becoming something else. Not coincidentally, the integration of these insights is what characterizes Lefebvre's own Marxism as developed in the second part of *Le Matérialisme dialectique*, titled "The Production of Man."

Correcting what he believes is a tendency to economic determinism on the part of Historical Materialism,[82] Lefebvre explains in the second half of *Le Matérialisme dialectique* that the 1857 rehabilitation of the Hegelian dialectic allowed Marx to analyze the "concrete process" by which man became alienated from himself and to demonstrate how man struggles through the "inhuman" to the "human." For Lefebvre, "alienation" is the most important analytic concept in Marxist philosophy because, with it, and by beginning from an analysis of "Praxis" or human activity, one can show how man's self-conception comes into being. One can also describe man as he is, as he was, and as he will become; one can describe "Total Man." As Lefebvre writes, alienation

> takes account both of the present drama and the historical drama of the human [and it shows that] the total man is both the subject and object of the Becoming. He is the living subject who is opposed to the object and surmounts this opposition. He is the subject who is broken up into partial activities and scattered determinations and who surmounts this dispersion. He is the subject of action, as well as its final object, its

products even if it does seem to produce external objects. The total man is the living subject-object, who is first of all torn asunder, dissociated and chained to necessity and abstraction. Through his tearing apart, he moves toward freedom; he becomes Nature, but free. He becomes a totality, like Nature, but by bringing it under control. The total man is "de-alienated man."[83]

As is obvious from this quote, the task of Humanist Materialism, as Lefebvre understood it, is that of elucidating and then transcending (by way of returning to him) those things constituting man's environment or "Nature" that are alienated from him. For Lefebvre, the combination of Historical and Dialectical Materialism performs this role by distinguishing in man's thought that which reflects "actual content" or "actual relations" and that which is only a reflection of man's alienation.[84] By making this distinction and basing it on the analysis of concrete realities, Lefebvre believed that Humanist Materialism should be able to envision solutions to man's alienation; this solution could then be realized through action. More specifically, given sufficient attention to man's determination by social objects (his job, family, church, even his furniture), the multiform alienation of man and community could be analyzed, understood dialectically as a combination of true and false conceptions, and eventually overcome. This analysis became the project for which Lefebvre is most famous, his *Critique of Everyday Life* and it is what he referred to in *Le Matérialisme dialectique* as "Materialist Humanism" or, simply, "Marx's philosophy."

Undoubtedly, there is much to say on behalf of Lefebvre's "Humanist Materialism" as it is presented in *Le Matérialisme dialectique*. The sheer dynamism that the emphasis on "Becoming" gives to his dialectical description of the progressive emancipation of man makes the reader want to go out and begin the conceptual critique of those objects that have been alienated from him. Lefebvre makes the dialectic come alive and he does so by emphasizing the continuities between Marx and Hegel, thereby giving Marx's dialectic a special urgency. However, as both his contemporaries and successive generations of critics have taken pains to point out, this dynamism is achieved at the cost of those elements of Marxist philosophy that distinguish him most from Hegel and that make Marx's philosophy original.[85]

As has already been noted, Lefebvre's interpretation of Marxist philosophy is heavily influenced by Marx's early works. Given that the juvenilia of the *1844 Manuscripts* and *The German Ideology* show

Marx wrestling to overcome Hegelian ideas and yet also reveal him to remain deeply indebted to Hegelian categories and concepts, it is to be expected that an interpretation of Marx like Lefebvre's that concentrates on these works would tend to show him as a Hegelian. However, it is also the case that these *oeuvres de jeunesse* document the integration by Marx of ideas that are not beholden to Hegel and that are crucial to an understanding of Marx's philosophy. Included among these are the two sources that Engels, Kautsky, and Lenin all cite in addition to Hegel as essential to an understudying of Marxism: nineteenth-century utopian socialism and classical political economy.[86] From the former, it is clear that Marx took the notion of the necessity of class struggle for the realization of political goals. From a study of the latter, Marx recognized the importance of monetary relations in the determination of social life and began the formulation of the concept of surplus value. In addition to these canonical roots, there is evidence in *The German Ideology* that Marx was also influenced by Moses Hess' concept of alienation and his description of money's role in this process.[87]

With the exception of Feuerbach, whose influence he minimizes to merely that of a correction of the "one-sidedness of the Hegelian dialectic"[88] and whose materialism he hardly mentions, Lefebvre barely acknowledges the importance and impact of any of these other sources. Perhaps most surprisingly given his audience, he never mentions Marx's French Utopian Socialist antecedents. These omissions tend to highlight the Hegelian influence on Marx's thought. Instead of justifying and making sense of the claim to be a revolutionary who "abandoned philosophy to realize it," Lefebvre's description of Marx's development shows him to be just another Left-Hegelian, a philosopher still dominated by and working within Hegelian categories and dynamics and specifically within the realm of pure thought. As Michael Kelly explains,

> Lefebvre's silence concerning the role of socialism and political economy in the development of Marxism is . . . a means of encompassing it within Hegel. Non-Hegelian influences are passed over, and so are important practical experiences, of political activity and growing capitalist economies. Without these important elements, there is no way of explaining Marx's development except as internal to Hegelian philosophy. Without an external materialist standpoint, how can Hegel be stood upright on his feet?[89]

In addition to encompassing Marx within the confines of the Hegelian system and dismissing his materialism and empiricism in all but name, Lefebvre's exaggeration of Hegel's influence on Marx's early works leads him to read Marx's later works as. likewise. essentially Hegelian. Thus, in *Capital*, Lefebvre fails to recognize an advance in Marx's thought in terms of its empirical description and explanation of the formation of the capitalist mode of production. Instead, he posits that the work is an improvement upon Marx's political and historical work only in that it represents a reintegration into Marx's thought of the Hegelian dialectic that Marx had abandoned with the *Theses on Feuerbach*. Believing that the "dialectic of Becoming" is later restored to Marx's analytic toolbox, Lefebvre reads Marx's later works just as he did *The German Ideology*, as narrative descriptions of man's alienation in objects and as a dialectical projection of the possibility that these objects will be restored to man. This interpretation is particularly evident in Lefebvre's tendency to use the concepts of "fetishism" and "alienation" interchangeably. He never recognizes that Marx's abandonment of the term "alienation," just like Marx's abandonment of the term "species-being" (which Lefebvre also preserves), might signal that Marx is perhaps up to something different in *Capital* than he was in the *1844 Manuscripts*.

What this emphasis on the Left-Hegelian revolutionary aspects of Marx's thought allows Lefebvre to do is posit Marxism as a theory of human liberation based on the "coming to consciousness" of those aspects of our species-being that are alienated from us. As Lefebvre understands the world, dialectical dynamism—the movement of Becoming—leads inexorably to the rational and practical organization of the human community, to what he terms "freedom."[90] Of course, action is needed for this to happen, but this can all be done conceptually through the dialectical elucidation of that which is alienating and that which is not. Short of being the proletariat's task, however, this practice is conceived by Lefebvre as the task of those representatives of "culture" such as the philosopher or artist who is able to grasp the "total content" yet not hypostasize it.[91]

Though Lefebvre's conception of Marxist philosophy as a Humanist Materialism is overly Hegelian and gives too much emphasis to the power of thought (and in this sense is not a materialism at all),[92] it does seem preferable to the Stalinism that his former colleagues Politzer and Nizan were simultaneously defending in 1938. Lefebvre's hypothesis that the world is infinitely rich and always in development leads him away from the conclusion that Marx gave a formula for the understanding of the world or that he described the way in which the revolution must occur. Also, because the dialectic of Nature is reflected in thought and largely moved forward by thought, his Marxism is neither subject to the crude economism of Stalin nor to Stalin's tendency to attribute true knowledge only to the working class or the party. In these ways, Lefebvre's efforts in *Le Matérialisme dialectique* were especially valuable because, written by a prestigious intellectual who was also a party member, they could possibly have served as a correction to these tendencies within the Communist Party and led to a consideration of Marx as a philosopher rather than as a scientist and prophet.

Unfortunately, Lefebvre's work was never to have this impact or at least was denied this impact until after World War Two. The reason for this is that, shortly after *Le Matérialisme dialectique*'s appearance, Stalin's *Short Course* was translated into French. This volume's appearance might not have been so bad if the party still tolerated the plurality of opinions it did during the Front Populaire era. A few of years earlier, Lefebvre's rich humanism might have been allowed to correct and be corrected by Stalin's formulation (as had happened to some extent with his and Guterman's *La Conscience mystifiée*). However, almost simultaneous with the appearance of the *Short Course* was a change in party direction occasioned by the signing of the Molotov-Ribbentrop agreement. Though strategically the non-aggression pact with the Germans may have been justified on the part of the Soviets, it was difficult for the French CP to defend to its membership the need to support a pact with the fascists whom it had supposedly been battling the last four years.[93] To enforce this new position, the party resorted to the hard-line tactics that had characterized the Front Uni era and squelched any heterodox political or theoretical positions, including those of Lefebvre. The nearly final blow to Lefebvre's *Le Matérialisme dialectique* came a few years later when, along with other works of Marxist philosophy, it was burned during the Nazi occupation.[94]

Notes

1. The scant availability of Marx's writings in France before the 1930s has already been remarked upon in the preceding chapter and will be examined in this one. For evidence of a hostile academic opinion on Marx from the 1920s see Henri Sée, *Matérialisme historique et interpretation économique de l'histoire* (Paris: Marcel Giard, 1927). In this book, Sée, a conservative historian, argues that Marxism is a strange combination of economic reductivism and utopian idealism that is efficacious as an *arme de guerre* for social agitators but does not constitute a philosophy.

2. For some, this tangential relationship with Marxism would not change. Many intellectuals such as André Gide and Anatole France went back to literature after a brief flirtation with Communism. Others like Barbusse, Aragon, and Vaillant-Couturier retained and deepened their interest in Marxist thought in the 1930s. Yet others continued to be involved in politics, but as liberals, socialists (even fascists), and critics of Marxism. Perhaps most interesting in this regard is the case of Boris Souvarine who after being expelled from the party made a point of discovering the "real Marx" that Stalin had betrayed but, in the end, became a Cold War apologist. See for instance Boris Souvarine, *Le Stalinisme: ignomie de Staline* (Paris: R. Lefeuvre, 1972).

3. Mark Mazower, *Dark Continent: Europe's Twentieth Century* (New York: Vintage Books, 2000), 22.

4. Bud Burkhard, *French Marxism between the Wars: Henri Lefebvre and the "Philosophies"* (New York: Humanity Books, 1999), 19. For much of my discussion of those philosophers associated with the Philosophies group I am indebted to Bud Burkhard's book. It provides the only in-depth analysis of the Philosophies activities from inception to dispersion and is really the first work to convincingly make the case that their work represents a significant contribution to Marxist thought.

5. For an extended discussion of this attitude and the intellectual creations it engendered see Stuart H. Hughes, *The Obstructed Path: French Social Thought in the Years of Desperation* (New York: Harper & Row, 1968).

6. Burkhard, *French Marxism between the Wars,* 21.

7. Paul Valéry, "La Crise de l'Esprit," *Nouvelle Revue Française,* no. 71 (August 1919): 322. As quoted in Burkhard, *French Marxism between the Wars*, 20.

8. Martin Jay, *Marxism and Totality: The Adventures of a Concept from Lucáks to Habermas* (Berkeley: University of California Press, 1984), 285.

9. George Lichtheim, *Marxism in Modern France* (New York: Columbia University Press, 1966), 66.

10. Burkhard traces this constructive movement to Marcel Arland and his 1924 call in the essay "Sur un Nouveau Mal du Siècle" for intellectuals to search for an Absolute capable of providing grounding for philosophy, science, and theology, an Absolute which would sate the "Crisis of Spirit." See Burkhard, *French Marxism between the Wars,* 22.

11. Burkhard, *French Marxism between the Wars*, 75.

12. Remi Hess, *Henri Lefebvre et l'aventure du siècle* (Paris: Éditions A.M. Métailié, 1988), 35.

13. One performative example of this denunciation, Lefebvre recounts in his autobiography that Politzer used to harass the aging Bergson by sitting opposite him at the bibliothèque Victor Cousin, noisily munching on sandwiches so as to demonstrate the discontinuity of experiences. The two also once took the trouble to release a tortoise they had nicknamed "Creative Evolution" to slowly cross Bergson's study table. Henri Lefebvre, *La somme et le reste* (Paris: Bélibaste, 1973), 41.

14. Hess, *Henri Lefebvre* , 35.

15. Burkhard, *French Marxism between the Wars*, 41-42.

16. Mark Poster, *Existential Marxism in Postwar France: From Sartre to Althusser* (New Jersey: Princeton, 1975), 15-117.

17. Henri Lefebvre, "Positions d'attaque et de defense du nouveau mysticisme," *Philosophies* 5/6 (March 1925): 472.

18. Henri Lefebvre, *L'existentialisme* (Paris: Editions du Sagittaire, 1946), 227.

19. Burkhard, *French Marxism between the Wars*, 61, 69.

20. Bruce Baugh, "Limiting Reason's Empire: The Early Reception of Hegel in France," *Journal of the History of Philosophy* 31, no. 2 (1993): 262, 268-69.

21. Burkhard, *French Marxism between the Wars*, 61-62.

22. Henri Lefebvre, introduction to *Recherches Philosophiques sur l'essence de la liberté humaine,* by Friedrich von Schelling, trans. Georges Politzer (Paris: Rieder, 1926), 51-52. See also Burkhard, *French Marxism between the Wars*, 62 and Hess, *Henri Lefebvre*, 65.

23. Burkhard, *French Marxism between the Wars*, 64.

24. Georges Politzer, introduction to *Esprit* 1 (1926): 70-71. As cited in Burkhard, *French Marxism between the Wars*, 65-66.

25. Burkhard, *French Marxism between the Wars*, 65.

26. Burkhard, *French Marxism between the Wars,* 66, 68.

27. Baugh, "Limiting Reason's Empire," 266.

28. Baugh mentions numerous courses by Alain at the Lycée Henri IV between 1923-1928 on Hegel as well as lectures by Charles Andler in 1928-1929 on Hegel's religious philosophy and the *Phenomenology* as instrumental in reviving Hegel as a philosophical force in France. However, he especially singles out Victor Baschi and his book *Les Doctrines politiques des philosophes classiques d'Allemagne: Leibniz-Kant-Fichte-Hegel* (Paris: Alcan, 1927) for its presentation of Hegel as a philosopher of freedom. He further argues that this mini-revival both preceded and led to the reconsideration and full-blown "Hegel Renaissance" of the 1930s and 1940s with Kojève and Hyppolite. See Baugh, "Limiting Reason's Empire," 270-272.

29. Burkhard, *French Marxism between the Wars*, 72.

30. Henri Lefebvre, *Le temps des méprises* (Paris: Stock, 1975), 49.

31. David Caute, *Communism and the French Intellectuals: 1914-1960* (New York: Macmillan, 1964), 97.

32. Pierre Morhange, "La Révolution d'abord et Toujours" in *Tractes surréalistes et declarations collectives, Tome 1 (1922-1939)*, ed. Jose Pierre (Paris: Terrain Vague, 1979).

33. Burkhard, *French Marxism between the Wars*, 76.

34. This is not counting conservative critiques such as that by Henri Sée mentioned in the first note to this chapter.

35. Caute, *Communism and the French Intellectuals*, 42.

36. Caute, *Communism and the French Intellectuals*, 77.

37. Michael Kelly, *Modern French Marxism* (Oxford: Blackwell Publishers, 1982), 29.

38. Sophie Coeuré, *La Grande lueur à l'est: les français et l'Union Soviétique, 1917-1939* (Paris, Éditions du Seuil, 1999), 192-95.

39. Baugh, "Limiting Reason's Empire," 263.

40. René Maublanc, *La Philosophie du marxisme et l'enseignement officiel* (Paris: PCF Bureau d'Editions, 1935), 24.

41. Maublanc, "La Philosophie du marxisme," 22, 29.

42. See particularly Henri Wallon's essay "Psychologie et technique" and Maublanc's "Hegel et Marx" in Volume 1 of Henri Wallon, *A la lumiére du Marxisme, essais* (Paris: Éditions Sociales Internationales, 1935).

43. Paul Labérenne, *Les Mathématiques et la technique* and particularly the section "Les mathématiques actuelles vues par les savants de l'U.R.S.S.," pages 30-37 in Henri Wallon, *A la lumiére du Marxisme,* vol. 1.

44. Kelly, *Modern French Marxism*, 30.

45. Martin Jay points out that though Lukács' reading of Marx in *History and Class Consciousness* (1926) was not influenced by a reading of Marx's early, explicitly Hegelian works, it was undoubtedly influenced by his tenure as a student in Heidelberg in the 1910s where he absorbed the German Rationalist tradition. See Jay, *Marxism and Totality*, 16.

46. Since at least the 1880s French intellectuals at the Sorbonne and at the E.N.S. had been attempting to trace the theoretical roots of German socialism to their source in Hegel and Left-Hegelian philosophy. For a listing of these accounts see Kelly, *Modern French Marxism*, 18.

47. Michael Kelly, "Hegel in France to 1940: A Bibliographic Essay," *Journal of European Studies* 11, no. 1 (March 1981): 19-52.

48. Auguste Cornu, "Karl Marx et la pensée romantique allemande," *Europe* (October 15, 1935): 199-216.

49. The publisher Alfred Costes began the publication of a sixty-plus volume "complete" works of Marx and Engels in 1924. During the 1920s and early 1930s the volumes that appeared had consisted principally of political and economic works. Exceptions to this were the publication in 1927 of *The Holy Family* (1844), Marx's doctoral dissertation on classical materialism (1841), and his *Contribution to Hegel's Philosophy of Right* (1843). In 1937 and 1938 volumes

were published containing the *1844 Manuscripts* and *The German Ideology*. See Kelly, *Modern French Marxism*, 21, 26.

50. The first issue of *Revue Marxiste* from February 1928 included, for example, Engels's *On the Dialectic* and Lenin's "On the significance of Militant Materialism."

51. G. W. F. Hegel, *Morceaux choisis de Hegel,* translated and edited by Norbert Guterman and Henri Lefebvre (Paris: Gallimard, 1938); V. I. Lenin, *Cahiers de Lénine sur la dialectique de Hegel,* translated and edited by Norbert Guterman and Henri Lefebvre (Paris: Gallimard, 1938); and *Karl Marx, oeuvres choisies tome 1 and 2,* translated and edited by Norbert Guterman and Henri Lefebvre (Paris: Gallimard, 1934).

52. Norbert Guterman and Henri Lefebvre, *La Conscience Mystifiée* (Paris: Gallimard, 1936).

53. Kevin Anderson, "Lenin, Hegel and Western Marxism," *Studies in Soviet Thought* 44, no. 2 (Spring 1992): 99.

54. Norbert Guterman and Henri Lefebvre, introduction to *Cahiers sur la dialectique de Hegel,* by V. I. Lenin (Paris: Gallimard, 1967), 52. There is evidence for this reading in the *Notebooks* of Hegel's *Science of Logic*, especially at the point where Lenin writes in his consideration of "The Idea" that: "The sum-total, the last word and essence of Hegel's logic is the *dialectical method*—this is extremely noteworthy. And one thing more: in this *most idealistic* of Hegel's works there is the *least* idealism and the *most materialism*." Depending on one's reading, this could be taken to show how close Lenin thought the materialist and idealist dialectics were. See V. I. Lenin, "The Idea" in *Conspectus of Hegel's Book "The Science of Logic"* (Lenin Internet Archives, 1993) www.marxists.org/archive/lenin/works/1914/conslogic/ch03.htm# LCW38_192 (accessed August 9, 2004).

55. Kelly, *Modern French Marxism*, 32.

56. Guterman and Lefebvre, introduction to *Cahiers*, 18.

57. Guterman and Lefebvre, introduction to *Cahiers,* 79. Translation is from Kevin Anderson, "Lenin, Hegel and Western Marxism," *Studies in Soviet Thought* 44, no. 2 (Spring 1992): 97.

58. Kelly, *Modern French Marxism*, 33.

59. Kelly, *Modern French Marxism*, 33.

60. Burkhard, *French Marxism between the Wars*, 86-87.

61. Hess, *Henri Lefebvre*, 95.

62. Kelly, *Modern French Marxism*, 45.

63. Burkhard in *French Marxism between the Wars* makes the point that this work should be seen as a collaboration with Guterman. Though Guterman at the time of its publication had already sought asylum in the United States, he contributed much to its content. Burkhard, *French Marxism between the Wars,* 224.

64. Henri Lefebvre, *Dialectical Materialism*, trans. John Sturrock (London: Jonathan Cape, 1968); originally published as *Le Matérialisme dialectique* (Paris: PUF, 1940), 25.

65. Lefebvre, *Dialectical Materialism*, 31.

66. Lefebvre, *Dialectical Materialism*, 33.

67. Lefebvre, *Dialectical Materialism*, 46, 47.

68. Lefebvre, *Dialectical Materialism*, 48.

69. Lefebvre, *Dialectical Materialism*, 49.

70. Lefebvre, *Dialectical Materialism*, 50.

71. Lefebvre, *Dialectical Materialism*, 56.

72. Lefebvre, *Dialectical Materialism*, 58.

73. Lefebvre, *Dialectical Materialism*, 61.

74. Lefebvre, *Dialectical Materialism*, 62, 63.

75. Lefebvre, *Dialectical Materialism*, 65.

76. Lefebvre, *Dialectical Materialism*, 81.

77. Lefebvre, *Dialectical Materialism*, 81.

78. Lefebvre, *Dialectical Materialism*, 81.

79. Karl Marx to Engels, 1 February 1858, *Selected Correspondence, 1846-1895*, trans. Dona Torr (Westport, CT: Greenwood Press, 1975), 105.

80. Lefebvre, *Dialectical Materialism*, 83.

81. Lefebvre, *Dialectical Materialism*, 84.

82. Lefebvre, *Dialectical Materialism*, 85.

83. Lefebvre, *Dialectical Materialism*, 162.

84. Lefebvre, *Dialectical Materialism*, 110.

85. For contemporary criticism of Lefebvre's idealism in the late 1930s from the perspective of the PCF see "H. Chassagne" [Charles Hainchelin], "Lefebvre et Guterman: La Conscience Mystifiée," *Commune*, no. 32 (April 1936): 1005-6. From a more academic perspective see Jean Grenier, "La Pensée Engagée," *Esprit*, no. 42 (March 1936): 959-64. For more recent critiques see Kelly, *Modern French Marxism*, 90; Jay, *Marxism and Totality*, 296; and Anderson, "Lenin, Hegel and Western Marxism," 99.

86. V. I. Lenin, "The Three Sources and Three Component Parts of Marxism," in *Collected Works* vol. 19 (Moscow: Progress Publishers, 1970), 23-28; Karl Kautsky, *Les Trois Sources du Marxisme: l'oeuvre historique de Marx* [1907] (Paris: Spartacus: 1947); as well as Friedrich Engels, *Anti-Dühring* (New York: International Publishers, 1939), 163-67. For more on the "Three Sources" and the suggestion that they may not be so canonical or as important to Marx's development as Lenin, Kautsky, and Engels argue see Étienne Balibar, *Philosophy of Marx* (New York and London: Verso, 1995), 7.

87. Dirk J. Struik, introduction to *Economic and Philosophic Manuscripts of 1844*, by Karl Marx (New York: International Publishers, 1993), 24.

88. Lefebvre, *Dialectical Materialism*, 68.

89. Kelly, *Modern French Marxism*, 37.

90. Lefebvre, *Dialectical Materialism*, 162.

91. Lefebvre, *Dialectical Materialism*, 165-166.

92. Lefebvre, *Dialectical Materialism*, 94.

93. Maxwell Adereth, *The French Communist Party: A Critical History (1920-1984): From Comintern to the Colours of France* (Manchester: Manches-

ter University Press, 1984), 92; and Yves Santamaria, *L'Enfant du malheur: le parti communiste Français dans la lutte pour la paix, 1914-1947* (Paris: S. Arslan, 2002), 261-62.

94. Burkhard, *French Marxism between the Wars*, 238.

Chapter 5

French Marxist Thought 1940-1956: Approaching Crisis

Immediately before World War II, the French Communist Party was in shambles and the state of Marxist theory in France was not much better. If the party's adoption of Stalin's "Dialectical and Historical Material- ism" as the final word on Marxist philosophy and the reversal of its poli- cies toward Germany in August 1939 had made it difficult to be a Marx- ist thinker, it became even more difficult when the party with which Marxist thought was singularly identified was persecuted by the French government for its support of the Molotov-Ribbentrop pact. Neither the *drôle de guerre* nor the occupation offered respite. Those few Marxist philosophers who had not silenced themselves in obeisance to the party line or who did not cease their intellectual production in disgust at the party's actions were effectively silenced when the prewar persecution of Communists gave way to the Vichy regime's suppression and burning of any literature that could be seen as possibly subversive.[1] Between late 1939 and the end of the war, there appeared basically no new Marxist philosophy.

Despite this voluntary and involuntary silencing, French Marxism did not emerge at the end of the war as neo-Kantianism and Bergsonism had emerged out of World War I, that is, on its last breath. Instead of being seen as decrepit, anachronistic, and in need of replacement, Marx- ist philosophy was hailed as the most salient, relevant, and true philoso- phy as well as the philosophy of the future. Of course, this is what the Philosophies group had been saying since 1929, but almost nobody in the academic establishment had listened to them. However, a few short years after the end of World War II, almost every intellectual in France had come to this conclusion.

What were the reasons for this new interest? Though some critics would say that Marxist philosophy suited the French intellectuals' perennial "taste for violent action" and "Manichean oppositions,"[2] the explanation for this new enthusiasm probably had less to do with inherited proclivities of the intelligentsia than with the political actions of the Communist Party. At the end of the war and as a result of the leadership position the party assumed in the resistance, the PCF appeared as one of the few identifiably progressive and moral forces at work during the war. By way of association, then, both progressive intellectuals as well as large swaths of the general populace came to Marxism because it was the philosophy that encouraged and allowed this resistance. This sympathetic identification with Communism led to a postwar boom in the exploration of Marxism, a boom that was to dominate French intellectual life for the next thirty years.

During the first 15 years of this explosion in popularity, Marxist philosophy took basically three forms.[3] Two of these are already familiar to the reader while the third is somewhat novel. The first of these is, of course, the philosophy of the French Communist Party. In the afterglow of resistance and liberation, the little philosophy made available by the PCF amidst postwar scarcity resembled the liberal Marxism that the party had encouraged during the Front Populaire era. However, by late 1948 and with the onset of the Cold War, party philosophers reverted to developing the implications of Stalin's formulation of the Materialist Dialectic. The second form that French Marxist philosophy took in the decade and a half after the liberation was that of an Hegelianized Marxism. This work is of interest in the postwar period both with regard to its internal development and with regard to the French Communist Party's hostile reception to the increasingly prominent role that culture and alienation came to play in the systems of Hegelian Marxists. The third variant of French Marxist philosophy pursued in the postwar theoretical boom is that of Existential Marxism. Like the thought of Henri Lefebvre, this was an intellectual and academic Marxism influenced by a particularly Hegelianized reading of Marx and that centered on problems of alienation. However, whereas Lefebvre's work emphasized the historical development of the social spirit into "Total Man," existentialist interpretations of Marx tended to focus more narrowly on problems within the subjective consciousness of the individual.

These three variants of French Marxist philosophy underwent significant development in the decade and a half following the second

World War. For their part, Existential Marxists busied themselves with the task of jury-rigging a phenomenology of individual consciousness to a philosophy of collective social action. Though not even in existence before the war, Existential Marxism quickly came to occupy a prominent place in French political and philosophical debates. In addition, unlike PCF theory and much more so than the Hegelian Marxism of the Philosophies group ever did, Existential Marxism was successful as an export. Though representative philosophers like Juan Axelos and Emanuelle Mounier never really achieved international prominence, the books of Jean-Paul Sartre and Maurice Merleau-Ponty found their way onto coffee tables and bookshelves from Brussels to Boston.

After the war, Hegelian Marxists also explored the relationship between consciousness and society. However, unlike the existentialists, they did so in a specifically historicist and culturalist fashion. As cultural critique began to assume a much more important theoretical role than economic analysis in their work, the research of Hegelian Marxists moved closer and closer to the "Western Marxism" of Gramsci, Benjamin, and Adorno (though not by conscious intent).

Moving in perhaps the opposite direction from Hegelian and Existential Marxism—philosophies that dealt mostly with culture and individual experience—PCF theory at the instigation of Andrei Zhdanov and the Cominform sought to apply the now formalized materialist dialectic to every aspect of life. Though there was much debate between these three variants as to who had found the "true" Marx, there was little to no collaboration between them. In keeping with the tenor of the Cold War, Existential Marxists, Hegelian Marxists, and the PCF each sought to carve out and define their own take on Marxist philosophy. The result of all this effort was not so much a creative flowering of French Marxist philosophy as the defense and formalization of its three principal tendencies.

The intellectual effort and resources that went into the development of these three strains of French Marxism were tremendous. Academics involved with Existential and Hegelian Marxism mobilized the usual resources of bookish people; seminars were devoted to the study of Marx and public debates about communism's contemporary political and philosophical relevance were engaged. Intellectuals also published numerous manuscripts devoted to Marxist thought and editors consecrated or reconsecrated journals like *Esprit* and *Les Temps Moderne* to the dissemination of Marxist-inspired work. Not one to fall behind where

Marxist philosophy was concerned, the PCF likewise invested much into philosophical research and education. The results of these efforts were published in its theoretical journals *Cahiers de Communisme, La Pensée,* and *La Nouvelle Critique,* as well as in numerous monographs issued by its house press, Éditions Sociales. In addition, party philosophers devoted much time to the development of courses and course materials for its Université Nouvelle, a free university intended to educate its new members in the philosophy of Marxism-Leninism.

Postwar Marxist Philosophy: Three Variations

PCF Theory 1945-1960

Whatever political and theoretical gains the French Communist Party had made during the Front Populaire era were forsaken with its 1939 decision to follow the lead of Moscow with regard to both theoretical and political protocols. While the directorate's endorsement of Stalin's *Short Course* cannot be seen as solely determinative of its policies, it is certainly the case that the willingness to sanction the Marxist-Leninist formula is symptomatic of the PCF's return to orthodoxy during this period. Further, it became clear during the period immediately leading up to the war and during the *drôle de guerre* that the decision to accept the *Short Course*'s chapter on "Dialectical and Historical Materialism" as the quintessential articulation of Marxist philosophy cemented already well-entrenched assumptions that Marxism scientifically demonstrated the inevitability of the revolution, the necessity of the dictatorship of the proletariat, and the party's claim to epistemological and hegemonic privilege.

Because in 1939 the success of the revolution to come was still identified with the survival of the Soviet Union, this identification meant that the PCF was willing to follow the directives of the Soviet-dominated Comintern even at the cost of its own organizational strength. Similarly, the analyses that the party itself provided world events were marked by a tendency to see the war, like World War I, as a conflict waged betweem imperialist powers. Even after the invasion of France in the spring of 1940, this reliance led the PCF to suggest that correct strategy would have been to make peace with the invading Germans so that a domestic revolution could be pursued, just as the Bolsheviks had done in 1918.[4]

This willingness to follow the directives of the Comintern and this tendency to fall back on classical Leninist formulas to understand world events explains the series of bizarre policy reversals in the fall of 1939. These started with the endorsement of the Nazi-Soviet pact and ended with the party's being banned after its antiwar position was taken as a pro-Nazi stance by the French government.[5] The former action led to the resignation of twenty-one of the party's seventy-two deputies, reducing party leadership once again to its Leninist core. The latter resulted in the party's forced dissolution by the French government and the persecution and imprisonment of thousands of its members and activists.[6]

Consequently, when the war did break out between Germany and France, the PCF was in its worst state since the early 1930s. Incapacitated and not really sure what to do, it responded to the Nazi invasion of France with a line similar to the one given by the Second International in 1914. It declared that the war was "imperialist on both sides" and that the best response to it was to work for peace.[7] This position of "hostile neutrality" did not last long. Though the party's rhetorical call for international peace was consistent both during and after the war, by early 1941 it had already begun to take action against the country's occupiers. Originally, these actions were not undertaken with the liberation of France in mind but, instead, consisted of acts of sabotage intended as a response to the increasingly violent persecution of its members by both the Vichy regime and by the Nazis.[8]

With the invasion of the Soviet Union in June 1941, it became apparent to both the PCF and to the Comintern that the Germans were a greater and more immediate threat to the survival of the Communist cause than any number of London bankers or monopoly industries. The party therefore shifted its targets from factory owners to France's Nazi occupiers. From this point on and until the end of the war, French Communists were responsible for the organization of the majority of resistance actions carried out during the occupation. Not limited to sabotage and armed insurrections, these activities also included the organization of strikes, the coordination of wide-based political initiatives, and the publication of political propaganda.[9]

Though during World War II the party could not resist its ingrained tendency to try and dominate any resistance coalitions it formed and though it consistently subjected the war to both an international and class analysis,[10] it did loosen up on some of its more divisive positions while organizing the resistance. For instance, rather than announcing that the party was fighting for the international liberation of workers from the most reactionary element of finance capital, it took the position that the resistance was engaged in the struggle for the national liberation of France from her oppressors.[11] This policy of putting France before the international worker was also shown in its willingness to cooperate with De Gaulle's "government in exile" both during the war and in the formation of a postwar government.[12] When the war ended, the combination of this Gallo-philic policy and the party's resistance record made the Communists appealing to the general French populace in a way they never were in the twenties and thirties when most of their energy was devoted to demonstrating that France was a nation irreconcilably divided along class lines and that it was an historical anachronism in comparison with the U.S.S.R.

Though some Trotskyist critics would later assert that the French Communist Party had failed to make good on the revolutionary situation that the end of the war and the party's popularity provided, the immediate aftermath of World War II left the PCF in a very good position.[13] Really, the French Communist Party was one of the few, if not the only, political organizations that could be identified as acting morally throughout the conflict. Unlike De Gaulle and the Comité Français de Libération Nationale, the PCF had never retreated and, unlike the SFIO and other political parties, it had never voted to support the Vichy regime.[14] What's more, it could claim itself to be the *parti des fusillées,* pointing out that it had lost 75,000 martyrs to the cause of France's liberation during a time when other political leaders were rounding up their towns' Jewry for deportation.[15] Given all these factors, the contrast between the actions of the Communists and of the majority of the population during the war was extreme. To those who wished to identify themselves with the resistance—even if they had not actively participated in it—the Communists were the obvious point of reference.

Postwar, this immense moral authority translated to political power and domestic prestige for the party. At least for a while, the PCF ran with its newfound approbation. By 1946, party membership had increased to 800,000, a figure more than twice as high as its previous apex in 1937. At the polls that same year, it commanded 28.6% of the vote, making it the largest party in France.[16] After these elections and for the first time, the party entered government in an executive capacity, placing six ministers in the Blum-led government. Although this coalition soon broke down and was replaced by a Radical government led by Ramadier, the party managed to retain ministerial representation for seventeen months. During this time it stayed consistent with its wartime policy of national unity and even went so far as to encourage workers to unite with the peasant masses and middle classes in rebuilding France.[17] As during the most liberal days of the Front Populaire, the party's enemy was no longer defined as every agency unsympathetic to its goals. Now it agitated only against the monopolists and financiers, the *"deux cent familles"* who were everybody's true oppressors. This concession to broad solidarity, though, had been made before during the Front Populaire. Perhaps the most surprising manifestation of the PCF's postwar liberalization was party leader's Maurice Thorez's statement in an interview with the *London Times* in November 1942. When asked about the continued necessity of the dictatorship of the proletariat, he replied that: "The progress of democracy all over the world . . . allows one to envisage the road to socialism by other paths than those taken by the Russian Communists."[18]

Though in 1946 such a sentiment might have been genuine on the part of Thorez, the party was never able to articulate a road to socialism that was particularly French nor even one that was particularly democratic. Instead, the Cold War intervened. At odds with the rest of the government over policies on Indochina and worker salaries, in early May 1947 Communist representatives refused to support the Ramadier government in a vote of confidence. Ramadier took the opportunity that this vote provided to dismiss all of the Communist ministers. Not coincidentally, this dismissal paved the way for the acceptance by France of United States aid under the auspices of the Marshall Plan.[19]

Alienated from government participation and vehemently against France's alignment with the United States, the French Communist Party was especially ready to accept the Soviet response to the Marshall Plan and to abandon its newly found nationalism and liberalism. As it was articulated by the Cominform in August 1947, this response demanded that all wayward European CP's return to orthodoxy, that they support the Soviet Union, and that they accept CPSU leader Zhdanov's analysis that the world now consisted of "Two Camps," one of imperialism and war, the other of socialism and peace.[20]

With their acceptance of the Cominform's declaration, French Communists found themselves in nearly the same situation that they had been in immediately before the war: calling for orthodoxy and returning to a Leninist hard line. Nonetheless, there were two big differences between 1939 and 1947. The first was that whereas the breakout of World

War II had found the French Communists effectively marginalized, the breakout of the Cold War found the Communists established as a domestic political force. The second difference was that whereas World War II was fought on conventional battlefields with conventional weapons, the Cold War in France was fought along ideological divides with propaganda—including Marxist thought—as its principal weapon. These two distinctions meant that whereas between 1939 and 1946 there was very little Marxist philosophy produced by the Communist Party, between 1947 and 1956 reams of it were produced. As propaganda, most of it was developed for the education of militants and to articulate and substantiate the "Two Camps" principle that the world is divided into two warring ideological and economic spheres. It is in these efforts that one really sees the worst that Stalinism has to offer in terms of an interpretation of Marx's philosophy. It is also where one recognizes the absurdity of a position that attempts to explain every phenomenon in terms of an impoverished and formulaic materialist dialectic.

Pragmatically forsaken for the thesis of "The Unity of International Science" both during the war and during the party's period of participation in the postwar government, the Cold War saw the claims to universal scientific knowledge implicit in Stalin's formulation of Marxist-Leninist philosophy again come to prominence in party pedagogical and theoretical texts. At first, this stance was rather mild. The party argued for instance that Marxist philosophy is an extension of the sciences that shares with them both a method and a concern with the concrete object.[21] However, as the Cold War heated up and the cult of personality around Stalin developed, the party in 1949 began to argue that, just as the political world was split into two camps, so were the sciences divided into two opposed systems of knowledge, only one of which was able to discover *"la réalité telle qu'elle est en elle-même"* [reality such as it is in itself].[22]

One especially polemical but not atypical articulation of the "two sciences" position was put forward by party intellectuals Francis Cohen, Jean Desanti, Raymond Guyot, and Gérard Vassails in a collaborative pamphlet entitled, *Science Bourgeoise et Science Prolétarienne*.[23] Though each contributor focused on a different problem, all were unanimous in the conclusion that, at least since the Greeks, there had existed two types of science: one materialist and revolutionary, the other idealist and conservative. Of the latter, they argued that it is fundamentally unable to provide knowledge of the world as it really is because its method is based on the mistaken positivist assumption that laws are discovered through empirical inquiry.[24] By way of contrast, proletarian science (or that which is alternately termed "scientific socialism") recognizes at the heart of its method the dialectical relationship between theory and practice and produces true knowledge about the world.

Though not above citing the *fusillées de la guerre* as proof of the superiority of proletarian over bourgeois science,[25] the pamphlet does offer support for its positions that there exist two sciences and that only one can correctly describe the world. For instance, Cohen in his contribution argues that bourgeois science cannot even account for its own history. Unlike proletarian history of science, which is able to scientifically reconstruct its development through the correlation of material practices to theoretical developments (the practice of Historical Materialism), bourgeois history of science can only attribute scientific discoveries to the work of individual savants. Galileo's theoretical advances, for example, are attributed by bourgeois historians to the Italian astronomer's genius rather than to the practical work done by navigators, manufacturers, and miners who actually deserve credit for the scientific advance. Though this may seem a surprising conclusion, Cohen argues that it was these *partisans* (partisans who in Renaissance Italy formed the revolutionary class and who were engaged in a practical struggle with the aristocracy) that enabled Galileo to overcome his era's dominant ideology and to make real scientific discoveries.[26] Of course, Galileo and his practice of experiment and observation had something to do with the advance. However, his contribution was really only the theoretical formulation of the practical wisdom that the bourgeoisie had developed in their struggle with the ruling class. Galileo's contribution to science and to history was thus, Cohen maintains, as one of the *"savants d'avant-garde"* who formulated the truths won by those struggling against the dominant ideology.

Through the course of *Science Bourgeoise et Science Prolétarienne*, example after example is given of how bourgeois science fails to adequately describe the phenomena that it studies. Without going into each of these examples, it should be possible to convey the thrust of the pamphlet's critique. Basically, the pamphlet argues that bourgeois science is a slave to the class interests that control it. Therefore, in capitalist countries, the sciences always work to confirm the ideology of the bourgeoisie. It is no surprise then to the authors of the pamphlet that physicists in capitalist nations find that atoms *"exprime en somme l'essentiel de toute constitution politique des démocraties occidentals"*[27] [expresses all that is essential about the constitution of political democracies] and that bourgeois biologists specify accident rather than fundamental laws as the motor of evolutionary change. These scientists come to these conclusions not because they are true (as the pamphlet notes, quantum physics and Darwinism are poor substitutes for mechanical atomism and Lamarckian evolution) but because they are forced to by the class interest that directs them.[28]

Like bourgeois science, proletarian science is also part of the super-structure and therefore serves a class interest. However, this determination does not invalidate or skew its results. This is because the intervention into the sciences by the proletarian or communist state is motivated by an essentially different interest. Because of the nature of the class that it serves, proletarian science is the only science that can understand objects in their objectivity as the manifestation of a fundamental law. To readers of chapter 3 of this work, the essential features of this argument will be familiar. However, its updating is of interest for the way in which Stalin's rigid formulation of the materialist dialectic came during the Cold War to justify the exclusive claim to knowledge of the Communist Party and the hegemonic mandate of the Soviets even after the "two sciences" policy was formally abandoned in the mid-1950s.[29] Though lengthy, a quotation by Desanti on the role of political leaders in proletarian states is here worth quoting as it succinctly captures this justification:

> . . . les hommes d'Etat prolétariens ne sont pas des hommes d'Etat commes les autres. La science fondamentale du prolétariat, le marxisme-léninisme, ils ont le devoir de la connaître afin d'en dominer les principes et d'en diriger l'application à la lutte quotidienne de la classe ouvrière. Entre les hommes d'Etat bourgeois et les hommes d'Etat prolétariens il y a une différence de nature. Les premiers sont les simples commis d'une classe désormais parasitaire. Les seconds sont les produits de la lutte du peuple lui-même, les plus conscients et les plus réfléchis des combattants prolétariens. Ils sont à l'avant-garde de la classe ouvrière qui est elle-même à l'avant-garde de la société tout entière. Les premiers ne peuvent intervenir dans la domaine de la culture et de la science: en tant qu'hommes d'Etat, ils sont etrangers au mouvement qui produit cette culture; ce mouvement se passe en dehors d'eux; il est en dehors de leur atteinte. Les hommes d'Etat prolétariens, les dirigeants des partis communistes, bien

au contraire, ont non seulement la possibilité, mais le devoir d'intervenir dans la science. Leur fonction, leur rôle historique, les rendent possesseurs d'une science sans laquelle ils ne seraient pas des hommes d'Etat et au nom de laquelle ils interviennent.[30]

[. . . statesmen of proletarian countries are not like the statesmen of other countries. They have the task of knowing the fundamental science of the proletariat, Marxism-Leninism, in order to dominate its principles and from this understanding to direct the daily struggle of the working class. There is an innate difference between bourgeois and proletarian statesmen. The former are the shop-assistants of a henceforth parasitic class. The latter are the products of the people's own struggle. They are the most aware and the most reflective unit of the proletarian army. They are at the avant-garde of the working class which is itself at the avant-garde of the whole society. The former can only intervene in the domains of science and of culture as statesmen. In so much as they are statesmen, they are strangers to the movement that produces culture; this movement takes place beyond them; it is outside their reach. Proletarian statesmen, the leaders of the communist party, like it or not, have not only the possibility but also the task of intervening in the sciences. Their function, their historic role, makes them possessors of a science without which they would not be statesmen and in the name of which they must intervene.]

In this quote, Desanti makes clear that the knowledge of the directorship of the Communist Party is superior to that of the leaders of bourgeois states. This superiority is not, however, due to better research or to technical facility. It is instead attributable to the different *natures* of the statesmen themselves. While the bourgeois statesman is only a *"commis"* or "shop boy" who carries out the commands of a parasitic class and whose knowledge is therefore tainted, the communist statesman is himself the product of the people's struggle. This is the guarantee of his knowledge for it is the case that he has been produced as "the most aware and reflective" element of a class which, in its struggle, embodies the unity of theory and practice that is the mark of a true science.[31] Because the Communist Party is that vehicle by which the proletariat realizes its destiny, the directors of the Communist Party who administer this action can thus be said to be the vanguard's vanguard. Unlike bourgeois statesmen whose role is accidental or merely functional, the "historic role" of party leaders has made them the possessors and the administrators of a science that understands the world in its truth. This truth is that the world is in the process of a dialectical transformation from capitalism to communism. Possessors of this knowledge and historically chosen agents of this transformation, party leaders therefore have, by nature, the ability to formulate and direct the revolution.

Although *Science Bourgeoise et Science Prolétarienne* stops just short of this conclusion, an article that appeared in the Communist theoretical journal *La Pensée* goes all the way with this line of thinking, identifying true knowledge not only with the leadership of the Communist Party but with the historical agent Stalin himself. In what could only charitably be called an argument, party philosopher and Paris bureau director Georges Cogniot states in a 1948 article, titled "Staline, Homme de Science," that, on the basis of Stalin's theoretical work on the dialectic in the *Short Course* and on the evidence of his masterful application of this work to the development of the Soviet Union, Stalin should be recognized as "*cet incomparable savant qui, dans une époque de l'histoire toute nouvelle . . . a su appliquer la méthode de la science, le marxisme, à un développement des choses totalement originales.*"[32] [that incomparable genius who, in a totally new epoch of history . . . knew how to apply the scientific method, Marxism, to totally new circumstances.]

That Cogniot's praise horribly overestimated Stalin's achievement and that the obsequiousness of the statement is due to the cult of personality surrounding the Soviet leader is obvious. However, Cogniot's laudatory article represented in an extreme fashion the extent to which Marxist philosophy had been immiserated in the postwar era by PCF theorists. No longer a philosophy attempting to describe the political world in the complexity of its historical development, Marxism or Marxism-Leninism was reduced to a scientific formula that guaranteed every aspect of the Communist program. All phenomena, be they natural or cultural, were reduced to a struggle of opposites in which quantitative change leads to qualitative transformation. That this fact was not universally accepted was itself taken as a proof of its veracity. For, if it was the case that bourgeois scientists could not recognize the dialectical processes at work in nature and bourgeois statesmen could not recognize dialectical processes at work in society, then this was only because their mistaken ideas were themselves the product of a dialectical development.

The bourgeois were simply on the wrong side of a dialectical struggle and the world had consequently not revealed its truth to them. The proletariat and most especially its theoretical vanguard, the Communist Party, were on the right side of the struggle. Because history had created them as a class that could recognize the world as being in the process of dialectical change, the party was certain of its historical mission and of the means to accomplish it. Having mastered the science of Dialectical Materialism and being certain of its historical role, the problem of revolution became not theoretical but technical; it was just a matter of applying a formula.

Hegelian Marxism 1945-1956

Because of the nature of the ties between Marxist intellectuals and the PCF, Hegelian Marxism only really flourished in France when, for strategic reasons, the Communist Party chose not to enforce its own Marxism-Leninism. This is true of the interwar period when it was only during the Front Populaire that Marxist intellectuals felt comfortable suggesting revisions to orthodox theory, and it is also true of the decade following World War II when Hegelian Marxism enjoyed a few years of development before the onset of the Cold War silenced all innovations. In this three-year period between the liberation and the Soviet rejection of the Marshall Plan, there appeared quite a few books and articles by philosophers like Henri Lefebvre and Auguste Cornu articulating a Hegelian Marxist position. These works reflected the liberal tenor of the time in which they were written. Though it is apparent that they were for the most part merely continuations of projects begun before the war, it is also the case that, because of the popularity of Communism and of Marxist thought in postwar France, these works enjoyed an audience and influence that they never would have were they published in the 1930s.[33] Such texts are therefore worth examining for their own sake as articulations of the Hegelian Marxist position and also because of the influence that these works exerted on later thinkers seeking to break with orthodox Marxism after the revelations of 1956 and who would look to these heterodox writings for inspiration.[34]

Exemplary of such texts are the two books that Auguste Cornu published in 1948. Both of these are of a part with his work from the early 1930s where he attempted to trace the roots of Karl Marx's thought back to its roots in the German romantic tradition. Though his dissertation and the first few articles he published on the subject were written without being able to consult Marx's early writings, his postwar works benefited from the incorporation of recently published materials like *The German Ideology* into their consideration of Marx's development. The first of these two books, *Karl Marx et la Révolution de 1848*, is principally a historical work (though the date of its publication suggests other avenues for interpretation). His other work from 1948, *Karl Marx et la pensée moderne*, attempts to show what Marx's thought owes to the native philosophical tradition from which it grew. Drawing on texts authored by Marx prior to 1846, Cornu traces Marx's thought back to its antecedents in German Romantic and Rationalist thinkers such as Goethe, Fichte, Schelling, and Hegel. Specifically to Hegel, Cornu concludes that the philosophy of Marx owes three things: first, the supposition of the "unity of thought and being"; second, the notion of reality's dialectical development; and third, the conclusion that reality is rational.[35] That this is more than Marx himself ever said that he got from Hegel is clear. Marx's admitted "borrowing" is limited to the dialectic and this he maintained was fundamentally transformed with the materialist inversion.[36] Of course, one should not always trust a philosopher's judgment of his own work, but what each of Cornu's attributions does is to bring Marx much closer to Hegel than is textually warranted. With the unity of thought and being, for instance, Cornu attributes to Marx's project the same telos as the Hegelian one: an understanding of the world in its totality. The attribution of a dialectical development to reality is consistent with the majority of Marx's texts. However, when it is combined with the supposition that reality is rational, Cornu seems to indicate that the realization of reason is inherent in the dialectic and that the self-development of reason is reality. Such a position would seem to run counter to Marx's consistent argument from as early as 1845 that reason is a product and not a cause of dialectical development. For instance, Marx and Engels write in *The German Ideology* that:

> this conception of history depends on our ability to expound the real process of production, starting out from the material production of life itself, and to comprehend the form of intercourse connected with this and created by this mode of production . . . as the basis of all history; and to show it in its action as State, to explain all the different theoretical products

and forms of consciousness, religion, philosophy, ethics, etc.,
and trace their origins and growth from that basis.[37]

By focusing mostly on Marx's writings before his break with Feuerbach, Cornu paints a picture of Marx as essentially a Left Hegelian. As a
response to accounts like Stalin's that overemphasize the economistic
and scientistic side of Marx, there was no doubt a strategic reason for this
account: it showed Marx to be involved with philosophical problems re-
lating to the relationship between being and thought rather than just as
pioneering a scientific method that could explain historical development.
Further, given the pre-1846 texts Cornu emphasizes, there is ample evidence for these connections. This is true even if a study of Marx's subsequent work suggests that many of these positions are later abandoned
with Marx's embrace of materialism and his rejection of speculative
philosophy for political practice. Cornu's Hegelianization of Marx is thus
defensible on two points: first, strategically, in order to open up Marxism
beyond Stalinist diamatics and, second, textually, because a reading of
Marx's work before 1845 justifies the discovery of an intimate link with
Hegel and the Left Hegelians.

The mough just as valid from a strategic standpoint, the work of Henri
Lefebvre during the three years following France's liberation is less tenable in terms of scholarship. This is so because even though, like Cornu,
Lefebvre concentrated on Marx's early work and emphasized its links to
Hegel, Lefebvre also insisted on the fact that this profound Hegelian influence continued all the way through the writing of *Capital*. As we have
seen, this argument also appears in Lefebvre's 1938 book, *Le Matérialisme dialectique*. However, it is continued and deepened in his immediate postwar work, *Logique formelle, logique dialectique* (1947), and in
his primer on Marxist thought written for the "Que sais-je?" series titled
simply *Le Marxisme* (1948).

As its title would suggest, *Logique formelle, logique dialectique* is
intended to be a philosophically rigorous work focusing on the relationship between formal and dialectical logic. As in the first section of *Le
Matérialisme dialectique*, Lefebvre maintains that the dialectical logic
developed by Hegel is superior to formal logics because it does not hypostasize logical categories but instead deals with them in their movement. Also as in *Le Matérialisme dialectique*, Lefebvre concludes that
Hegel's categories, as idealist, are inadequate to deal with *la réalité concrète* and that Marx's materialist inversion corrects this shortcoming
even as it preserves Hegel's essential insights. More interesting than the

book's argument as a whole. though, is its introductory chapter on epistemology. In this chapter, Lefebvre argues against the crude "reflection"
theory of knowledge typical of Marxism-Leninism. In its place, Lefebvre
proposes that the production of knowledge is an active process, "distinct
from, but bound to, nature."[38] As Lefebvre depicts this process, it is one
of reciprocity: man, interacting with nature and organizing it in thought,
eventually produces true knowledge of it. On this point, Lefebvre's
epistemology is undoubtedly superior to the crude mechanical accounts
he implicitly challenges. Typified by party-produced educational materials for the Université Nouvelle, these accounts specify that production
determines consciousness in a one-way relationship. However, Lefebvre's theory of knowledge also brings him very close to the position
that the material world has no priority over thought. Therefore, his position is closer to the Hegelian and objective idealist position that thought
is itself the world.

Le Marxisme goes even further than *Logique formelle et logique
dialectique* in ascribing to Marx an objective idealist position. As in
Cornu's work, this ascription is accomplished by arguing that the most
important parts of Marx's philosophy are taken from Hegel. However, he
goes beyond Cornu in maintaining that this remains the case in Marx's
mature works. The first chapter of *Le Marxisme* is the only one devoted
to Marx's philosophy (the others are devoted to Marxist ethics, sociology, economics, and politics). In it, Lefebvre argues that "*considéré
philosophiquement, le marxisme . . . apparaît sous deux aspects princi-
paux*" [considered philosophically, Marxism . . . appears under two principal aspects].[39] No surprise, both of the "principal aspects" of Marxist
philosophy are taken from Hegel. The first (specified by Lefebvre as essential), is the "*aspect méthodologique*," the dialectic that Hegel developed in his *Logic* and which Marx validated with his scientific research.
The second principal feature of Marx's philosophy is that which Hegel
sketched in his *Phenomenology of Spirit*: "*une histoire générale de la
Conscience humaine*" [a general history of human consciousness]. As
Lefebvre explains the process, Marx took Hegel's story, transformed it
into a "*théorie concrete*," and arrived at the concept of alienation. Because these are the only two aspects of Marx's thought that Lefebvre argues are essential, they are worth considering individually for what they
reveal about what Lefebvre believes Marxism to be.

As far as method goes, Lefebvre maintains that Marx follows Hegel
in specifying that a full analysis of reality demands that the real be rec-

ognized as an ensemble of contradictory elements.[40] For Hegel, Lefebvre believes that this analysis starts with the intuitive but correct recognition of the *"importance primordiale de la contradiction dans tous les domaines (nature et histoire)"* [primordial importance of contradiction in both domains (nature and history)]. Following from this recognition, the dialectic was specified by Hegel as the only logic capable of describing these contradictions in their relations and transformations. This was all correct. However, from this point, argues Lefebvre, Hegel went too far. Believing that he could define this contradiction in general, Hegel took this logical structure as the structure of reality and then reconstructed the necessity of the development of reality in thought. Because of this unwarranted ambition, Hegel's *Logic* culminated in a system that started and ended with thought and that *"n'avait de sens que dans la tête du philosophe,"*[41] [only made any sense in the head of a philosopher].

Though Marx embraced the concept of the dialectic, he did not take it as sufficient within itself for the explanation of all reality. Rather, Lefebvre contends, Marx took the dialectic merely as a method for the analysis of a specific reality. What the dialectic did for Marx then was provide a *"cadre générale"* rather than an *"idée générale."* This "general framework" allowed Marx to investigate the elements of reality and, after sufficient research, to understand it in its own proper movement. This emphasis on the production of knowledge exclusively through the analysis of the *concrète* (that is, of reality's specific historical determinations) is, Lefebvre believes, Marx's main contribution to philosophy and his principal difference from Hegel.

Despite this identification of the principle difference between Marx and Hegel, it is not so obvious that the end result of Lefebvre's "concrete analysis" is that dissimilar to Hegel's speculative one. Though it is apparent that the former differs from the latter in that it departs not from the structure of thought itself but from the analysis of concrete determinations such as the *"formation économique sociale,"* the end result of these analyses is very similar. What Lefebvre believes Marx's dialectical method does is:

> . . . permet [l'analyste] . . . de retrouver le mouvement réel dans son ensemble, donc d'exposer et de comprendre la totalité concrète, actuellement donnée, c'est-à-dire la structure économique et sociale actuelle. La connaissance de cette totalité, à travers ses moments historiques et son devenir, est un résultat de la pensée, mais n'est en rien une reconstruction ab-

straite obtenue par *une pensée* qui accumulerait des concepts
en dehors des faits, des expériences, des documents.[42]

{. . . allow [the analyst] . . . to recover the movement of the
real in its whole and therefore to expose and understand the
actually given concrete totality. This is to say that it allows
one to comprehend the actual economic and social structure.
The knowledge of this totality, through its historical moments
and its becoming, is a result of thought, but it is nothing but an
abstract reconstruction obtained by *a thought* that has accu-
mulated these concepts outside of facts, outside of experiences
and deeds.}

At least as Lefebvre explains the results of the application of Marx's
dialectical method, it is not so different from Hegel's. Really, it is only
their approach that differs. Both produce full knowledge of the world in
its totality, one just does so from the vantage point of pure thought while
the other requires the dialectical analysis of the socioeconomic whole.

In that it mistakes thought about the world for the world itself, there
is another difference specified by Lefebvre between Marx's result and
Hegel's in that Hegel's conclusion is incorrect. Starting and ending with
thought, Hegel specifies a closed system. Because Marx starts with the
infinite determinations of the *concrète* and develops his dialectical understanding of the world out of this, he makes no such error. Rather,
Marx provides the tools to understand and eventually direct this development. Of course, Hegel came very close to this conclusion and developed all of the categories necessary for this elaboration. However, he
failed to make the crucial step from thought to the concrete. According to
Lefebvre, though, this failure can itself be explained by a Hegelian concept that was, like the dialectic, in need of Marx's correction. This concept is that of alienation.

In *Le Marxisme*, Lefebvre's description of alienation does not differ
tremendously from the one given in *Le Matérialisme dialectique*. It still
consists of the supposition that, in his daily activity, man separates off
aspects of himself that then control him. As Lefebvre writes: "Les pro-
duits de l'homme échappent à sa volonté, à sa conscience, à son contrôle.
Ils prennent des formes abstraites . . . des réalités souveraines et oppres-
sives."[43] [The products of man escape from his will, from his consciousness, from his control. They take on *abstract* forms, . . . realities both
sovereign and oppressive.] Simplifying this formula yet further, Lefebvre

specifies that alienation is the process by which a human becomes inhuman. However, because this process, like all processes, is dialectical, it is not man's fate to be forever alienated from himself. Eventually, that which is alienated from us will be restored in a higher unity when *"l'être humaine devient capable d'organiser consciemment et rationellement son activité,"*[44] [the human being becomes capable of organizing consciously and rationally his own activity]. When this happens, Lefebvre argues, we will be fully human.

By combining the concrete theory of alienation with Marx's method, Lefebvre believes that one should be able to trace the natural progress of this alienation, to direct it, and, eventually, to restore man to himself. Shying away from the words "Historical Materialism" and indeed from materialism altogether, Lefebvre argues that the application of the dialectical method to history results in an account of how social production has led to the progressive development of culture and, what is the same thing, to man's increasing alienation.[45] What this analysis of necessity concludes with is the knowledge that this alienation can be ended by the practical recuperation of the human, of the powers that man has turned against himself.[46] This practice, Lefebvre writes, is communism or scientific socialism and its goal is the *"dépassement de l'aliénation"*[47] [overcoming of alienation].

As in the epistemology developed in *Logique formelle, logique dialectique* where there is almost no mention of the priority Marx assigns to the material over thought, in Lefebvre's discussion of the overcoming of alienation there is almost no mention of the class struggle as the process that drives this transformation. Similar to Cornu's identification of the unity of thought and being and the supposition that reality is rational, these conclusions can be attributed directly to both philosophers' tendency to read Marx as a Hegelian. Consequently, most of their work overemphasizes the power of thought and critique to be productive of social change. Especially with the theory of alienation, these postwar Hegelian Marxist works end up ascribing to Marx a philosophical anthropology that makes it seem like a revolution can and will occur when thought has analyzed, understood, and communicated the problem of alienation sufficiently. In Lefebvre's case especially, this leads to the conclusion that the work needing to be done to encourage the revolution is essentially cultural: artists and philosophers need to show what is alienated in culture and then to creatively show ways to overcome this alienation.[48]

Though Lefebvre's endorsement of an artistic revolution seems particularly at odds with a Marxist-Leninist orthodoxy specifying that the revolution will be undertaken by the proletariat and led by the party, between the years 1945 and 1948 the French Communist Party was quite happy to have philosophers and party members like Cornu and Lefebvre busy developing their own variants of Marxist philosophy. Besides echoing the spirit of unity and liberalization that the party wished to foster while in government, such work by prominent intellectuals added to the party's prestige. During this time, Lefebvre was even explicitly recognized as the "Party Philosopher" and hailed as representing *"le marxisme vivant."*[49] However, after the start of the Cold War and with much encouragement from Moscow, the PCF again felt the need to enforce its own understanding of Marxism.

For a Communist Party whose chief ideologues were again emphasizing the priority of material practices over thought and the dogma that universal knowledge was only available to the proletariat and its representative party, the work of the Hegelian Marxists did not sit well. In fact, just mentioning Hegel was seen as a suspicious activity.[50] Representing the start of a trend that would become commonplace during the Cold War era for Marxists both political and intellectual, both Cornu and Lefebvre were in 1949 compelled by the party to author self-critiques of their philosophical positions.[51] For Cornu, this meant admitting that his analysis of the development of Marx's philosophy in *Marx et la pensée moderne* was overly theoretical and that he failed to recognize the role that history (such as the events of 1848) had played in Marx's development.[52] In his autocritique, Lefebvre castigated himself for "thinking too much like a philosopher" and for making Marx into an epistemologist. Like Cornu, he also regretted focusing on the early Marx to the exclusion of the mature economic works and the *hegelianisation* that resulted from this emphasis.[53]

In the case of Cornu, it is apparent that this exercise in self-criticism had some effect. In his subsequent work, he acknowledges Marx's diverse theoretical legacy and attempts to understand Marx as more than a Left Hegelian.[54] For Lefebvre, however, the exercise in self-critique did not steer his work away from its emphasis on alienation, the power of thought, and the role of culture. Though for a time Lefebvre curtailed his more heterodox statements on Marxist philosophy and retreated into writing literary analyses, he never really gave up the argument that he had begun developing in the 1920s that Marxism was a philosophy of human liberation and that this liberation could be accomplished by cultural and artistic means. Evidence of Lefebvre's reluctance to assimilate his work to the party line even during the darkest days of the Cold War came in 1952 when his party membership was suspended after he attributed a fabricated statement to Marx. Following a quote by Zhdanov on music (that, like politics and science the head of the Soviet Communist Party had divided into bourgeois and proletarian camps), Lefebvre inserted into his *Contribution à l'esthetique* (1949) a quote from Marx which read: *"L'art est la plus haute joie que l'homme se donne à lui-même."* [Art is the highest joy that man can give to himself.] Obviously, this fabricated statement conflicts with orthodox aesthetics which held that the idea of art as a "higher pleasure" was a decadent bourgeois prejudice. Party leaders demanded that Lefebvre produce his references and expelled him when he could not. Of course, such a pronouncement on the joy of art was not something that Marx himself would ever have written, but it was very much the kind of statement that the Hegelianized Marx that Lefebvre developed might have set down in one of his more idealist moments.[55]

Existential Marxism 1945-1956

Like the academic Marxisms of Henri Lefebvre and Auguste Cornu, Existential Marxism owed its unique character to a particularly Hegelian reading of Marx. However, unlike the Marxism of the Philosophies group which was inspired equally by Hegel's *Logic* and by the full sweep of the *"histoire générale de la Conscience humaine"* described in *The Phenomenology of Spirit*, Existential Marxists like Maurice Merleau-Ponty and Jean-Paul Sartre took their inspiration almost exclusively from the section in the *Phenomenology* having to do with "The Truth of Self-Certainty." The reason for this particular focus can be traced to Merleau-Ponty's and Sartre's involvement with German phenomenology and, specifically, to their absorption of Husserl and Heidegger, philosophers concerned almost exclusively with the project of describing the relationship of individual consciousness to the world. To this foreign influence may also be added that of a particularly French tradition of reading Hegel inaugurated in the 1930s by Alexandre Kojève and Jean Hyppolite. This tradition influenced not only Merleau-Ponty and Sartre but also had a profound influence on two generations of French philosophers.

Though the French "Hegel Renaissance" has been described as an almost spontaneous occurrence,[56] it should be apparent from this book's discussion of the Philosophies group and its "discovery" of Hegel in the late 1920s that the flurry of interest surrounding Hegel during the years leading up to World War II was not without antecedent. Like that of the Philosophies group a few years before, the readings of Hegel which Ko-jève began offering in lectures at the École Practique des Hautes Études in 1933 and that Hyppolite gave in a series of articles that started appearing in the late 1930s emerged (particularly in Hyppolite's case) out of an established tradition of French Hegelianism.[57] Further, like the work of the Philosophies group, these readings of Hegel were motivated by a postwar desire to overturn the philosophical establishment as this was represented by the idealism of Brunschvicg and other neo-Kantians. As it had since the nineteenth century, the embrace of Hegel thus represented a countertendency in French thought and an effort to expand beyond its native resources.

Despite the fact that Kojève's and Hyppolite's readings of Hegel are not sui generis, it is true that both these philosophers appropriated Hegel in a manner radically different from most previous French efforts and even in a substantially different way than that of the Philosophies group, with whom they shared much the same motivation for reading Hegel. Whereas most previous French philosophy considered *The Phenomenology of Spirit* to be little more than a veiled justification for the Prussian state and had therefore concentrated on Hegel's Greater and Lesser Logics (if at all), Kojève and Hyppolite followed Jean Wahl and the Philosophies group in looking to the *Phenomenology* as an antidote to the atemporal moral idealism characterizing the dominant strain of French academic philosophy as well as to its positivism. Like the Philosophies group, then, they were concerned with locating reason in history and with the resources this situating offered for theorizing social and moral progress without recourse to "eternal reason." However, unlike the Philosophies, whose reading of Hegel's *Logic* and embrace of Marxism led to the development of a worldview encompassing and explaining the dialectical transformation of the social-historical totality, Kojève's and Hyppolite's near exclusive concentration on Hegel's *Phenomenology* tended to focus their attention on the development of individual consciousness.

Though this tendency is more pronounced in Kojève than in Hyppolite, the emphasis on individual consciousness leads both philosophers to ignore or downplay in their readings those aspects of *The Phenomenology of Spirit* which suggest that Hegel's account represents the necessary development of reason through a world-historical synthesis. Instead, each narrows in on sections of the *Phenomenology* that provide descriptions of the relationship of individual consciousness to the world. Thus, in their interpretations, Hegel becomes primarily a phenomenologist of individual experience rather than a dialectical logician or a chronicler of the development of the absolute spirit through its self-alienation.

In the works on the *Phenomenology* for which they are best known, Kojève's *Introduction à la lecture de Hegel* (1939) and Hyppolite's *Genèse et structure de la Phénoménologie de l'esprit de Hegel* (1946), both philosophers pick out an element or stage from Hegel's narrative that is concerned with self-consciousness and that they believe essential to understanding the movement of Hegel's dialectic. For Kojève, this essential stage of dialectical development is that of the contest of wills depicted by Hegel in the dialectic of Lordship and Bondage. The primordial demand for the recognition of one's own status as a desiring, self-conscious being through the active subjugation of another for Kojève holds the key to understanding all of the subsequent developments described in the *Phenomenology*.[58] From this understanding of the motor of the dialectic, the world as Kojève understands and describes it unfolds as essentially a violent place. Consequently, history for him is seen to consist of the successive struggles of individuals toward their own self-realization as free agents in a free society.[59]

Like Kojève, Hyppolite's reading of *The Phenomenology of Spirit* tends to focus on the problem of individual consciousness. However, whereas Kojève locates the essential feature of Hegel's dialectic in the individual's battle for recognition, Hyppolite emphasizes the experience of "unhappy consciousness."[60] Because self-consciousness is only able to constitute itself through the recognition of others, to be self-conscious is to be alienated; it is to simultaneously assert and deny what one is. For Hyppolite, the ontological given of alienation finds its reflection in the experience of unhappy consciousness. In this stage of the dialectic, the individual consciousness recognizes that there is something in the world that it can neither negate nor deny but that it must recognize as greater than itself. Thus the alien in one's own consciousness is reflected in the fundamental otherness and estrangement of the absolute. Though Hyppolite describes this forlorn attitude as that which typifies Western culture, he does not believe that it is permanent.[61] Rather, just as conscious-

ness once alienated itself into self-consciousness in order to realize a
higher synthesis, the spirit of the absolute as the once alienated human
spirit is in the process of being re-assimilated through the progress of
culture.[62]

In that both Kojève and Hyppolite relate philosophical anthropolo-
gies in which individuals, through history, realize their true nature and
their true freedom, it is easy to see how the readings of Hegel that each
promulgates might be assimilable to certain French Academic readings
of Marx. Despite this affinity and even though Kojève and Hyppolite
both explicitly recognize the connection between their philosophies and
that of Marx, when these authors' writings exploded in popularity following World War II, they were met with hostility by the party and by
Marxist philosophers associated with the party. Undoubtedly, this hostile
reception was due to these works' emphasis on Hegel at a time when just
mentioning the German academician's name in a positive light was
viewed by the party as evidence of idealist heterodoxy. However, Kojève's and Hyppolite's thought was also anathema because of its association with the philosophy for which the Communist Party and its philosophers reserved the bulk of their bile during the immediate postwar
years: existentialism.

At least as represented in its secular variant by Maurice Merleau-
Ponty and Jean-Paul Sartre, existentialist philosophers took the work of
Kojève and Hyppolite on Hegel's dialectic of consciousness quite seriously. Despite this attention, French Existentialism as it developed between 1936 and 1945 did not deal much with the historical aspects of the
dialectic, an area of major concern for Kojève and Hyppolite.[63] Instead,
Sartre and Merleau-Ponty chose to concentrate almost exclusively on
those parts of *The Phenomenology of Spirit* that outlined an ontology of
individual experience. Though Kojève and Hyppolite also demonstrate
this concentration, they did so because they believed that the concept of
recognition provided the key to understanding all of the dialectical transformations that constitute the total historical movement described in
Hegel's tome. Sartre's and Merleau-Ponty's concentration on the ontological constitution of the individual as a split subject cannot therefore be
solely attributable to their influence. Rather, it seems to be the case that,
at least while writing *L'Être et le néant* (1943) and *Phénoménologie de
la perception* (1945), the main influence on both Merleau-Ponty and
Sartre was prewar German Phenomenology and particularly the onto-

logical descriptions of being-in-the-world provided by Heidegger and Husserl.

Given the scope of this study, a thorough consideration of Sartre's and Merleau-Ponty's existential philosophies in relation to French Hegelianism and German Phenomenology is precluded. However, in that Merleau-Ponty's and Sartre's subsequent forays into Marxist philosophy cannot be understood except as an attempt to graft Marxism onto this earlier work, it will be helpful to outline these works' general features. In addition, because Merleau-Ponty's *Phénoménologie de la perception* (1945) can be read as a response to the dualistic ontology developed by Sartre in *L'Être et le néant* (1943), it is probably best to start with Sartre's description of individual experience in that work before specifying how Merleau-Ponty's *Phénoménologie* amended this description and certainly before going into how both perspectives were changed by their authors' considerations of Marx and Marxism.

In *L'Être et le néant*, Sartre does not hide the debt that his thought owes to Hegel, Husserl, and Heidegger. Rather, he emphasizes that his ideas about the nature of consciousness, about the need for phenomenological description, and about the primacy of Being all have their antecedents in these philosophers' ideas (albeit also representing significant corrections of them).[64] Broadly considered, what Sartre presents in *L'Être et le néant* is an ontology that attempts to describe the basic features of reality and of consciousness without recourse to essences. He thus follows Husserl in rejecting the use of nature/appearance dualisms in ontological description because he believes that they "embarrass philosophy."[65] Not wishing to continue reddening philosophy's countenance, Sartre insists that reality is only as it is found in human consciousness, as appearance. Starting then from phenomena, from things as they appear, Sartre attempts in *L'Être et le néant* to examine being as it appears to us. As with Heidegger in *Being and Time*, he begins this examination with the positing of a question. Sartre wonders, "What kind of attitude reveals the relation of man to the world?" His answer to this question is that it is itself the asking of questions that reveals the fundamental relation of man to being. This attitude of questioning, he maintains, expresses the permanent possibilities of non-being which are to be found in being. For, when we question, we express both a lack in ourselves (we do not know the answer) and the possibility of negative replies to our query.

Being, Sartre maintains, does not experience this same attitude. The attitude of questioning, of wondering what may not be, is a human characteristic. A curious attitude is thus the fundamental relation of human being to world and it can only be explained as the expression of a lack that is a part of one's being. To illustrate this point, Sartre describes how negation only arises in the world through human consciousness. For example, there is no such thing as destruction or the changing of something into nothing in the physical world. However, we, as humans, give meaning to the concept of nothingness by positing that something once extant is no more. Sartre concludes from this that "the *not*, as an abrupt, intuitive discovery appears as consciousness [of being]."[66]

As humans, our primary awareness is a pre-reflective consciousness of something that is not us. In other words, even before we are conscious of being conscious (the second stage of awareness), we are aware of an object that is not us. From this examination of the relationship of self to world, which shows that that which is most fundamental to us is the attitude of negation, Sartre concludes that negativity is at the heart of consciousness. It is only when one establishes that one is "not" this chair, "not" this glass of pastis, "not" this mother's body that one becomes self-aware. This negativity, this "not" (which is what we are) is that which Sartre terms the *pour-soi* or "for-itself." It is one aspect of our being. The other aspect of our being is what the for-itself relates itself to and it is that which the for-itself is constantly in a process of denying. Sartre terms this component of the self the *en-soi* or "in-itself."

The in-itself is the non-conscious aspect of one's being. It is given and exists as a plenum: it is everywhere full. The in-itself lacks nothing and it desires nothing. It is contingently the way that it is. The in-itself is what the for-itself relates itself to when it speaks of having a past. The past is that which the for-itself was but is no longer because of its negation.[67]

As opposed to the in-itself which is non-conscious, the for-itself is pure consciousness. It is related to the in-itself but only in the mode of not being it. The in-itself provides a referent which the for-itself constantly negates and abhors.[68] The for-itself is lack; it is the continuous nihilation of the in-itself. Differently put, the for-itself is oneself as freedom. It is the denial of what one was, the possibility associated with what one is, and the projection to what one could be. Because one aspect of our being is this ability to affirm or deny anything, Sartre maintains that we are ontologically constituted as radically free individuals, always presented with a choice.[69]

Though the for-itself and the in-itself compose the self and define its dynamic as one of self-overcoming through action, the two do not constitute a complete self. A complete self would be one that could unite in-itself and for-itself and that could thereby provide its own foundation. Because the for-itself is lack, it desires being in the way that the in-itself has being and is complete unto itself. However, if the for-itself were able to become identical with the in-itself, then it would cease to exist as consciousness. Nevertheless, the impossible union of the "in-itself-for-itself" is its goal.

The unfulfillable desire of the self to be united as in-itself-for-itself Sartre terms the desire to be God.[70] This is the desire to be one's own cause or to be one's own foundation. Because the split in being is an ontological feature, the for-itself will never achieve this goal and the self will remain fundamentally a failure. The conscious realization by the self that this failure is perpetuated by each action of the for-itself and that the goal of becoming in-itself-for-itself will never be achieved makes the character of the self essentially one of dissatisfaction. The for-itself is creative; as it nihilates it makes choices about itself and its relation to others. As a creative being, the for-itself desires to perform the ultimate creative act, which is to create itself. Because this desire is unattainable, the self finds itself an unhappy consciousness: aware of something bigger than itself with which it must reconcile, but unable to achieve this union without giving up what it essentially is.

Though sketchy, this account of Sartre's phenomenological description of consciousness in *L'Être et le néant* has hopefully delineated some of its more prominent characteristics. Among these, what perhaps stands out most to the reader of this book after so much emphasis in Marxist theory on the production of consciousness through work and social structures is the fact that Sartre takes consciousness not as produced, but as an ontological given. As he depicts the structure of reality and of consciousness, it is just a fact that there exist individuals whose essence is to be conscious of that which they are not. Unlike Hegel or the early Marx where the divided or unhappy consciousness is shown to be the result of a process which is itself subject to overcoming, Sartre hypostatizes the dialectic; one is always in the process of negating what one is, yet this negation will never lead to a greater synthesis. In terms of experience, this given translates to the fact that, though one is essentially free, this freedom comes at the price of being always uncomfortable with our past, with our bodies, with our relationships with others, and even with each choice that our consciousness makes in order to realize itself as freedom.

Though the existential philosophy of Merleau-Ponty agrees both in method (phenomenological description) and in its basic ontology (that man is essentially negation) with that of Sartre, Merleau-Ponty attempts to correct some of the conclusions to which Sartre's insistence on the dualistic nature of human consciousness had led. Thus, though Merleau-Ponty agrees with Sartre (and with Kojève) that man, in choosing, is essentially transcendence, he specifies in *Phénoménologie de la perception* that this movement always takes the form of the historical transcendence of a specific situation in the world. For Merleau-Ponty, it is this contingency with which man must interact and which determines the meaning and context of the choices that man makes in asserting his freedom.[71]

The recognition of the importance of contingent factors in giving meaning and direction to the choices of a negating consciousness lead Merleau-Ponty to a rejection of the radical separation of the individual from himself, from other people, from the world, and from history that is characteristic of Sartre's position in *L'Être et le néant*. In place of this radical separation of for-itself from in-itself, Merleau-Ponty provides a phenomenological description of the "space in between: the intersubjective space of perception and the body."[72] Thus where Sartre posits a radical separation between mind and body, insofar as the body is in-itself and frustrates the desires of the conscious for-itself, Merleau-Ponty recognizes that the body is the locus of sensations which allow the for-itself to operate in the world. How it operates, he explains, is as an embodied subject whose being is defined through its relation with others. Subjectivity, Merleau-Ponty concludes, is an intersubjective, dialectical process and not just an ontological given.

Finally, Merleau-Ponty takes issue with Sartre's notion of freedom. Though he recognizes that the subject is always in the process of negating that which she is, this negation always takes the form of committing to some future on the basis of the situation which the past and its contingency provides. This is not determinism. What is given does not compel the subject's choice. However, it does mean that, by choosing, the subject commits herself, to a certain relationship, to a certain understanding of what her choice means in relation to others, to herself, and to history. Of course, she is free to choose again, but this choice will again be constituted and given meaning by the relationships between herself and the others that the choice affects.[73]

After France's liberation, the existentialist philosophies of Sartre, Merleau-Ponty, Camus, Mounier, and others came into popular vogue. Not only were their writings read by philosophers and other academics, but their work was also broadly discussed by the popular media and heralded as the philosophy that captured the zeitgeist of the era. Given this popularity, it is no surprise that the Communists (who were themselves convinced that Marxism and not existentialism was the true philosophy of the postwar age) met the existentialists with hostility. Though it is not necessary to detail the attacks made by philosophers like Cogniot, Desanti, and Lefebvre on the existentialists, it is worth mentioning the general line that these attacks took.[74] At its base, the Communists argued, existentialism was a bourgeois philosophy and it represented bourgeois ideology. This, they ascertained, could be the only reason that a philosophy like Sartre's could emphasize that the individual is radically free, that he is estranged from his community, and that his acts have no meaning in history. To a worker who is daily confronted with the "choice" of having his labor stolen or starvation and who finds meaning in the struggle to end his estrangement, such a position is inconceivable. In this aspect, existentialism was simply the old liberal dream masquerading under a facade of radicalism. As such, Communist critics of existentialism judged that it provided an apology for things as they are and for the Gaullist state.[75]

Given the acrimony between the existentialists and the communists that existed in the years immediately following World War II, it is somewhat surprising that both Sartre and Merleau-Ponty as well as the journal they edited, *Les Temps Moderne*, would embrace the philosophy of Marxism. The reasons for this embrace are complex and are not the same for either philosopher. However, it seems to be the case that, about 1945 but perhaps much earlier,[76] Merleau-Ponty became convinced that the only chance for history to advance and for man to become free was a revolutionary movement. Further, he decided that the vehicle for this revolution was most probably (but not definitely) the Soviet Union. Similarly, but under different circumstances, in 1952 Sartre was swayed to investigate the philosophy of Marxism and the politics of Communism. He did so because they seemed to provide the only genuine alternative to the bourgeois state and because this was the only theory and the only program that seemed capable of securing the individual a field for authentic self-realization.

While Sartre in 1945 was busy proclaiming that existentialism was a humanism and that the philosophy of Marxism was superseded by his insights into the radical duality of human beings,[77] Merleau-Ponty took it upon himself to investigate what resources Marxism had to offer existential philosophy. Unlike Sartre's subsequent conversion to Marxism, which seems capricious and motivated almost wholly by moral indignation, Merleau-Ponty had already taken up certain Marxist themes in *La Phénoménologie de la perception*. Though in this book he had critiqued Marxism for its economic determinism—an assumption that he felt missed the fact that all people are in their consciousness free—he substantially agreed that social conditions and history give meaning to revolt.[78]

The three years following the publication of *La Phénoménologie de la perception* saw Merleau-Ponty move closer and closer to a Marxian perspective and to an endorsement of communist politics. This movement is evidenced in his critiques of liberalism, which juxtapose its timeless abstractions and ideals to the values that arise out of history and social situations. His sympathies with Marxist thought were also acknowledged explicitly in a number of essays written for *Les Temps Moderne* and gathered in the book *Sens et non sens* (1948) that assimilate his existentialism to Marxism. As might be expected given his background and his earlier work, the Marx with whom Merleau-Ponty attempted to merge his existentialism is the early Marx who theorized the possibility of man's liberation. Rejecting economic deterministic aspects of Marx's thought, Merleau-Ponty maintains in these essays that Marx was involved in the study and critique of "general forms of existence."[79] The materialist method for Merleau-Ponty is therefore not concerned with the discovery of ineluctable laws but with the description of historical structures in all their complexity and variety and in their tendencies and direction. At least in this aspect, Merleau-Ponty believes that Marxism comes very close to phenomenology as both philosophies "conceive of history as the dialectical process in which general structures emerge."[80]

Hardly mentioning the role of economic structures, Merleau-Ponty argues in *Sens et non sens* that it is man and his decisions that constitute history. It is not the case for Merleau-Ponty that Marxism describes the economic movement that produces a revolutionary class. What it does is provide an analysis of the general socioeconomic structures from which man can then make a decision about how and in what way to act. Marxism thus becomes the method of critique by which revolutionary leaders can reveal to the proletariat the possibilities for liberation inherent in their contingent situation. Given this information, the individual proletarian is then free to make a choice about whether or not she will realize this possibility in praxis or political acts.[81]

An occasion for a deep consideration of the meaning of political acts came for Merleau-Ponty with the publication of Arthur Koestler's *Darkness at Noon* (1946, in France as *Le Zéro et l'infini*). Written as a fictitious first-person account of the Moscow show trials, to many liberal and even not-so-liberal ideologues, this book represented the last word on the brutality and horror inextricably associated with communist regimes. As would be expected, the novel was immediately attacked as a work of bourgeois propaganda by the Communists. In two of the essays that formed *Humanisme et terreur* (1947), Merleau-Ponty also attacked Koestler's work. As he believed that the fictionalized details of the trials that Koestler provided were substantially correct, he did not attack it as the PCF did, for its falsity. Rather, through a rather complex argument that owes much to the Kojèvian thesis that all action is inherently violent and that it is only through violence that man realizes himself and creates history, Merleau-Ponty argued that Koestler failed to understand the historical situation that made the trials comprehensible as anything more than meaningless political purges. Where all that Koestler could see was terror without reason, Merleau-Ponty argued that, from another perspective—that of the proletariat engaged in revolution, this violence might be judged quite differently. As he wrote,

> Within the U.S.S.R. violence and deception have official status while humanity is to be found in daily life. On the contrary, in democracies the principles are humane but deception and violence rule daily life. Comparisons only make sense between wholes taking into account their circumstances. It is useless to confront a fragment of Soviet history with our practices and laws.[82]

Merleau-Ponty's critique of Koestler and of liberalism should not be read as an endorsement of Communist practice or of Marxist-Leninist philosophy. While he argues in *Humanisme et terreur* that the proletariat is the only class that is in a position to end its alienation and seize its freedom, he takes pains to demonstrate that there is not necessarily an identification between this "universal" class and the Soviet Union. What Merleau-Ponty apparently believed that he was doing with his critique of Koestler was making an argument from within Marxist philosophy that would allow both liberalism and communism to be understood and critiqued. Further, it was hoped that this critique might permit both communists and liberals to come to terms with the fact that human freedom is neither an ontological nor a historical given but that it is realized in the determinate actions and choices of individuals in the social structure. If neither the communists nor the liberals allow people to be in a position to choose this freedom, then Marxism is needed as a means to diagnose the problem and to give people a context in which to act and to move toward the full recognition of man by man.[83]

In the years following the publication of *Humanisme et terreur* and *Sens et non sens*, Merleau-Ponty moved further and further away from his conviction that Marxist philosophy held the key to human liberation. Helped along by events such as the Soviet Union's actions with regard to the Korean war, Merleau-Ponty retreated from his argument that the dialectic of consciousness promised any sort of total liberation.[84] The last gasp of his attempt to understand the human condition through Marxist logic and concepts came with his book *Les Aventures de la dialectique* in 1955. In this work, he argues that—over the hundred or so years of its existence—Marxist philosophy has itself undergone a dialectical transformation. As it existed in 1848, the proletariat gave Marxism and the dialectic a historical subject. As history advanced and the proletariat and its role became more nebulous, Marxist philosophy likewise became more nebulous and detached from its object. It is to this development that Merleau-Ponty traces the advent and rise of "Western Marxism." As he explains it, thinkers like Korsch, Lukács, and Lefebvre progressively found it harder to empirically identify the rigid polarization of the social body into working class and bourgeoisie. Because of this difficulty, they increasingly concerned themselves with how to create or identify forces in the superstructure—in culture—that might suggest revolutionary possibilities.[85] The final result of this process was the formulation of a Marxism where an ideal proletariat is still identified with the future of humanity but no actual proletariat can be found that corresponds to this ideal. The realization of this occurrence leaves Marxism without a historical subject and thus without a purpose for existing. For Merleau-Ponty, however, this development was fine. He had come to the conclusion that what was wrong was not the dialectic (which did indeed provide a means for analyzing human relations), but the "pretension of terminating it in an end of history or in a permanent revolution, in a regime that, being the confrontation of itself has no need of being challenged from outside."[86] Marxism as a philosophy of the advance of history was thus a failure but the dialectic of consciousness remained unchallenged. With this conclusion, Merleau-Ponty moved back almost to where he had started in the mid-1940s, that is, filling in a phenomenology of consciousness.

At the same time that Merleau-Ponty was in the process of rejecting Marxism as a philosophy which held the key to the realization of human freedom, Jean-Paul Sartre began accommodating it to his own existentialism. Though neither years of scathing critiques by Marxist philosophers associated with the party nor his associate Merleau-Ponty's embrace of Marxism had made him revise the opinion that Marxism made man into an effect rather than acknowledging him as a cause,[87] Sartre was abruptly converted to Marxism and to communist partisanship in 1952. The occasion for this conversion is attributable to various causes, none of which were philosophical. The first and antecedent cause seems to be Sartre's frustration at the failure to realize his own political and ethical program through the vehicle of the political party he founded along with other noncommunist leftist militants. Known as the Rassemblement Democratique Révolutionnaire, this party's failure by early 1952 had left him feeling that there was really no alternative between communism and capitalism. Further, after Korea, Sartre felt that the East in general and communist states in particular were increasingly the victims of a "war-mongering West."[88] What seemed to be the proximate event that put him decidedly in favor of Marxism and of Communism was the arrest of the Communist Parliamentarian Jacques Duclos on espionage charges in May 1952. Both the absurdity of the arrest—two dead pigeons and a car radio were seized by French authorities as spy gear—and the perception that the arrest had been made as a Cold War gambit in an attempt to placate the United States apparently tipped the balance for Sartre.[89] Almost immediately after the arrest he set about writing a series of articles for *Les Temps Moderne* under the heading *Les Communistes et la paix*. In between polemical attacks on the bourgeoisie as "*beaux enfants*" and "*chers rats visquex*," these articles represented the first attempts by Sartre to graft his existentialism onto a Marxian framework.[90]

As in *L'Être et le néant*, Sartre in *Les Communistes et la paix* concentrated on the individual and his freedom. However, instead of arguing that the only restrictions placed on man's freedom are those that he allows by acting in bad faith, Sartre now recognized that history somewhat determines one's ability to act. Thus while the proletarian individual might choose to end his alienation, it was now understood by Sartre that this choice could only be realized in action inasmuch as there was a sociopolitical situation that allowed this to happen. For the bourgeois individual, the capitalist system seemed to work just fine. The worker, however, found that any solo attempts to realize his own freedom were frustrated. What the worker needed therefore was to organize himself politically as a class and to reject bourgeois institutions that did nothing but separate him from his fellow workers.[91] This done, he could then set about achieving the end to his own alienation through political or revolutionary means.

Though Sartre probably could have stopped at this conclusion and ended up offering an interesting version of a Humanist Marxism, he went further in his analyses and argued that not only did workers need to organize themselves as a class to realize their authentic freedom, but that the communist party was necessarily the vehicle that enabled this organization and transformation. Without the party, Sartre reasoned, workers were—like the bourgeoisie—"atomized" and incapable of acting creatively. Each act was destined to end in frustration. However, the party was that vehicle, that pure subject, which overcame the isolation of individuals, unifying them as a creative force, and allowing the lone prole to act for the good of all humanity.[92]

As could be expected of a piece written by a prominent intellectual who was previously their enemy but who had now endorsed every aspect of their program, the reaction of the French Communist Party to *Les Communistes et la paix* was quite positive. Of course, if the party had bothered to look closely at his argument, it would have recognized how far from Stalinist orthodoxy Sartre's theory of liberation through free choice actually was. However, it seems that, in 1952, they were just happy to have him as an ally. He would remain so until the events of 1956 led him to change his position once again. Though he did not show the same good sense as his partner Merleau-Ponty in forsaking the attempt to force together an ontology of individual freedom with a philosophy of history, he did at least abandon the opinion that the Communist Party was the only and necessary vehicle for the realization of this freedom.

Notes

1. Michael Kelly, *Modern French Marxism* (Oxford: Blackwell, 1982), 50.

2. Tony Judt, *Marxism and the French Left* (Oxford: Clarendon Press, 1986), 178.

3. Sunil Khilnani in the introduction to *Arguing Revolution* (New Haven, CT: Yale University Press, 1993) argues against this type of classification. Quoting Richard Rorty, he derides it as an "attempt to impose a problematic on a canon drawn up without reference to that problematic." The fact remains, however, that even though participants in a philosophical movement may not have answered to a particular name or subscribed to a particular doxology, these participants can, in retrospect, be categorized according to their shared positions and separated from others according to their distinctive positions. This is not to say that there will be no overlap between individuals, but that a finite number of positions around a certain issue can be identified and that those who hold those positions but do not hold others can be roughly grouped together. This is especially the case if one takes the care to detail why and how certain positions develop and why some persons would likely share certain arguments but resist others.

4. Yves Santamaria, *L'Enfant du malheur: le parti communiste Français dans la Lutte pour la paix, 1914-1947* (Paris: S. Arslan, 2002), 265; and Roger Bourderon, *La Négociation: été 1940, crise au PCF* (Paris: Éditions Syllepse, 2001).

5. See D.S. Bell and Byron Criddle, *The French Communist Party in the Fifth Republic* (Oxford: Clarendon Press, 1994): and Maxwell Adereth, *The French Communist Party: A Critical History: From Comintern to the Colours of France (1920-1984)*, (Manchester: Manchester University Press, 1984), 51.

6. Neill Nugent and David Lowe, *The Left in France* (New York: St. Martin's Press, 1982), 32.

7. Adereth, *The French Communist Party*, 111.

8. Adereth, *The French Communist Party*, 113.

9. Ronald Tiersky, *French Communism 1920-1972* (New York: Columbia University Press, 1974), 114; and Adereth, *The French Communist Party*, 117-120.

10. Nugent and Lowe, *The Left in France*, 33.

11. Adereth, *The French Communist Party*, 119.

12. Santamaria, *L'Enfant du malheur,* 277-78; and Adereth, *The French Communist Party*, 122-24.

13. Adereth, *The French Communist Party*, 127.

14. Judt, *Marxism and the French Left,* 327.

15. Santamaria points out that the number of casualties was undoubtedly exaggerated by the PCF. Bell and Criddle add, however, that the more accurate

number of approximately 10,000 members executed by the National Socialists "is impressive enough." See Santamaria, *L'Enfant du malheur,* 276; and Bell and Criddle, *The French Communist Party in the Fifth Republic,* 75.

16. Nugent and Lowe, *The Left in France,* 137; and Judt, *Marxism and the French Left,* 327.

17. Adereth, *The French Communist Party,* 141.

18. Kelly, *Modern French Marxism,* 144.

19. Jacques Fauvet, *Histoire du parti communiste Français* (Paris: Fayard, 1977), 387-88.

20. Bell and Criddle, *The French Communist Party in the Fifth Republic,* 78.

21. Cécile Angrand, introduction to *Cours de Philosophie* (Paris: Éditions Sociales, 1945), 6.

22. Jean Desanti, "La science idéologique historiquement relative," in *Science bourgeoise et science prolétarienne,* Casanova et al. (Paris: Les Éditions de La Nouvelle Critique, 1950): 7-14.

23. For similar arguments, through less extreme, see Roger Garaudy, "À propos de la position de parti dans les sciences," *Cahiers de Communisme* no. 5 (May 1955): 590-611; and Georges Cogniot, "La loi économique fondamentale du socialisme," *Apprendre,* no. 22 (Feb/Mar 1953): 4-23.

24. Raymond Guyot, "Conclusions," in *Science bourgeoise et science prolétarienne,* 45.

25. Laurent Casanova, introduction to *Science bourgeoise et science prolétarienne,* 5.

26. Gerard Vassails, "Atome et Politique," in *Science bourgeoise et science prolétarienne,* 20.

27. Gerard Vassails, "Atome et Politique," in *Science bourgeoise et science prolétarienne,* 28; and Francis Cohen, "Génétique classique et biologie mitchourienne," in *Science bourgeoise et science prolétarienne,* 42. Examples of the "illumination" provided by membership in the French Communist Party exist across scientific disciplines. However, as in the Soviet Union and with the case of Lysenko, the science of biology provides some of the most egregious examples. For instance, the scientific researcher and popularizer Marcel Prenant went in the span of a few months from arguing strongly and explicitly that neo-Darwinism proves the theory of nature espoused by Marx and Engels to a posture of total vacillation, willing neither to endorse the neo-Darwinist position nor to condemn it. Having even less of a scientific conscience, party intellectuals like Georges Cogniot went so far as to decry as absurd the hypotheses of Weismann, Morgan, and Mendel that hereditary information governs all of an organism's traits and that the environment has no effect on this hereditary matter at the level of the individual. Of course, then as now, these hypotheses were taken by most biologists as established. It is no wonder then that even biologists who were also committed communists could not in good conscience endorse such

rhetoric. Upon being pressured to second it with their researches, many biologists and other scientists resigned their memberships in the PCF. See Georges Cogniot, *L'Histoire du Parti bolchevik et ses enseignements actuels* (Paris: Éditions Sociales, 1949), 39-46; and Eva Shandewyl, "Tensions Between Scientific Ethos and Political Engagement: Belgian University Professors and the Lysenko Case" (paper presented at the 19th International Congress of Historical Sciences, Oslo, Norway, 11 August 2000, www.oslo2000.uio.no/univhist/ presentation.html (accessed August 11, 2004), 9, 10. For more on biology and on what may be the most ridiculous claim of Soviet science, that of "dialectical genetics" and the fight against the use of hybrid grain see Dominique Lecourt, *Lysenko* (Paris: Maspero, 1976) and Remi Hess, *Henri Lefebvre et l'aventure du siècle* (Paris: Éditions Métailié, 1988), 135-39.

28. Jean Desanti, "La science idéologie historiquement relative," in *Science bourgeoise et science prolétarienne,* 10.

29. Embarrassed by its conclusions, in October 1951 the "two sciences" thesis was abandoned by the party. However, its influence was still apparent as late as 1966 in articles such as Michel Langevin's "L'enrichissement du Marxisme à partir des resultats du developpement des sciences de la nature." In this article the C.N.R.S. researcher and party pedagogue argued that developments in nuclear arms substantiate the superiority of Engels's dialectics of nature over that of bourgeois science. See Michel Langevin, "L'enrichissement du Marxisme à partir des resultats du developpement des sciences de la nature: 'la dialectique de la nature,'" in *Cahiers de l'Université Nouvelle* series "Esquisse d'une Histoire de la Pensée Scientifique," no. 412 (February 1966): 4.

30. Jean Desanti, "La science idéologique historiquement relative," in *Science bourgeoise et science prolétarienne,* 9.

31. Raymond Guyot, "Conclusions," in *Science bourgeoise et science prolétarienne*, 45.

32. Georges Cogniot, "Staline, Homme de Science," *La Pensée* (November-December 1948): 3.

33. For instance, Lefebvre's 1947 book, *Le Marxisme*, sold over 250,000 copies and by 1974 was in its 16th printing.

34. Althusser, for instance, references Cornu's work on the young Marx favorably in some of his personal letters and Garaudy's humanistic turn evidences the influence of Lefebvre.

35. Auguste Cornu, *Karl Marx et la pensée moderne: contribution à l'étude de la formation du marxisme* (Paris: Éditions Sociales, 1948).

36. Karl Marx, "Afterward to the Second German Edition," *Capital* vol. 1, (Great Britain: Lawrence and Wishart, 1960), 19.

37. Karl Marx and Friedrich Engels, *The German Ideology* (New York: International Publishers, 1989), 58.

38. Kelly, *Modern French Marxism*, 58.

39. Henri Lefebvre, *Le Marxisme* (Paris: PUF, 1974), 23.

40. Lefebvre, *Le Marxisme*, 29.

41. Lefebvre, *Le Marxisme*, 31.

42. Lefebvre, *Le Marxisme*, 35.

43. Lefebvre, *Le Marxisme*, 41.

44. Lefebvre, *Le Marxisme*, 44.

45. Lefebvre, *Le Marxisme*, 119.

46. Lefebvre, *Le Marxisme*, 43.

47. Lefebvre, *Le Marxisme*, 46.

48. See for example Henri Lefebvre, *Contribution à l'esthétique* (Paris: Éditions Sociales, 1953).

49. Remi Hess, *Henri Lefebvre et l'aventure du siècle* (Paris: Éditions A.M. Métailié, 1988), 117.

50. Kelly, *Modern French Marxism*, 81.

51. For more on the practice of autocritique see Pierre Juquin, *Autocritiques* (Paris: Grasset, 1985).

52. Félix Armand and Auguste Cornu, "Critique et Auto-Critique," *La Pensée* (September-October 1949): 84-88.

53. Henri Lefebvre, "Auto-Critique: contribution à l'effort d'èclaircissement idéologique," *La Nouvelle Critique* vol. 4 (March 1949): 41-57.

54. See for instance Cornu, Auguste, *Karl Marx et Friedrich Engels*, 3 vols. (Paris: Éditions Sociales, 1955).

55. For more on this episode and for Lefebvre's critique of Lyssenkism see Hess, *Henri Lefebvre*, 120-40.

56. Mark Poster, *Existential Marxism in Postwar France: From Sartre to Althusser* (New Jersey: Princeton University Press, 1975), 3. Though I disagree with Poster's conclusion that there was an "utter absence of interest in Hegel by academic philosophers," I am indebted in my consideration of Kojève, Hyppolite, Sartre, and Merleau-Ponty to his 1975 work on Existential Marxism and to his 1982 book, *Sartre's Marxism* (Cambridge: Cambridge University Press).

57. Though overemphasizing one aspect of French Hegelianism, Bruce Baugh's recent *French Hegel* (New York: Routledge, 2003) is the work that best demonstrates the influence of Hegel on French thought as perennial and pervasive.

58. Alexandre Kojève, *Introduction to the Reading of Hegel* (New York: Basic Books, 1969), 15.

59. Kojève, *Introduction,* 29.

60. Jean Hyppolite, *Genèse et structure de la phénoménologie de l'esprit de Hegel* (Paris: Aubiers, 1946), 184.

61. Poster, *Existential Marxism*, 26.

62. Poster, *Existential Marxism*, 27.

63. While all Marxist philosophy was banned and Marxist writers were forced underground during the war, existentialist philosophers such as Merleau-

Ponty, Sartre, and Camus continued with their work and their books were allowed to be published.

64. Jean-Paul Sartre, *Being and Nothingness* (New York: Washington Square Press, 1966), 315-40. See also Pietro Chiodi, *Sartre and Marxism* (Sussex: Harvester Press, 1976), 8-10, 29-32.

65. Sartre, *Being and Nothingness,* 3-5.

66. Sartre, *Being and Nothingness,* 43.

67. Sartre, *Being and Nothingness,* 173.

68. Sartre describes this flight of consciousness from being in *Nausea* through his protagonist Rocquentin, who thinks: "I am the one who pulls myself from the nothingness to which I aspire: the hatred, the disgust of existing, there are many ways to make myself exist, to thrust myself into existence" (Norfolk, CT: New Directions, 1964), 100.

69. Sartre, *Being and Nothingness,* 567.

70. Sartre, *Being and Nothingness,* 764.

71. Maurice Merleau-Ponty, *Phénomenologie de la perception* (Paris: Gallimard, 1945), 197; and Barry Cooper, *Merleau-Ponty and Marxism: From Terror to Reform* (Toronto: University of Toronto Press, 1979), 17.

72. Poster, *Existential Marxism,* 147.

73. Cooper, *Merleau-Ponty and Marxism,* 20.

74. For a detailed consideration of the party's attacks on Sartre and his response see Poster, *Existential Marxism,* 109-60. For a consideration of the party and Merleau-Ponty see Sonia Kruks, *The Political Philosophy of Merleau-Ponty* (Atlantic Highlands, NJ: Humanities Press, 1981), 57. Also for a general critique that follows the party line but also reflects on his own youthful existential proclivities see Henri Lefebvre, *L'existentialisme* (Paris: Éditions du Sagittaire, 1946).

75. Laurent Casanova, introduction to *Science bourgeoise et science prolétarienne,* 6.

76. Jean-Pierre Clero and Olivier Bloch, "Maurice Merleau-Ponty et la Guerre: Philosopher en France (1940-1944)," *Revue philosophique de la France et de l'etranger* 3, no. 127 (2002): 315-31.

77. Jean-Paul Sartre, *Existentialism and Humanism* (London: Methuen, 1948).

78. Merleau-Ponty, *Phénomenologie de la perception,* 442-43.

79. Maurice Merleau-Ponty, *Sens et non sens* (Paris: Nagel, 1948), 108; and Kruks, *Political Philosophy,* 49.

80. Kruks, *Political Philosophy,* 50.

81. Kruks, *Political Philosophy,* 56.

82. Maurice Merleau-Ponty, *Humanism and Terror: An Essay on the Communist Problem* (Boston: Beacon Press, 1969), 180.

83. Merleau-Ponty, *Humanism and Terror,* 111-12.

84. Clero and Bloch, "Maurice Merleau-Ponty et la Guerre," 315.

85. Maurice Merleau-Ponty, *Adventures of the Dialectic* (Chicago: Northwestern University Press, 1973), 53.

86. Cooper, *Merleau-Ponty and Marxism*, 132.

87. From 1945 to 1952 Sartre was consistent in this position. See for examples "Materialism and Revolution" (1946) in *Situations VI* (Paris: Gallimard, 1964), 17; and "Faux savants ou faux lièvres" (1950) in *Situations VI* (Paris, Gallimard, 1964), 23-68.

88. David Archard, *Marxism and Existentialism: The Political Philosophy of Sartre and Merleau-Ponty* (Belfast: Blackstaff Press, 1980), 65, 72.

89. Adereth, *The French Communist Party*, 151-52.

90. Jean-Paul Sartre, *Les Communistes et la paix* (1952) in *Situations VI* (Paris, Gallimard, 1964), 80-384.

91. Poster, *Existential Marxism*, 167.

92. Poster, *Existential Marxism*, 169, 170.

Chapter 6

The Purification of Theory

The Response of French Marxism to the Events of 1956

Though they by no means put an end to the postwar popularity of Marxist thought, two events in 1956 occasioned a serious rethinking of the directions that PCF theory, Existential Marxism, and Hegelian Marxism had taken in the decade after the war. The first of these was the February Congress of the CPSU during which Khrushchev gave his "secret speech" detailing the abuses of the Stalin era. The second event was the Soviet invasion of Hungary in November. The effect of these two occurrences on Marxist thought in France was enormous. With the exception of the Trotskyist minority, almost every variant of French Marxism before 1956 was wedded to the position that the Soviet state and the Communist Party were the embodiment of the truth of Marxist philosophy. For the PCF, this identification was so definitive that the party routinely sacrificed its own best interests to the Soviets' whims. Because they believed that the Communist Party held the only hope for the type of total revolution they still desired, academic Marxists were also not immune to this equation.[1] From the thirties to the fifties, Hegelian Marxists had held so steadfastly to this identification that, like Nizan and Politzer, they had either abandoned their own philosophical research or, like Lefebvre and Cornu, had subjected to scathing self-criticism projects suggesting that changes in culture rather than Soviet hegemony might lead to revolution.[2] Existential Marxists such as Sartre and Merleau-Ponty, who even before 1956 had had a difficult time swallowing many Soviet initiatives, took pains developing elaborate apologias designed to explain how these actions—even if they appeared heinous and unjust—were actually essentially positive because they moved history along to a higher moral state.[3]

Despite the show trials and rumors of purges, famine, and mass incarcerations in the Soviet Union, both French Intellectuals and the French Communist Party felt comfortable during the depression of the 1930s pointing to the Soviets as proof of the superiority of the communist system over Western capitalism and, by association, to the superiority of Marxist over bourgeois philosophy. The Soviet victory over "reactionary capitalism" in World War II reinforced these notions. Even during the Cold War and despite the theoretical poverty of scientific socialism and increasing international awareness of Soviet atrocities, many French intellectuals routinely engaged in thoughtless pro-Soviet polemic.[4]

In 1956, the revelation by the Soviet Premier of millions murdered in the name of progress and the demonstration by invasion a few months later that this revelation had not fundamentally changed Soviet practice made it very difficult, if not impossible, to carry on with the identification between Marxist philosophy, the PCF, and the political program of the Soviet Union. Many fellow travelers used these revelations as a final excuse to break with Communism and Marxism altogether.[5] Others, especially those in the party, tried to go on as if nothing had changed. However, for some philosophers the events of 1956 occasioned a rethinking of Marxist philosophy and of the assumptions undergirding the correlation between this philosophy, the Communist Party, and political practice.

It would be nice to say that the majority of these rethinkings were inspired and their conclusions revelatory. However, for the most part, the responses by the PCF, by Existential Marxists, and by Hegelian Marxists were limited by the theoretical resources that each brought to the project. Thoroughly Stalinized and with party secretary Maurice Thorez administering his own cult of personality, it really took the PCF four years to even entertain changes to its orthodox positions.[6] In the early 1960s, when PCF presses tentatively offered Roger Garaudy's works on Humanist Marxism as an alternative to Stalinism, his was a minority voice.[7] Even so, it appeared that the best Garaudy and his fellow Communist Party thinkers could offer in terms of a challenge to Marxist-Leninist orthodoxy was an anemic approximation of Lefebvre's theory of alienation coupled with a willingness to admit anyone, including Catholics and middle managers, into the workers' struggle. Though at times seconded rhetorically, the actual effect on the party of this revision was virtually nil.[8]

Never without its problems, the fusion of existentialism and Marxism offered by some leftist academics was much easier when philosophers such as Maurice Merleau-Ponty and Jean-Paul Sartre had the benefit of popular sentiment or at least self-righteousness on their side. After the wartime experience of resistance (real or imagined), a philosophy of individual action and communal goals just seemed to go together. Further, the link with the Soviet project as an identifiable moral good followed from the latter emphasis. When in 1956 this link was irreconcilably compromised in 1956 by Soviet actions, it threw the problems of the relation of existentialism's individualist ontology of freedom to Marxism's deterministic dialectic of history into relief. The response of the existential Marxists to these events was mixed. While Maurice Merleau-Ponty recognized the awkwardness of his position and retreated further from political philosophy and into phenomenological analysis and psychoanalytic studies, Sartre just worked harder at his speculative gymnastics designed to force Marxism and phenomenology together. The success of this project "to constitute a structural, historical anthropology" can be judged both by its failed completion and by the extent that *La Critique de la raison dialectique* (1960) is referenced favorably today by political philosophers, by students of anthropology, or by phenomenologists.[9]

Though representing an even further retreat from the problems of communist practice than his writings from the late thirties, some of the best work resulting from French Marxism's attempt to deal with the revelations of 1956 was that accomplished by Henri Lefebvre. Representative of the projects undertaken by Edgar Morin, Juan Axelos, and Pierre Fougeyrollas, his fellow contributors to the interdisciplinary journal *Arguments*, Lefebvre's post-PCF philosophy showed a willingness to incorporate methods from sociology and political science. It also evidenced a continuing eagerness to question the fundamental tenets of orthodox Marxism-Leninism, including its long-standing emphasis on work and on the dictatorship of the proletariat.[10] For a time abandoned by and abandoning the PCF, Lefebvre drew on the critical apparatus first sketched out in *La Conscience mystifiée* to further develop the project known as *Critique de la vie quotidienne*. In these studies, he systematically attempted to describe the way in which the modern world constitutes subjects as passive consumers of culture through their alienation by everyday objects and habits.[11] Still cited by cultural critics and architects as well as recognized as one of the inspirations for both May 1968 and for the Situationist movement, this work has had a lasting impact.[12] However, representing a retreat from the endemic problems of Marxism-Leninism, like the revisionist projects of the PCF and Sartre, it cannot be judged to have really suggested productive alternatives to the three ways of theorizing Marxism that characterize the postwar era.

While the responses of Existential Marxism, Hegelian Marxism, and the PCF can retrospectively be recognized as an interesting retreat, an impotent miscegenation, and a dead end, there was one response to the events of 1956 that appeared to offer resources for reconstructing Marxism as something other than a Left Hegelianism or as the state philosophy of the Soviet Union. This was the response to the crisis in Marxist thought articulated by Louis Althusser, first in a series of articles appearing primarily in the journal *La Pensée* between 1960 and 1963 and then in the collaborative work *Lire le Capital*, from 1965. Written by an academic philosopher who was also a committed Communist Party member, it would have made sense that Althusser's work shared with Garaudy, Lefebvre, and the *Arguments* group the tendency to respond to 1956 by opening up to the resources that non-Marxist philosophies and methodologies offered. In some ways, such as his reading Marx through Spinoza, he did just this.[13] However, as a communist deeply committed to the belief that, with Marx, philosophy had become something radically different from what it was before, Althusser took a different path. Instead of mixing Marx with Teilhard de Chardin, Hegel, or Husserl, he advocated a return to Marx's original texts. From these, he hoped to distill a pure theory of Marxism, uncovering those essential elements that made Marx and Marxism different from all the philosophers and philosophies that had preceded it.

Althusser's Assessment of French Marxism in 1956

To fully comprehend the rereading of Marx that Althusser began in 1953 with his article "À propos du Marxisme" and which reached its culmination in *Lire le Capital* in 1965, it is first necessary to see how this project is simultaneously a combination, a rejection, and a reformulation of the traditions of reading Marx in which he was immersed as a professor at the École Normale Supérieure (E.N.S.) and as a Communist Party Mem-

ber. It is within these theoretical traditions (traditions that he believed
had become moribund) that Althusser made his intervention and suggested a solution to the failures of Marxist philosophy in each of its variants.

Publicly, these interventions took the form of critical exegeses of
classical Marxist texts published in academic journals. More privately,
they took the form of seminars and reading groups at the E.N.S. con-
ducted with interested students. Both of these platforms for the development and exposition of Althusser's thought were intended for a philosophically sophisticated audience, and it is this work for which he is best
known. Less well known is the fact that Althusser also authored *vulgari-
sations* of his research meant for the edification of Communist Party
members. Fitting in nicely with the well-established genre of party educational texts in which the same five or so hackneyed quotes from Marx
are combined with three from Engels and two from Lenin (all of which
are then summarized by confident pronouncements that the future be-
longs to communism), these essays, letters, and even drafts of entire
books are helpful in showing how Althusser's thought complements and
is meant as a response to established party tropes and formulas. They
also reveal his philosophy to be neither sui generis nor as simply pastiche
and combination (e.g., Marx + Spinoza + Mao + Lèvi-Strauss = Althusser). Instead, they show Althusser to be a part of and responding to
an established tradition that includes not only the erudite academic
Marxism originating from the rue d'Ulm and published by Gallimard and
Éditions du Seuil but also the vulgar Marxist philosophy issued by Éditions Sociales and disseminated from 64, boulevard Auguste-Blanqui.

The largest unpublished text by Althusser intended for a communist
audience is *Théorie Marxiste et Parti Communiste* (1966-1967). In his
archive, its drafts comprise hundreds of typed and edited pages. If completed, the resulting book would have been Althusser's largest. Written
in response to the party's desire that Althusser reconcile his philosophy
with the thesis of the union of theory and practice, it was also written in
accord with Althusser's belief that party political reform would prove
fruitless without widespread and deep theoretical reform. This work then
was his attempt to change the party by reinterpreting its basic philosophical principles. Due to historical circumstance, to the reluctance of
party presses to publish his thought, and, finally, due to Althusser's radical revision of his project (a revision that rendered this work obsolete),
this text and others similar to it were never published.[14] Nonetheless, by

examining works such as *Théorie Marxiste et Parti Communiste* alongside *Lire le Capital* and classic early articles like "Sur le jeune Marx"
(1961), "Contradiction et surdetermination" (1962), "Sur la dialectique
matérialiste" (1963), and "Marxisme et Humanisme" (1964), one can get
a very good picture of what Althusser believed French Marxism had become by the early 1960s, what dead ends it had run into, what assumptions he believed that he was rejecting, and what problems he was trying
to solve.

In the English translation of *Pour Marx*, the work that gathers the
articles listed above, Althusser provides two introductions. One of these,
"Aujourd' hui," was included in the original 1965 French edition and
was intended to situate his work in the time in which the articles that
comprise it were written and within the traditions of French Marxist
thought. The second introduction, written in 1967 and titled "To My
English Readers," likewise directs his British and American readers to
consider the "conjuncture" in which the articles that comprise it were
authored. The later introduction differs from the earlier one in that it provides a more schematic and less Gallocentric explanation of the motivations for his "interventions." Taken together, the two introductions provide quite a bit of insight into what Althusser thought was wrong with
French Marxism (and with Marxism in general) and what he thought his
reevaluation of Marx accomplishes both politically and philosophically.

Overall, Althusser's estimation of the history of Marxist philosophy
in France, both academic and communist, is that it was abysmal. In his
introduction to the 1965 François Maspero edition of *Pour Marx* he
characterizes it as a "void" and notes the "absence of any real *theoretical*
culture in the history of the French workers' movement."[15] As for the
PCF, he observes that for most of its existence it made do on the meager
theoretical resources bequeathed it by the Comintern and the Cominform.
This starvation diet led the party first to reduce philosophy to science and
then, during the height of the Cold War, to reduce science to ideology.[16]

Why was the party so easily led to these reductivist conclusions? In a
perhaps too simplistic explanation, Althusser reveals that it was easily
swayed to this position because there was no native tradition of French
Marxist thought equivalent to that of Antonio Gramsci in Italy or Rosa
Luxembourg in Poland. Such a tradition might have allowed it to resist
Stalinist domination. Further, there had always been structural and historical obstacles to the development of Marxist thought in France. Due to
the legacy of the revolution of 1789, most radical intellectuals believed

that they could have an effect on the political process by persuading the bourgeoisie to come to their opinion. Most consequently felt no need to identify themselves with the working class in order to foment social change.[17] Those few intellectuals who did identify with the working class and who came to the party were then abused for the crime of not being workers and were driven away. Thus, for the most part, the French party never attracted or was unable to retain the first-rate intellectuals who might provide it with the theoretical labor it so badly needed. Those few exceptional thinkers that it did attract were, like Georges Politzer, "sacrificed to urgent economic tasks" or, like Auguste Cornu, were simply ignored by a party too impatient to get on with its political agenda to spend any time considering the philosophical justification for its actions.[18]

As for academic Marxists, those "intellectuals of petty bourgeois origin" who were attracted to Marxist philosophy, Althusser argues that the work of these *compagnons de la route* was severely compromised by both the "debt they thought they had contracted by *not being proletarians*" and by the poverty of the theoretical material with which they had to work.[19] Jean-Paul Sartre perhaps best represents this type of sympathetic intellectual because he sacrificed the integrity of his own thought "to political and ideological conflict" and ended up destroying any worth that his philosophy had on its own.[20] As for those academic Marxists who did not sacrifice their philosophy to the party, Althusser notes that they instead made a habit of sacrificing Marx to another philosopher. Thus in the writings of thinkers like Henri Lefebvre, Maurice Merleau-Ponty, and Lucien Goldmann, Marx became Hegel, Marx became Husserl, or Marx became the "ethical and humanist Young Marx."[21] What they, however, lost in these transformations and rebirths was Marx as Marx.

Due to the abuse of the party, the poverty of their theoretical resources, and the miscegenations undertaken to compensate for these deficits, when the worldview-shattering events of 1956 came, French Intellectual Marxism was left in just as awkward a position as the PCF: both traditions lacked the theoretical resources to deal with the fact that the Soviet Union could no longer be identified with the truth of Marxism. On the PCF's part and unlike the intellectuals whose relationship to the party and party theory was often strained, at this late date, too much intellectual and political capital had been invested by the party in the support and reinforcement of the link between Marxist philosophy and the Soviet Union to simply give it up. The result of these factors was that

while many intellectuals could simply abandon Marx or, like the Socialisme ou Barbarie group, rework their Marxism until it was largely indis-
tinguishable from other forms of critical social theory, neither of these
paths was an option for the PCF.[22]

However, for many party theorists there was a silver lining to this
cloud. Unlike artistic and intellectual fellow travelers who saw 1956 as a
curse or as a wake-up call, many party thinkers accustomed to self-
censorship tended to view the breakdown of Stalinist authority in quite
the opposite way, that is, as a sort of theoretical liberation. party intellectuals saw in the events of 1956 and the discrediting of Stalin's philosophy an opportunity: they could now write what they believed and
what their intellectual consciences led them to, not what the party demanded! Althusser explains that when this sentiment combined with
their theoretical handicap, Communist Party theorists turned to the clos-
est interpretation of Marx at hand that could account for this sensation of
liberty. Following the path already well worn by petty bourgeois intellectuals, they turned directly to Marx's Early Work and to its theory of
human liberation. For the most progressive of party theorists, Stalinist
Marxism was thus fast converted to Humanist or Hegelian Marxism.
Though not singled out by Althusser in his introduction (and this probably for political reasons), Roger Garaudy perhaps best represents this
trend. In 1948, the PCF's "Party Philosopher" followed the Stalinist line
and argued that "humanism" was the ideology of slaveholders and capitalists.[23] A year after the Twentieth Congress of the CPSU, however, he
was heavily involved in the project for which he would become most
well known: that of showing how Marxism is not only a humanism but a
theory of human liberation compatible with Judeo-Christian notions of
emancipation.[24]

Short of being any kind of advance, though, Althusser identifies this
movement by Communist theorists to Humanist Marxism as a regression
to a philosophy that is idealist, ideological, and resolutely pre-Marxist.
Though this atavism is the result of a specific historical conjuncture and
thus must be understood in the historical context of 1956, Althusser notes
in his introduction that such a regress in Marxist thought had happened
before. Further, he believes that it was possible to combat such a slide
using the resources that Marxism itself offered. Concisely put, this was
his motivation for turning from authoring studies of eighteenth-century
political philosophers such as Montesquieu and Locke to addressing
questions in Marxist philosophy directly.[25] In that he saw this effort as a

type of combat, he understood his work as functioning in the tradition of the polemics Marx launched against Feuerbach, Engels against Dühring, and Lenin against the Russian Populists and Empiriocritics. As with these antecedents, Althusser believed that he was engaged in the struggle to articulate the difference between idealism and materialism.[26] So, just as Lenin sought to differentiate Marxism from the "spontaneity" of the Russian populists and Marx his own philosophy from the anthropology of Feuerbach, Althusser sought to show how Humanist Marxism was a philosophical and political dead end, a dead end that must be contested both theoretically and politically if Marxism was to preserve and reconstruct itself in its integrity and efficacy as a philosophy of political practice.

When Althusser wrote the articles that would comprise *Pour Marx*, humanism was in vogue. Because of this, he reserves a lot of rhetorical ammunition for its critique. This is especially the case because Althusser's principal intention in writing articles like "Marxisme et humanisme" was to provoke changes in the French Communist Party. As humanism was the only alternative that the PCF seemed willing to entertain in lieu of Stalinism, his critique implied that the party had fundamentally made no theoretical progress and had even regressed. While in its rhetoric the party admitted that Stalinist dogmatism could no longer serve as a theoretical guide, its actions—especially in regard to the Soviets—belied this conviction and showed the party to still be quite Stalinized.[27]

To change the party, Althusser believed that he must correct its understanding of Marxist theory, demonstrating how Stalinist and humanist positions were inconsistent with the party's own principles and also with the classical texts of Marxist thought. The most well known examples of this critique are to be found in *Pour Marx* and *Lire le Capital*. Given the theoretical sophistication of these texts and their enthusiastic reception among intellectuals, it is understandable why some critics have argued that Althusser was guilty of aspiring to Leninist vanguardism.[28] That only graduate students would have the time, patience, and theoretical sophistication to work through *Lire le capital* seems to lend credence to the charge that Althusser subscribed to the idea that a small, theoretically sophisticated cadre should direct the revolution. However, these are not the only texts that Althusser authored. The compendiums of his thought that he put together for popular audiences made many, if not all, of the same points.

In this vein, one sees Althusser in an unpublished but widely circu-lated manuscript from 1964 urging communist militants interested in Marxist philosophy to dismiss humanist Early Works such as *The Holy Family*, to read *Capital* and the preface to *A Critique of Political Econ-omy*, and to critically compare these last two works to the exposé of Marxist philosophy given by Stalin in the *Short Course*.[29] One also sees him in *Théorie marxiste et parti communiste* making analogous claims to those in *Pour Marx* and the first edition of *Lire le Capital*. For instance, contra Stalinist tendencies, Althusser insists on the crucial importance of Theory for political action and argues plainly that Marxist Philosophy is not a theory of teleological economic evolution. Contra humanist tenden-cies, he also takes pains in this work to highlight and define the scientific nature of Historical Materialism and to demonstrate the ideological char-acter of concepts endorsed by party philosophers such as the "'*fin de l'aliénation*,' '*l'avènement de 'l'homme totale*,' *et de la 'liberté cré-atrice*'" ["'end of alienation,' the advent of 'Total Man,' and of the 'freedom that creates'"].[30] For Althusser, then, at all levels and in all its instantiations, it was clear by the early 1960s that both Stalinism and Humanist Marxism needed to be critiqued and overcome if the "worker's movement" was to survive. Further, he believed that this critique needed to proceed via a rereading of Marx. In line with this belief, Althusser characterized his overall project at the time as two interventions both designed to make the party rethink its positions vis-à-vis Stalinism and humanism and to answer the singular and fundamental question: "What is Marxist philosophy?"[31]

One of the interventions that Althusser indicates he needed to make in order to discover Marx's philosophy in its specificity and its integrity is that of "'drawing a line of demarcation' between the true theoretical bases of the Marxist science of history and Marxist philosophy on the one hand, and, on the other hand, the pre-Marxist idealist notions on which depend contemporary interpretations of Marxism."[32] In other words, Althusser wished to make a distinction between Dialectical and Historical Materialism and idealistic interpretations of Marxism as a "philosophy of man" or as a "humanism." In his definition of the term, such humanist interpretations would include "objective idealistic" read-ings of Marx such as Lefebvre's, Cornu's, and Garaudy's, that hold that history is the journey of the human spirit to end its alienation. It would also include "subjective idealisms" like those of Sartre and Merleau-Ponty, which hold that the dialectic describes the individual's attempt to end his alienation by realizing his freedom in the human community. Althusser maintains that what both interpretations of Marx miss in their concentration on Marx's Early Work and on the theory of alienation is that, at a certain historical juncture, there is an "epistemological break"[33] in Marx's thought when he no longer begins to think of the dialectic in terms of human liberation. What therefore must be demonstrated in order to define Marx's philosophy in its specificity and originality is that there is a fundamental difference between Marx's Early Work (which evidences exactly this kind of idealism) and his Later Work (which indicates that a "scientific" and "materialist" understanding of development has replaced the earlier idealistic one). Further, it must be shown what this advance consists of and what the recognition of this advance means for an understanding of Marxist philosophy and Marxist political practice. This intervention, designed to prove that there is a real and definitive difference between the Early and Late Marx, is the first aspect of Althusser's project in the early 1960s.

The other intervention into Marxist theory that Althusser specifies as necessary to reform Marxism philosophy and practice encompasses in its critique not only Humanist Marxism but also Stalinist Marxism. Although before 1965 Althusser never really criticizes the Communist Party directly, this intervention can be recognized as an attempt to suggest to the party that its Stalinism is a deeper tendency than it might be willing to admit and that some of its most fundamental assumptions about what Marxism is need to be questioned in order to purge party theory and practice of these residues. Specifically, Althusser is bothered by the party's formula for revolution as this is cast in terms of an economic determinism and a reflective epistemology. In that this formula specifies the necessary transformation of the world according to predetermined laws, this "materialist" dialectic is, Althusser believes, only a veiled form of idealism. In this respect, even though the party talks of the economic and material determination, its theory is no better than that of Humanist Marxism: both are metaphysical teleologies that take seriously neither science as it is actually practiced nor the materialist dialectic as Marx (but not Engels) articulated it.[34] Althusser labels both interpretations of Marx "philosophical subjectivisms" or "empiricisms" because both take it for granted that the essence of an object (be this object a thing, a psychological state, or a historical process) can be known as it is by a subject.[35] With the exception of Spinoza, this subjectivism is the hallmark of modern philosophy and it is that from which Marx struggled to break away. In that Humanist Marxism and Marxism-Leninism in their classical formulations are both empiricistic, both end up ascribing laws to history and essences to historical "subjects" (whether this be the party or Man). Althusser therefore lumps them together for making the twin mistake of economism/humanism. To overcome this mistake and to stop Historical Materialism and the dialectic from sliding into a formalistic method and an idealism, Althusser indicates that one needs to again deal with the problem of Hegel, demonstrating exactly what the difference is between his idealism and Marx's materialism.

The Purification of Theory: Althusser's Interventions

As a trained philosopher and as an active party member, Althusser knew that there were abundant problems—both theoretical and practical—with "Diamatics" and with its reduction of Marx's thought to a series of crude formulas. In addition, and perhaps also again because he was an active communist, Althusser suspected that there was something wrong with humanist interpretations of Marx that valorized his Early Work as the key to and truth of his philosophy.[36] Put succinctly, Althusser in the early 1960s believed that most contemporary readings of Marx were incorrect and that they served to misrepresent Marx's philosophy. In that this was Marxist philosophy and therefore theory in the service of the revolution, these theoretical errors also led to misguided political practice (a fact unfortunately repeatedly demonstrated by the PCF). Althusser was convinced that these misrepresentations occluded what was truly original in Marx's thought: his founding of the science of history and his materialist philosophy. It was then in an attempt to uncover the truly original aspect of Marx's thought and to set Marxist theory on firm foundations that Althusser began his systematic rereading of Marx's texts.

Against the Marxist humanist position that the key to reading and understanding Marx's philosophy lies in early works such as the *Critique of the Philosophy of Right* (1843) and the *Economic and Philosophic Manuscripts of 1844*, Althusser vehemently argues in *Pour Marx* and *Lire le Capital* that these writings are juvenilia and that they do not reflect Marx's "true" philosophy. What such interpretations do is make Marx into a Left Hegelian who, like Bruno Bauer and Ludwig Feuerbach, is concerned only with philosophical anthropology.[37] As a reasoned alternative to the contention that the key to understanding Marx's oeuvre is as a philosopher always concerned with the development of man into an unalienated subject, Althusser proposes that there is a radical break in Marx's thought. At a specific juncture, Althusser maintains, Marx abandons metaphysical speculations on the telos and essence of man and replaces this speculation with an analysis of the materialist logic of economic and social structures in history. Althusser identifies this break as occurring with *The German Ideology* in 1845 or, alternately and a bit earlier, with the sixth thesis on Feuerbach.[38] This thesis states that:

> Feuerbach resolves the religious essence into the human essence. But the human essence is no abstraction inherent in each single individual. In its reality it is the ensemble of social relations.[39]

This break, when Marx ceases to think in terms of human essence and begins to think of the individual as socially produced, signals the simultaneous development of Marx's true philosophy and the inauguration of a new science. This science is the science of history and it consists in the retrospective analysis of social production. This philosophy is the necessary, if not yet explicit, theoretical background for the science. Though neither Marx nor Engels used these terms, this new philosophy in Marxist-Leninist circles came to be called "Dialectical Materialism" while the science of history which corresponded to it was termed "Historical Materialism."[40] The relationship between philosophy and science was described as such that the former provided the theoretical support and justification for the latter. The catch was that while Marx had done much in works like *The Eighteenth Brumaire of Louis Bonaparte* (1852) to develop the science,[41] the philosophy that articulated its possibility lagged behind or—in the case of *Capital*—remained implicit and needed to be teased out through an attention to the text's problematic, to the conditions of its production.[42]

In all of his work from the early to mid-1960s, Althusser chooses to preserve the distinction between Dialectical Materialism and Historical Materialism while clarifying just exactly how these two knowledges are related to each other and how they relate to philosophy and science in general. It is in the articulation of these differences that one can get into a detailed discussion of what science and philosophy are for Althusser and how this informs his project of rereading Marx.[43]

One of the problems that Althusser sees with traditional Marxist theory is the distinction it makes between theory and practice. This separation of mental from physical and social labor is, he argues, a bourgeois conception that occludes Marx's original insight from *The German Ideology* that no human activity can be separated off from the ensemble of forces that produce it. Althusser's original position on science and philosophy is thus comprehensible only if one sees that he is consistent in maintaining that all human activity consists of practice and that Marx was the first to identify this truth. As he explains it, Marx's singular contribution was to replace "the old postulates [of essences and subjects] . . . by a historico-dialectical materialism of *praxis*: that is, by a theory of the different specific *levels of human practice* (economic practice, political practice, ideological practice, scientific practice) in their characteristic articulations, based on the specific articulations of the unity of human society."[44]

Starting then from the insight that all of human activity consists in the production and reproduction of social life (that is, practice), Althusser contends that Marx makes it possible to think about and analyze these practices in their specificity and in their relation to the social totality. *Capital* is such an analysis: it is an exposition of the practices of a social unity that is characterized by its relation to the production of surplus value. However, though a theoretical and methodological framework for this analysis is latent in *Capital* and apt to be drawn out by the proper reading, Althusser argues that the philosophy that would justify such an analysis never in *Capital* becomes explicit. Althusser's project in *Lire le Capital* is to make this framework explicit, to define the different levels of practice (economic, political, ideological, and scientific), and to show the way in which they interact or fail to interact. In this way, Althusser hopes to answer the question of "What is Marx's philosophy?"

For Althusser, philosophy and science, like ideology, work, and politics, are all practices and must be understood as such. But what is it that makes them all practices? What is the concept that unites them? The feature that they all share in common is that each practice consists of the alteration through labor of preexisting and real objects by specific methods in order to produce a new product.[45] At the level of economic practice, this process is rather obvious: naturally occurring materials are subjected to labor power which, utilizing the available means of production, creates a new product. The level of political practice is a bit more abstract but can be typified as the process of taking given social relations and doing political work (making arguments, organizing, protesting) that results in new social relations.

After political practice and economic practice, the characterization of practices becomes a bit more difficult. This is especially the case because things like ideology, philosophy, and science are usually considered conceptual or theoretical, not practical. Take ideology: it is not traditionally defined as something which we as subjects do but as that in which we are immersed. Contrary to this definition, Althusser argues that ideology exists as real only in the sense that it is performed and enacted. It consists of the "existing modes of representation by which our experience is organized."[46] Ideology is our *lived* experience in the world. We practice ideology when we use the stock of concepts it provides us with to make our way in the world. To borrow and perhaps to pervert a Gadamerian formulation: ideology is the production and reproduction of social life at the level of prejudice;[47] it is the necessary background that allows us to function in the world. As such, ideology is a sort of knowledge, a knowledge that is always present and is always being used.[48] This does not mean, however, that ideology is static. It is also quite clear that specific ideologies can change when they are confronted with a different (and contradictory) ideology or, what may be the same thing, when the material modes of production that are themselves productive of ideologies change. The result will not however be no ideology (the Marxist-Leninist dream); it will be a new ideology. Ideology is a structural constant. This is Althusser's first salvo against the humanists and economists. Neither the proletariat, nor the Communist Party, nor the individual will ever be free from ideology. However, it is possible that the specific ideology in which they are immersed will be transformed.

For Althusser, science and philosophy are—like ideology, politics, and work—practices. But, in terms of their relationships to their objects and in terms of their effects, they are much closer to ideology than they are to politics and work. This is the case because science and philosophy are conceptual and social practices that—like ideology—are productive of knowledges. Unlike ideology, however, science and philosophy recognize their provisional status and are capable of creating new knowledges instead of merely reproducing prejudices. In the case of science, Althusser argues that it is capable of producing new knowledge when, drawing from a preexisting body of concepts (be they scientific or ideological), these concepts are organized into a new theory which has its own internal criteria of verification.[49]

This process of organization is easy to see in sciences like mathematics that do not necessarily require the application of their theorems in order to prove their validity. It is less readily apparent in the experimental sciences that do seem to draw their validity from external sources. Despite this appearance, Althusser argues that external verification is not where truth is found. Rather, proof and demonstration are said to be "the product of definite and specific material and theoretical apparatuses and procedures internal to each science."[50] It is thus the internal production of new theory that allows questions to be posed which, in turn, allow for the further definition and development of a science. The shift from Ptolemaic to Galilean astronomy provides one example of such a production. In this practice, already existing and sometimes contradictory concepts are organized into a new science: that of modern physics. Along with this shift, Althusser identifies two others that best exemplify the founding of a new science: that of Thales and his "discovery" of irrational numbers, which inaugurates the science of mathematics, and that of Marx and his discovery of economic determination, which inaugurates the science of Historical Materialism.[51]

But is internal verification sufficient guarantee of the veracity of these scientific knowledges? An oft-repeated critique of Althusser's philosophy of science is that, because science is defined only by criteria internal to itself and consists only of concepts, the knowledge that it produces has no external check.[52] A science is what the scientists who practice it say it is. That which it calls "true" is merely that which meets the criteria for truth established by that science's problematic. This seems to be both an extremely rationalist and an extremely conventionalist view of science. Althusser adds fuel to this argument when he makes statements like "the production of knowledge which is peculiar to theoretical [scientific] practice constitutes a process that takes place entirely in thought, just as we can say *mutatis mutandis* that the process of economic production takes place entirely in the economy."[53] When a production takes place entirely in thought and the objects that it works with are exclusively concepts, it is hard to see how such a practice can be externally verified. Consequently, Althusser's materialism, in this sense, drifts dangerously close to an idealism of the type that he wished to criticize.

The way in which Althusser attempts to get around the problem of external verification is by suggesting that philosophy is the practice which guarantees the internal coherence of science. As he defines it, philosophy is a theoretical practice whose objects are scientific concepts. Philosophy does its work of transformation on them. However, philosophy does not change scientific concepts in order to create new scientific concepts. Instead, it clarifies and makes explicit a science's internal logic and sorts true scientific concepts out from the ideological concepts in which they are embedded. Because it performs this role, Althusser identifies it as "the Theory of theoretical practices" or, less frequently, "the Science of sciences."

At least in his work from the early 1960s, most of the descriptions Althusser provides of philosophy acting as the Theory of theoretical practices have to do with the work of Marxist philosophy (Dialectical Materialism) in clarifying the science of history (Historical Materialism). As Althusser tells the story, Marx, in the process of writing *Capital,* was too involved in scientific research to do anything but hint at the philosophy that underlay the work's analysis and conclusions. This does not mean however that this philosophy is not there. As he notes in *Théorie Marxiste et Parti Communiste*:

> la tradition marxiste affirmée sans équivoque par Marx, Engels et Lénine, ne nous laisse aucun doute sur l'existence d'une *philosophie marxiste distincte* de la science de l'histoire. Mais d'autre part cette philosophie ne nous est, la plupart du temps, donnée et donc accesible, *qu'indirectement.*[54]

> [the marxist tradition affirmed without equivocation by Marx, Engels, and Lenin leaves us with no doubt about the existence of a *marxist philosophy distinct* from the science of history. However, this philosophy is for the most part presented to us as given. Therefore it is accessible *only indirectly.*]

Though unfortunately not explicit, it is Althusser's contention that Marx's philosophy can be teased out of *Capital* and other classic texts with a hermeneutic sufficiently attuned to the text's "problematic," that is, by a reading that is attentive to the author's intent, to the conditions of its production, and to the prejudices of the reader. In the case of the science of Historical Materialism, then, it is the work of Marxist theoreticians to discover in works such as *Capital* "[b]y means of what concepts, or what set of concepts, it is possible to think the new type of determination" that Karl Marx identified.[55] By doing exactly this type of philosophic work, Althusser thinks he is able to make explicit concepts like "contradiction," "structural causality," "uneven development," and "overdetermination," which are not clearly articulated in Marx's texts but which constitute his philosophical achievement and mark the distinction from both Hegel and from his juvenilia.

The concepts of contradiction, overdetermination, uneven development, and structural causality are used by Althusser to explain the framework for thinking the socioeconomic totality that he believes is latent in *Capital*. Contrary to the Stalinist model which holds that the totality is one wherein the economic processes of capitalism dictate and determine historical and cultural progress, this conception of the "whole" is one marked by a complex and sedimentary structure. This structure is complex not only because a distinction is maintained between economic, political, ideological, and scientific practices, but also because the totality cannot be understood as the complex and varied expression of a simple Idea (as it is in Hegel) or as the complex and varied expression of a simple Material Law (as Stalin explains it). Instead, Althusser insists that real difference exists. By "real difference," Althusser means that the differences that constitute any social formation are expressions of a socioeconomic structure which has a material basis that is not the expression of an antecedent essence but which constitutes its own essence.[56] Freed from Hegelian jargon, Althusser means to argue that, for Marx, *there exist real and diverse material conditions*. The upshot of this is that one society can simultaneously contain and be characterized by multiple modes and levels of production. Further, these real modes of production cannot be reduced to the expression of one bare essence or principle. Rather, in their real and material specificity and diversity, they constitute the essences of a certain structure or society. The recognition that any totality will necessarily include in itself the sum of these differences is what Althusser terms "uneven development."[57]

Uneven development describes the diverse reality of a complexly structured totality. The reality and materiality of uneven development determines the social formation as a site of differences or contradictions. All this is to say that the contradictions in any society's structure can be understood as the effect of the unevenness of that structure. This is not a simple relation. Though the economic is, in the last instance, determinative of the way in which every contradiction arises, given that the economic is itself uneven and structured according to relations of dominance, the contradictions that the infrastructure manifests will never be simple and heterogeneous. It is not even clear that economic practices need to be dominant in every epoch. Further, every contradiction of a given social formation is also a necessary manifestation and reflection of every other contradiction that the structure contains. A contradiction is thus "inseparable from the total structure of the social body in which it is found, inseparable from its formal *conditions* of existence . . . and determined by the various *levels* and *instances* of the social formation that it animates."[58]

In an attempt to clarify these "Marxian" concepts of uneven development and contradiction, an example from Althusser's work might help. Addressing in the essay "Contradiction et surdétermination" the question of why the Russian Revolution succeeded and why the revolution in Germany envisioned by the Social Democrats failed, Althusser notes that the Russian Revolution succeeded precisely because the sum of the contradictions of Russia's internal and external uneven development was such that a revolution was possible. On the one hand, Russia enjoyed a situation in which its uneven development (as typified by the contradictions shown by the weakness of its state and bourgeoisie, its lack of imperialist practices, its relative isolation, etc.) was amenable to revolution. On the other hand, Germany failed to achieve revolution because—though it appeared stratified along class lines (and thus fit the vulgar conception of the necessary prerequisites for revolution)—its uneven development was such that a revolution could not occur: the contradictions of Germany were that its bourgeoisie had given up their role as uninhibited consumer and ceded their prerogative and profits to the state in order to protect itself and to ensure the expansion of imperialism. The sum of Germany's contradictions thus did not, as did Russia's, constitute themselves as revolutionary.[59] With this historical example, Althusser illustrates how contradictions manifest themselves in interrelation to one another. The unevenness of Russian economic development manifested a plenum of diverse contradictions which, in relation to one another, set up the necessary conditions for revolution. The unevenness of German development manifested itself in diverse contradictions that prevented, or more precisely, could not produce a revolution.

Because for Althusser every contradiction is both inseparable from its formal conditions of existence (conditions which include not only its economic determinants but also the consort of other material contradictions which compose the social formation: ideology, laws, ethics, politics, family structures, etc.), Althusser states that every contradiction is "overdetermined." By overdetermined he means that every contradiction—whether this contradiction is embodied by the social totality, a state, a class, or a subject—is not simple and can thus not be reduced to

such categories as "capitalist state" or "true proletariat." A specific contradiction is always overdetermined and "specified by the historically
concrete forms and circumstances in which it is exercised."[60] Overdetermination thus can be said to be the point at which the ensemble of contradictions that make up a "whole" system are reflected on an individual
contradiction. For example: a political state is overdetermined in that it is
an individual contradiction which "focuses'" and represents the contradictory expressions of both its internal uneven development (its domestic
contradictions) and its external uneven development (its relations in
dominance to other states). Thus the individual contradiction that is a
state is made actual by the "forms of the superstructure (the state, dominant ideology, religion, political movements, etc.) that determine it on
the one hand as a function of the national past and on the other as functions of the existing world context (what dominates it)."[61] Insofar as it is
determined by a multiplicity of specific and real differences, a state, a
subject, or any other "individual" can, for Althusser, be said to be overdetermined.

This conception of Marx's totality as contradictory, overdetermined,
and unevenly developed is deployed by Althusser against both the crude
"infrastructure/superstructure" analyses of the socioeconomic totality
made by Stalinist theorists and the slightly more sophisticated dialectico-
historical models advanced by Humanist Marxists. Both the former conception (which suggests that knowledge of the social whole is produced
by the economy and known in its reality only by the party) and the latter
(which speculates that true knowledge of the social whole will come
about when man or the proletariat has restored the products of his labor
to himself), Althusser argues, miss the distinction between Marx and
Hegel. In Hegel's conceptions of the dialectic, the parts of a whole are
seen as manifestations of a central essence that causes or determines
them. Althusser juxtaposes to this notion of causality the "scientific"
concept of "structural causality" where the parts of the totality are not
determined but "overdetermined" because:

> [t]he structure is not an essence *outside* the economic phe-
> nomena which comes and alters their aspect, forms, and rela-
> tions and which is effective on them as an absent cause . . .
> [E]ffects are not outside the structure, are not a preexisting
> object, element, or space in which the structure arrives to *im-
> print its mark.* [T]he structure, which is merely a specific
> combination of its elements, is nothing outside its effects.[62]

The thrust of Althusser's argument here is that Marx's conception of the world and of the dialectic is fundamentally different from that of Hegel. Following Marx in his "Afterword to the second German edition of *Capital*," Althusser maintains that Hegel's dialectical whole is mystified while Marx's dialectical totality is rational. By "mystified" he means that Hegel's dialectic is still governed by a central idea that explains all of its appearances and transformations. Marx's "rational" dialectical totality, in contrast, describes nothing but actual social formations in their historical development.[63] This scientific and materialist understanding of the dialectic and its effects is, Althusser argues, latent in Marx's texts. Further, such an articulation of the socioeconomic totality is apt to be drawn out by a reading of Marx's writings that is sufficiently attuned to their problematic. Indeed, this is the project that Althusser specifies he undertook in *Lire le Capital*.

Though this is an example of how philosophy supposedly works to clarify science by articulating its concepts even after the science has begun to be practiced, it in no way provides an adequate response to the criticism that Althusser's description of science and philosophy are both excessively rationalist and excessively conventionalist.[64] That these charges are warranted is fairly obvious. Lending further support to this contention is the fact that Althusser himself eventually recognized that both his philosophy of science and his meta-philosophy were inadequate. In his *auto-critique* from 1972, he repudiated this explanation of how philosophy functions exactly for its "theoreticist tendencies" and he revised those aspects of his philosophy of science that could be called conventionalist. It is with this emendation to his original position that the next chapter will concern itself. However, before turning to this discussion, it may be helpful to defend Althusser's original position, just as he did during his 1975 doctoral defense at the University of Amiens, as a political act meant to combat other philosophies of science that made even worse errors.[65] Doing so should help to clarify the reasons for Althusser's original position on philosophy and science as well as provide a transition to an understanding of his revised position where he makes the claim that philosophy is a political intervention in the field of theory.

As Althusser describes them in his *Soutenance d'Amiens*, the arguments that he made in *Pour Marx* and *Lire le Capital* were explicitly meant to preserve a certain autonomy for Marxist theory and for theory in general. This autonomy would "allow [theory] to develop in alliance with political and other practices without betraying its own needs" and without becoming a "slave to tactical political interests."[66] What did he mean by this "enslavement"? As we have seen, Althusser was referring both to Stalinist dogmatism and to the critique of this dogmatism by Humanist Marxism.[67] The enslavement of Marxist theory by Stalinist dogmatism is rather easy to describe, that of Humanist Marxism a bit more subtle. The philosophy of science dogmatically decreed by Stalinist Marxism and subsequently theoretically justified by Soviet scientists such as Trofim Lyssenko was based on two assumptions. The first assumption was that Engels was correct in his argument from *The Dialectics of Nature* that the laws of nature are dialectical. The second assumption is the Stalinist position that there are two sciences: one, a bourgeois science which is ideological; and two, a proletarian science which can discern the truth of nature. Were this to be correct, there would be a law of gravity for workers and one for stockbrokers. Further, this law would have to be described as working according to a dialectical logic; universal attraction would have to be characterized as a battle between opposites. The absurdity of such a claim needs no refutation, though, as has been noted in the previous chapter, precisely analogous claims were made by Soviet and French scientists throughout the 1950s. In claiming autonomy for theory, that is, for science both Marxist and traditional and for philosophy both Marxist and traditional, Althusser wanted to avoid precisely this type of absurdity. Dogmatic theory, he believed, should no more drive scientific research than it should mandate political action. That he combated this theory with his own type of absurd theory, he would later admit.[68]

The way in which Humanist Marxism "enslaved" Marxist theory is a bit harder to define in terms of its philosophy of science. This is perhaps because Humanist Marxism really did not have a philosophy of science. As we have seen, Sartre, Lefebvre, and Cornu were always much more involved with existential concerns revolving around human subjectivity than they were with scientific ones.[69] This lack of involvement with or even an active shunning of science was precisely where Althusser saw a problem. Althusser believed that Marxism was a science and that this science had an object. This object is the social structure as a totality, its contradictions, and its history. He did not argue that the analysis of subjectivity was an illegitimate philosophical pursuit—this was precisely what his research on Ideological State Apparatuses concerned itself with.[70] However, he believed that this analysis could not be undertaken, as Humanist Marxists wished, that is, from a subjective position conceptualized in terms of alienation. For Althusser (and he would argue for Marx as well) the subject can only be comprehended in its relation to and overdetermination by the social totality. Put differently, the subject can only be understood in terms of subjectivization and not by way of a phenomenological analysis of human subjectivity. To ignore this structure and its effects, or to posit them as somehow external and unknowable, is to slip into the sorts of subjective and objective idealisms typical of French Academic Marxism that give lip service to Marxism but which ignore its status as an objective science of social formations in history.

Were Althusser's Interventions Successful?

To combat Humanist Marxism's denial or discounting of the scientific status of Marxism as well as to counter Stalinist philosophy, Althusser retrospectively maintained that he developed his radical theses on scientific and philosophical practice as a way to change the balance between these positions and to open up debate within the French Communist Party about these issues.[71] More ambitiously, he hoped with his interventions to restore Marxism to its proper position as a science that, like other sciences, produced true (if still fallible) knowledge of the world and that gave real reasons for political action.

So far as the goal of opening up debate, Althusser was inarguably successful. The publication of *Pour Marx* and *Lire le Capital* precipitated an explosion of academic literature debating the merits of his positions. These responses ran the gamut from those condemning his positions as Stalinist to those citing his researches as the only real future for Marxist philosophy.[72] Probably more important—at least for Althusser—was that his "intervention" encouraged real discussion and soul-searching in what was still in the mid-1960s a very much Stalinized French Communist Party. For the first time since the Popular Front, real debates about issues of dogmatism and humanism as well as about Communism's relationship to the broader left were taken up by the Communist Party and at the highest levels.[73] This opening was in large part attributable to Althusser's influence. That this intervention as well as a subsequent one in 1978 had little to no real effect in terms of changes to party philosophy and policy was not really his fault. As Althusser himself could probably have pointed out had he only undertaken the necessary analysis, the Parti Communiste Français had at this point already been overdetermined and had overdetermined itself such that it was incapable of any trenchant self-critique and policy adjustment.[74]

But what about Althusser's own stated goals of articulating Marx's "real" philosophy such that it could serve as the basis for political practice and of challenging the theoretical errors of Humanist Marxism and Stalinist dogmatism? On the attribution of complete success to the first goal, there is reason to be cautious. Indeed, there may be reason to separate out the aim of articulating Marx's real philosophy from that of (re)constituting Marxist philosophy such that it is both theoretically tenable and fit to serve as the basis for political practice. The next chapter will address specific concerns regarding these aspects of Althusser's project. As for the twin objectives of combating the most pernicious aspects of Stalinist dogmatism and Humanist Marxism, there is ample reason to judge his project successful at the theoretical level in terms of its distinctive differentiation of Marxism from the economism/humanism dyad.

If there is one central theoretical problem with Marxism as formulated by Lenin and Stalin and as adopted by the PCF, it is the emphasis put on economic practice as being strictly determinative of a culture's ideas and institutions. It was this emphasis that led to or at least justified the most outrageous of Soviet practices, including the liquidation of bourgeois intellectuals, mass imprisonments, show trials, the abuse of psychology, the elimination of the Kulaks, and even (if less directly) the famines resulting from planification. In his conception of the social totality as a complexly structured series of effects in which no structure or practice can be identified as determinative of the rest, Althusser avoids the crude infrastructure/superstructure arguments that justify Stalinism's crude scientism and its dialectical teleology. With this conception, Althusser reasserts the primacy of the material and suggests a way to study it, not as a process with a goal, but in its integrity for what it actually does or has done, that is, by its effects. Finally, by redefining the relationship between ideology and scientific theory, he takes away the epistemological privilege of the working class and therewith the justification for theories of vanguardism and dictatorship in both their Leninist and Lucàksian forms. Despite these successes, there is a flaw in his conception of "levels of practices" that leads Althusser to excessively rationalistic and conventionalist conclusions about philosophical and scientific practice. Nonetheless, his insistence that ideology must be understood as one practice among many also opens up the door for what is one of Althusser's most penetrating and potentially productive projects, that of the critique of Ideological State Apparatuses.

As for the critique of Humanist Marxisms and the proposition of an alternative to them, this venture may also be judged positively given the theoretical superiority of Althusser's alternative to Existential and Hegelian Marxisms. To "objective idealist" philosophies like those of Lefebvre and Cornu, Althusser demonstrates the radical difference between Marx and Hegel in terms of their conceptions of the dialectic. With his argument that the dialectic must (if one wishes to remain a materialist and a scientist) be understood as nothing but the abstract description of actually occurring contradictions, Althusser shows why it is necessary to resist seeing history as a process for man. To believe that history had a beginning with man's original alienation and to believe that it will have an ending when man's powers are returned to him is to overstep available material evidence and to attribute a "spirit" or "reason" to history. Looking at history as materialists and scientists, one can only say that human beings are not as they once were and then demonstrate why and how human beings and human communities have actually changed. From this study, one might even be able to argue on the basis of apparent tendencies that human beings will not be as they are now and that they and their forms of organization might change in specific ways given specific economic and political developments. However, there is no "necessary law" of transformation to be found in capitalism, nor is there the possibility that, at the end of this transformation, we will find ourselves unalienated and fully human. Hegel's categories from the *Phenomenology* simply do not apply anymore except as they accurately describe actual occurrences (which is not often).

In Althusser's interpretation of Marx's dialectic, there is no beginning and no end. History is simply not for us, even if it is always our history. In contrast to objective idealisms that see in Marx's dialectic the promise of a utopian future, Althusser insists that all Marxist philosophy provides us with are the conceptual tools to give a scientific analysis of the development of capitalism and to determine its effects such that we might be able to change them. The prospect of "Total Man" is not even on the far horizon.

To the humanism of the Existential Marxists, Althusser proposes his theoretical anti-humanism.[75] This position is derived from an analysis of the social structure and of the relationship of the individual to this structure. If, as the Existentialist Marxists suggest, there exists a "self-negating" consciousness which feels radically other to the material world, then Althusser shows that such a subject must be a symptom of a particular socioeconomic structure that compels him to believe this.[76] However, in that this notion *"possède un sens* pratique, *qu'il indique l'*existence *d'une réalité sans donner le moyen de la* connaître" [possesses a *practical* sense, indicating the *existence* of a reality without providing the means of *knowing* it]," this belief is ideological, not scientific.[77] The bourgeois subject is then quite right that he feels alienated. However, he is not alienated from any "essence" of man or from any desired ontological equilibrium. He is alienated for the same reason that the Microsoft Corporation, liberalism, and procedural democracy also exist: all are effects of the social structure of capitalism and each expresses the logic of the system and the structure in dominance that determines its effects (but which is not its essence).[78] This is not to say that, for the subject, this is an easy or untroubled relation (though for some it may be), but that this relation of the totality to its part (the structure to the individual subject) is somewhat explainable given sufficient analysis. This explanation is possible, however, only through the analysis of socioeconomic structures in their complexity and interaction and cannot be extrapolated or articulated fully through the phenomenological analysis of any individual consciousness (as Existential Marxism is wont to do). Such a project would always only ever be epiphenomenal. Althusser thus demonstrates the theoretical superiority of his recasting of Marxism as an anti-humanism by virtue of its ability to explain both our conscious experience of the world and the objective structures that demand or allow this subjective experience.

If there is one thing that unites each of Althusser's critiques of humanism and "subjectivisms," it is that they all emphasize the fact that formulas and laws cannot substitute for analysis and theory in Marxism. The materialist dialectic is not just Hegelian categories turned on their head: there is no essence that is the truth of history and that motivates its progress. Rather, the dialectic is nothing but the actual appearance of differentiated social structures in history, the sum of contradictions that constitute an epoch. In some of his writings from the late 1970s, Althusser goes so far as to abandon the notion of the materialist dialectic completely. He prefers instead the descriptive title "Marx's materialist philosophy," a notion purged of any eschatological baggage. In an unpublished work from the mid-1970s titled *Textes sur la philosophie marxiste,* one can actually see direct evidence of this shift. While the original typescript has Althusser using the term "Dialectical Material-ism," in subsequent revisions he has crossed-out the term by hand and replaced it with the phrase "the philosophy of Marx."[79] The tendency exemplified here to abandon idealist notions in all of their guises repre-sents a decisive advance for Marxism over the "pre-scientific" theories that Althusser wished to critique and which were driven more by the imaginary demands of the dialectic than by the exigencies of the real world.

The theoretical success of Althusser's critique of Stalinist and Hu-manist Marxism is attributable to his identification of a radical break between Hegel, the Young Marx, and the Mature Marx. More specifi-cally, this success is achieved by attributing to Marx the founding of a science and an epistemology based on the structural articulation of levels of practice (economic, political, ideological, and theoretical) that have no discernible relation one to the other. This structural articulation allowed Althusser to preserve the autonomy of theory from both crude economist and from the more sophisticated humanist interpretations of Marx. How-ever, it also trapped Althusser in his own sort of idealism where "The-ory" existed in the mind, enjoying no discernible and direct relation to the other levels of ideological and political practice. These relations, however, were precisely that which theory needed to effect if it was to be a theory for practice. It is this flaw and its overcoming in Althusser's work from the late 1960s up until 1978 that will be addressed in the next chapter.

Notes

1. Tony Judt, *Marxism and the French Left: Studies in Labour and Politics in France, 1830-1981* (Oxford: Clarendon Press, 1986), 185.

2. Nizan and Politzer have already been discussed in this regard. As for Le-febvre and Cornu see Auguste Cornu and Félix Armand, "Critique et Auto-Critique," *La Pensée* (September-October 1949): 84-88; and Henri Lefebvre, "Auto-Critique: contribution à l'effort d'èclaircissement idéologique," *La Nou-velle Critique* 4 (March 1949): 41-57.

3. See Jean-Paul Sartre, *Les Communistes et la paix* (1952) in *Situations VI* (Paris: Gallimard, 1964), 80-384; and Maurice Merleau-Ponty, *Humanism and Terror: An Essay on the Communist Problem* (Boston: Beacon Press, 1969).

4. Sunil Khilnani points out that, during the postwar years, the only vo-cabulary really open to Left intellectuals was a Marxist-Leninist one and that the only opportunity for Left political action seemed to be one mediated through the

party of revolution, the PCF, which, in turn, identified with the Soviet Union. Sunil Khilnani, *Arguing Revolution: The Intellectual Left in Postwar France* (New Haven, CT: Yale University Press, 1993), 44-45.

5. David Caute, *Communism and the French Intellectuals* (London: André Deutsch, 1964), 228-33.

6. Michael Kelly disputes this and traces reform attempts back to 1953. Most other accounts, including those of Adereth, Judt, and Bell and Criddle agree with this characterization.

7. Maurice Cranston, "The Thought of Roger Garaudy," *Problems of Communism* 19, no. 5 (September/October 1970): 11-13.

8. Robert Geerlandt, *Garaudy et Althusser: le débate sur l'humanisme dans le parti communiste Français et son enjeu* (Paris: Presses Universitaire de France, 1978), 129-30; and Geoffrey M. Goshgarian, "Introduction to *The Humanist Controversy and Other Writings*" (London: Verso, 2003), xxv-xxxi. In his authoritative account of the 1966 Central Committee debates at Argenteuil between Althusser and Garaudy, Geerlandt shows that, though the party ended up seemingly endorsing Garaudy's Humanism, its statement on the matter was equivocal and ceded very little authority to either philosopher's revisions. Goshgarian adds to this account, showing that, though party General Secretary Waldeck Rochet and other party leaders endorsed Garaudy's humanism, the net effect of the debate was that of closing off discussion and limiting further discussions.

9. Jean-Paul Sartre, *Search for a Method*, trans. Hazel Barnes (New York: Knopf, 1963), xxxxiv.

10. For an extended consideration of the *Arguments* group see Mark Poster, *Existential Marxism in Postwar France: From Sartre to Althusser* (New Jersey: Princeton University Press, 1975), 209-63.

11. Henri Lefebvre, *La vie quotidienne dans le monde moderne* (Paris: Gallimard, 1968).

12. For a bibliography of recent work on Henri Lefebvre and of recent work inspired by his ideas see Robert Shields, "Henri Lefebvre," Carleton University, 2004, www.carleton.ca/~rshields/lefebvre.htm (accessed August 19, 2004).

13. Louis Althusser, *Essays in Self-Criticism* (London: New Left Books, 1976), 187-95.

14. For more on these works and their political context, see Goshgarian, "Introduction to *The Humanist Controversy*," xxxiii-xxxiv. The only part of this project that saw publication was a small section taken from *Théorie Marxiste et Parti Communiste* that appeared, unsigned, in the Maoist journal *Cahiers Marxistes-Léninistes* published by some of Althusser's students. See "Sur la Révolution Culturelle," *Cahiers Marxistes-Léninistes* (1966): 5-16.

15. Louis Althusser, *For Marx* (London: New Left Books, 1977), 23.

16. Althusser, *For Marx*, 22.

17. Althusser, *For Marx*, 24-25.

18. Althusser, *For Marx*, 26-27.

19. Althusser, *For Marx*, 27. Emphasis is Althusser's

20. Further substantiating Althusser's work from this time as a critique of Sartre's is the subtitle to the essay "Sur le jeune Marx" from 1960. Here, the subtitle *"Question (au pluriel) de théorie"* parodies Sartre's introduction to his *Critique de la raison dialectique* wherein the *habitué* of the Deux Magots raises a "Question (au singulier) de méthode." Pierre Macherey, "Althusser et le jeune Marx," *Actuel-Marx* 31 (2002): 159-63.

21. Althusser, *For Marx*, 28.

22. Judt, *Marxism and the French Left,* 189-91.

23. Roger Garaudy, *Le Marxisme et la Personne Humaine* (Paris: Éditions Sociales 1948), 31

24. Roger Garaudy, *Humanisme Marxiste* (Paris: Éditions Sociales, 1957).

25. Louis Althusser, *Montesquieu, la politique et l'histoire* (Paris: PUF, 1959); and "Sur Raymond Polin, La Politique Morale de John Locke," *Revue d'histoire moderne et contemporaine.* vol. 9, no. 2, (April-June 1962): 150-55.

26. Althusser, *For Marx*, 10, 11.

27. For instance, in regard to the invasion of Hungary the PCF limited its objections to the use of military force and did not object to the intervention itself or to the installation of a hard-line regime to replace Dubcek. See D. S. Bell and Byron Criddle, *The French Communist Party in the Fifth Republic* (Oxford: Clarendon Press, 1994), 92-93. Also on the PCF*'s* rhetorical efforts to distance itself from its Stalinist legacy see Maurice Thorez and Roger Garaudy, "Les Tâches des philosophes communistes et la critique des erreurs philosophiques de Staline," supplement to *Cahiers du Communisme*, nos. 7-8 (July/August 1962).

28. Khilnani, *Arguing Revolution,* 116.

29. Louis Althusser, unpublished typescript, "Éléments sommaire de bibli-ographie pour l'étude du matérialisme historique" [1964], ALT 2. A10-04.05, Fonds Althusser, Institut Mémoire de l'Édition Contemporaine, Paris, France.

30. Louis Althusser, unpublished typescript, *Théorie Marxiste et Parti Communiste ('Union théorie/pratique')*[1966-1967], ALT2. A7-01.09, Fonds Althusser, Institut Mémoire de l'Édition Contemporaine, Paris, France.

32. Althusser, *For Marx*, 31.

32. Althusser, *For Marx*, 13.

33. On what of this notion Althusser owes to the philosophies of science developed by Gaston Bachelard and Georges Canguilhem see Étienne Balibar, "From Bachelard to Althusser: The Concept of Epistemological Break," *Economy & Society* 7, no. 3 (1979): 24-47; and Peter Dews, "Althusser, Structuralism, and the French Tradition of Historical Epistemology," in *Althusser: A Critical Reader*, ed. Gregory Elliot (Cambridge, MA: Blackwell, 1994), 104-42.

34. Althusser thus criticizes the citations from Engels that the party uses to justify this position even after the Stalinist quotes it formerly cited to make the same points have become anathema. Louis Althusser, unpublished typescript

(photocopy), "Sur Engels: Feuerbach et la fin de la philosophie allemande," ALT2. A10.05.05, Fonds Althusser, Institut Mémoire de l'Édition Contemporaine, Paris, France.

35. Althusser, *For Marx*, 12, 251.

36. Althusser, *For Marx*, 52.

37. Althusser, *For Marx,* 227.

38. Althusser, *For Marx*, 32. The quote that Althusser cites to justify this contention is from Part 1 of *The German Ideology* where Marx and Engels write: "we resolved . . . to settle accounts with our erstwhile philosophical conscience."

39. Karl Marx, "Theses on Feuerbach," in *Selected Writings,* ed. David McLellan (Oxford: Oxford University Press, 1977), 157.

40. Étienne Balibar, *The Philosophy of Marx* (London: Verso, 1995), 3.

41. Louis Althusser, Unpublished typescript, "Éléments sommaire de bibliographie pour l'étude du matérialisme historique" [1964], Alt 2. A10-04-05, Fonds Althusser, Institut Mémoire de l'Édition Contemporaine, Paris, France, 3-4.

42. Althusser points out that it is not unusual for the articulation of a philosophy adequate to a science to lag behind its discovery and the articulation of its results. For instance, the theoretical advances by Copernicus and Galileo had to await Kant and Newton for their philosophical articulation. See "Lenin and Philosophy," in *Lenin and Philosophy and Other Essays* (New York: New Left Books, 1971), 40-42.

43. Étienne Balibar, "Althusser's Object," *Social Text* 39 (1994): 161.

44. Althusser, *For Marx*, 229.

45. Althusser, *For Marx,* 183-87.

46. Steven Smith, *Reading Althusser: An Essay on Structural Marxism* (Ithaca, NY: Cornell University Press, 1984), 10.

47. Hans-Georg Gadamer, *Philosophical Hermeneutics* (Berkeley: University of California Press, 1977), 9.

48. Louis Althusser, "Ideologie et Appareils Idéologiques d'État (notes pour une recherche)," *La Pensée* no. 151 (April 1970).

49. Robert Paul Resch, *Althusser and the Renewal of Marxist Social Theory* (Berkeley: University of California Press, 1992), 160.

50. Louis Althusser, *Philosophy and the Spontaneous Philosophy of the Scientist and Other Essays* (London: Verso, 1990), 209.

51. Althusser, *For Marx,* 14.

52. See for instance Donald Lee, "Althusser on Science and Ideology," *Southwest Philosophical Studies* 7 (April 1982): 68-74; or Alex Callinicos, *Althusser's Marxism* (London: Pluto Press, 1976), 72-75.

53. Louis Althusser and Étienne Balibar, *Reading Capital* (New York: Verso, 1970), 42.

54. Althusser, *Théorie Marxiste et Parti Communiste.*

55. Althusser and Balibar, *Reading Capital*, 186. This new determination is that of "the determination of a given region by the structure of that region."

56. Althusser, *For Marx*, 93.

57. Althusser, *For Marx*, 212.

58. Althusser, *For Marx*, 101

59. Althusser, *For Marx*, 98.

60. Althusser, *For Marx*, 106.

61. Althusser, *For Marx*, 106.

62. Althusser and Balibar, *Reading Capital*, 188-89.

63. Michael Emerson, "Althusser on Overdetermination and Structural Causality," *Philosophy Today* 29 (Fall 1984): 203-14; and Althusser, *For Marx*, 90-91.

64. For others who have commented on these tendencies see D. Atkinson, "The Anatomy of Knowledge: Althusser's Epistemology and Its Consequences," *Philosophical Papers* 13 (October 1984): 1-19; and Lee, "Althusser on Science and Ideology," 68-74.

65. Louis Althusser, "Soutenance D'Amiens ou 'Est-il simple d'être marxiste en philosophie?'" in *Solitude de Machiavel et autres textes*, ed. Yves Sintomer (Paris: PUF, 1998), 199-236.

66. Louis Althusser, "Is It Simple to Be a Marxist in Philosophy?" in *Philosophy and the Spontaneous Philosophy of the Scientists* (London: Verso, 1990), 208.

67. Althusser, "Is It Simple," 208.

68. Althusser, "Is It Simple," 208.

69. Lefebvre authored a work on science that was to be the follow-up to *Logique formelle, logique dialectique* and which was part of a proposed multi-volume series called *À la lumière du matérialisme dialectique*. Though announced in the Éditions Sociales catalog, this volume on the *Méthodologies des Sciences* was censored by the party after its publication and never appeared on the market.

70. See Louis Althusser, *Sur la Reproduction* (Paris: PUF, 1995) for the most complete collection of Althusser's writings on Ideology and the State.

71. Althusser, "Is It Simple," 208.

72. Some of the more prominent French respondents included Raymond Aron, *D'une sainte famille à l'autre* (Paris: Gallimard, 1969); Jean-Luc Nancy, "Marx et la philosophie," *Esprit* 349, (1966); Nicos Poulantzas, "Ver une théorie marxiste" *Les Temps Modernes* 240 (1966); Andréa Glucksmann, "Un Structuralisme ventriloque," *Les Temps Modernes* 250 (1967); Jean Hyppolite, "Le 'scientifique' et l' 'idéologique' dans une perspective marxiste," *Diogène* 64 (1968); and Henri Lefebvre, "Sur une interpretation marxiste," *L'Homme et la société* 4 (1967). After the intitial review article that introduced Althusser to English readers authored by E. J. Hobsbawm, "The Structure of Capital," *Times Literary Supplement* (December 15, 1966), 1161-63, the three most prominent

English-language responses came from John Lewis, "The Althusser Case," *Marxism Today* (January and February 1972); E. P. Thompson, *The Poverty of Theory* (New York: Monthly Review Press, 1978); and V. Gerratana, "Althusser and Stalinism," *New Left Review* 101/102 (1977), 110-21.

73. For balanced records of these debates see Geerlandt, *Garaudy et Althusser* and Goshgarian, introduction to *The Humanist Controversy*, xxiv-xxxi. For an alternative interpretation of the stakes involved and its effects (one that wrongly represents these debates as merely being a matter of careerist posturing between intellectuals), see Sudhir Hazareesingh, *Intellectuals and the French Communist Party: Disillusion and Decline* (Oxford: Clarendon Press, 1991), 99-100.

74. In the past decade, many historians have offered explanations as to why the PCF was unable to adapt to changing times such that it may have remained a viable political party. Though emphasizing different facets of PCF experience, most agree that the Party's identification with the Soviet Union and with the principles of Marxism-Leninism (particularly those of democratic centralism and of class-based revolution) left it ill equipped to deal with a world in which the U.S.S.R. did not exist, and in which the possibilities for revolution (and thus the justification for democratic centralism) seemed increasingly remote. Sophie Coeuré in *La Grande lueur á l'Est* is particularly good at showing how an idealized image of the Soviet Union combined with the dream of revolution to play a constitutive role in the PCF*'s* identity. Marja Kivisaari suggests how the party's educational system reproduced these identifications and ultimately led to its inability to conceive of any other set of goals and values. See Coeuré, *La Grande lueur á l'est: les Français et l'Union Soviétique, 1917-1939* (Paris: Éditions du Seuil, 1999); and Kivisaari "The Decline of the French Communist Party: The Party Education System as a Brake to Change, 1945-90," (Ph.d. diss., University of Portsmouth, 2000).

75. Marta Harnecker, "Althusser and the 'Theoretical Anti-Humanism of Marx,'" *Nature, Society, and Thought* 7, no. 3 (1994): 325-29.

76. Bernard Rousset, "Althusser: la question de l'humanisme et la critique de la notion de sujet," in *Althusser Philosophe*, ed. Pierre Raymond (PUF: Paris 1997), 137-54.

77. Louis Althusser to the Comité Central d'Argenteuil, March 11-13, 1966, ALT2. A42-04.01, Fonds Althusser, Institut Mémoire de l'Édition Contemporaine, Paris, France. In an irony that Althusser could only chuckle at, the Communist Party daily *l'Humanité* debuted an advertising campaign in 2002 built around the concept that the newspaper exists because oppression exists and hinging on the line: "Dans un monde ideal *l'Humanité* n'existerait pas." [In an ideal world, *l'Humanité* would not exist.] One can anticipate Althusser's rejoinder: "*Non, dans un monde reel, l'humanité n'existe pas.*" [No, in the real world, humanity does not exist.]

78. Michael Emerson, "Althusser on Overdetermination and Structural Causality," *Philosophy Today* 29 (Fall 1984): 203.

79. Louis Althusser, Unpublished typescript, "Textes sur la philosophie marxiste" [1975 or 1976], ALT 2. A22-01.02, Fonds Althusser, Institut Mémoire de l'Édition Contemporaine, Paris, France.

Chapter 7

Theory for Practice

Though there is sufficient evidence to argue that Althusser's interventions against Stalinist dogmatism and Marxist humanism correct some of the worst tendencies of these traditions' interpretations of Marx, it is subject to debate whether or not Althusser's writings on science and philosophy from the early 1960s accomplish the greater goals of his project. As detailed in chapter 6, these goals were to articulate Marx's real philosophy and to defend Marxism as a science that produces objective knowledge of the world, knowledge that, in its resistance to ideology, provides real direction for political action.[1] Regarding the goal of articulating Marx's real philosophy, it is clear that his early critics were right in asserting that, even though Althusser might be up to something philosophically interesting with his rereading of Marx, it is not the case that the philosophy he ended up articulating was the true Marx. As Eric Hobsbawm pointed out in one of the first English-language reviews of *Pour Marx* and *Lire le Capital*, Althusser was an extremely selective reader of Marx.[2] In choosing to emphasize *Capital* and the preface to the *Critique of Political Economy* and to deny or disavow the importance of the *Grundrisse* and other philosophically substantial texts, Althusser turned a blind eye to developed aspects of Marx's thought in order to emphasize those aspects that fit with his anti-humanist interpretation. His insistence on the existence of an epistemological break in Marx was likewise an interpretation only authorized by a selective reading of Marx. That toward the end of his career Althusser himself expressed agreement with Raymond Aron's view that what he had produced between 1960 and 1966 was an "imaginary Marxism" and that he gradually backed away from claiming an epistemological break in Marx's development[3] would lend further support to the criticism that Althusser's goal of uncovering the "real Marx" was not met. In retrospect, these positions appear to be strategic (if still sincere). To a party that claimed Marx, Engels, and Lenin as the ultimate authorities on issues of theory, one way to influence that party as a philosopher was to provide exegeses of the same sources that it dogmatically used to justify its actions and to demonstrate that they could not consistently be read in this way.[4] Certainly, this was a better tactic than asking the party's political bureau to read Spinoza.

If one needs more reason to argue that Althusser failed to uncover the real Marx, then there is also an immanent one; Althusser's consistently maintained hermeneutic provides good reason to suspect any reader's claim to articulating the real meaning of a given text. In *Lire le Capital*, Althusser argued that Marx's major work must be understood as a product, combination, and critique of the most advanced theoretical discourses of his day. As such, Marx's text could properly only be understood as a product of a certain confluence of historical events; that is, as overdetermined in a complex though still analyzable way. Given that this rule of production applies to all material practices, it is hard to understand how Althusser's reading of Marx (itself making use of concepts borrowed from Lacan, Lévi-Strauss, and Bachelard) can be understood as anything but the product of a later historical conjuncture. Thus, though this work can be said to constitute a new reading of Marx and therefore a new Marxist philosophy, it cannot be said, even on Althusser's own terms, to articulate the real Marx.

Despite this failure to articulate the real Marx, Althusser's later writings do provide the rudiments for a contemporary understanding of Historical Materialism as a science that produces objective knowledge of the world such that it might serve as the basis for political practice. These writings also provide for the possibility of a renewed practice of Marxist philosophy now understood as a discourse capable of articulating a critique of contemporary political and scientific practices and thereby changing them. This reconstructed Marxism, however, provides neither the exactitude nor the certainty that Althusser originally intended his intervention to produce.

In order to demonstrate how Althusser achieved this reconstruction and to define its limits, this chapter will show how the understanding of philosophy that Althusser develops in the late 1960s in works such as *Philosophie et philosophie spontanée des savants* and *Lenine et la Philosophie* solves the problems that his earlier theory had with rationalism and conventionalism. It will also reveal how this is accomplished while still providing for the (now relative) autonomy of scientific knowledge and while maintaining the distinction between Marx's philosophy and the science of Historical Materialism.[5] Further, it will suggest how these revised definitions go a long way toward clarifying the way in which Marxist philosophy functions politically and how Historical Materialism informs politics. Merely showing how Althusser's later philosophy overcomes some of the theoretical problems associated with its first formulation does not, however, accomplish the larger goal of this book. This goal is to ascertain what today remains of Marxist philosophy that is of philosophical and political value. In an attempt to answer this question, this chapter and the book will conclude with some thoughts on what remains of Marx's thought such that it might serve as a political philosophy adequate to today's exigencies.

Althusser's Revisions

In his book, *Althusser and the Renewal of Marxist Social Theory* (1992), Robert Paul Resch makes the point that there is a consistent tension throughout Althusser's career between his "conventionalist view of science" and his "realist and materialist ontology."[6] The last chapter discussed how Althusser's early philosophy of science can be termed conventionalist in that proof and demonstration are said in it to be the product of procedures internal to each science. Less was said about Althusser's realism except to mention that it is one of his basic assumptions. It is definitely the case, though, that even in Althusser's most theoreticist texts of the early 1960s, he never wavers in his realism.[7] The obvious conflict between this realism and this view of science is that whereas a conventionalist would have it that scientists rationally define their object and name its truth, a realist holds that scientific truths exist independently of our thoughts about them and that scientists work to provide a description of the laws or regularities that underlie appearances. In his work from 1960 until the summer of 1966, Althusser resolves the tension in his thought between realism and conventionalism with a solution already criticized as excessively rationalistic and possibly idealistic: science is validated internally by philosophy.

When Althusser begins in the mid-1960s to critique his theoreticism, one might expect that his conventionalism might also be subject to revision. However, this is not the case. What does happen is that his understanding of the process of science and its relationship to philosophy gradually changes such that he is willing to promote the position that reality itself provides an external check on science's findings.[8] What is gained in this revision is the possibility for correction of conventionalist errors, not the renunciation of conventionalism. What is lost is the notion of epistemic truth for science. It is replaced with the concept of "correctness" or "*justesse.*"[9] Correspondingly, the attribution of autonomy to science is replaced with the supposition of relative autonomy.[10]

Just as conventionalism and realism are preserved in Althusser's later philosophy of science, so too is the distinction between science and ideology. In both *Lenine et la Philosophie* (1968) and *Marx dans ses limites* (1978), ideology remains a source of error in the knowledge process and science is still the only practice capable of correcting these errors. What has changed from his earlier writings in self-critical works such as these is the relationship of philosophy to science and ideology. The three are all still considered real practices. However, he now argues that they are much more integrated than they were in the original descriptions of each provided in *Pour Marx* and *Lire le Capital*. Then, these practices were found to be totally separate and only structurally related. Now, ideological structures are said to cover everything, including philosophy and science.

The omnipresence of ideology does not, however, mean that there is no way to "escape" from ideology and to do science (be it physical, social, or theoretical). Inherent in the concept of ideology is the presupposition that we enjoy both a "real relation" and an "imaginary" or "lived" relationship between ourselves and the world and that there is a difference between these two relations.[11] It is this difference which science is able to uncover and it is able to do so by the formulation of rules about the world that, unlike ideological truisms, are testable and subject to revision.[12] With this work, science does not produce "truth" as it formerly was understood to do so, that is, in the sense of epistemic certainty. However, it does allow the scientist to begin to know the world-as-it-is, apart from ideology.

But what is philosophy's task if it is no longer understood as the guarantor of truth, if it is no longer the "Theory of theoretical sciences"? As Althusser describes it, philosophy should now be a handmaiden to science. In this somewhat Lockean position, Althusser argues that the role of philosophy is to help to distinguish for science which of its concepts are ideological and to make sure that a science's results are not perverted in their reception.[13] Philosophy is no longer that practice which guarantees a theory's truth nor is it that logical framework which undergirds and allows scientific research.[14] Philosophy still works on concepts but it does not guarantee their veracity. Instead, philosophy is theory that intervenes in theory, marking divisions within it and producing theses. What this intervention does is "to draw . . . a line of demarcation that separates, in each case, the scientific from the ideological."[15]

But how does it perform this operation? As Althusser describes the problem whose solution is the intervention of philosophy, science would do quite well if it weren't for the scientists who practice it. Because of the nature of their work with the real scientists are, after all, "spontaneous materialists." The problem with these lab-coated Lucretiae, however, is that they cannot help but be products of a specific socioeconomic and historical conjuncture, inhabiting and instantiating the ideologies that typify and reproduce it. With the hypotheses scientists pose and in the interpretations of results they offer, they bring into their research and conclusions the ideology of the wider culture. In fact, it is this ideology that permits certain questions to be posed and certain answers to be understood. Because they are working on the material real, some of this ideology will inevitably begin to be dispersed. This is why science can be said to progress. However, ideology or error will never be totally excised from the body of concepts that allow the science to be established and developed.[16] Philosophy, though, can help with this excision, analyzing scientific results and demonstrating in them what is ideological and what is scientific.

An example of this process applied to a physical science is given by Louis Althusser in an analysis of a lecture given by the French biologist Jacques Monod at the Collège de France in 1967.[17] In this example, Althusser shows how Jacques Monod is essentially correct in his argument that the discovery of DNA must cause us to rethink teleological assumptions in evolutionary science and to now think in terms of the emergent complexity of biological organisms as aleatory. Monod is correct in these assertions, Althusser argues, because there is abundant and real material evidence for this claim. Monod does not, however, stop with this analysis but goes on in his lecture to assert that "humanity is born" when the

> latest of these [biological] accidents could lead to the emergence in the heart of the biosphere of a new realm, the *noosphere*, the realm of ideas and knowledge which was born on the day when the new associations, the creative combinations

in an individual could be transmitted to others through language, rather than dying with him.[18]

It is this move, when Monod transposes the logic of biology onto human society with the argument that "language created man," that Althusser sees ideology enter into and distort what was theretofore a scientific analysis. What this move does is to "arbitrarily impose upon another science—which possesses a real object, different from that of the first—the materialist content of the first science."[19] As Althusser points out, this is a classic idealist and therefore ideological move to make. What Monod does is to assume that there is a universal logic or content (in this case biological) that describes each and every process no matter how materially or functionally disparate. At this point, it is the job of philosophy to step in. Its task is to mark out that which in Monod's argument is ideological and that which is philosophical.

The intervention by philosophy in science is, Althusser specifies, always political. It is an attempt to control the way in which scientific knowledge is received by the wider social sphere. However, it seems a long way from the assertion that philosophy always makes a political intervention to the claim Althusser makes in his *Reponse à John Lewis* (1972) that "philosophy is the class struggle in theory." Nonetheless, it is a consistent claim, albeit one that is obscured and injured by the excessively Leninist rhetoric Althusser tends to adopt in his more polemical pieces. It is also an argument that only makes sense in the context of Althusser's ontology and in line with his understanding of class. If one follows Althusser, though, and considers the world to be constituted exclusively of practices and if one rejects essentialist notions of class for one that views it as an abstract scientific category, then saying that "philosophy is the class struggle in theory" begins to sound less like a Leninist apologia than like a viable apologia for philosophy. By this claim, Althusser means to assert that philosophy always takes a theoretical position and that it defends this position against other theoretical positions.[20] If the theoretical terrain is thereby reconstituted by this intervention, it cannot help but affect other practices, including those of scientific, ideological, political, and economic reproduction. Philosophy is thus able to transform the relations between classes (and is thus "the class struggle in theory") because "philosophical discourses are related to ideological practices, thus to political practices, thus in the last analysis to the class struggles that transform the world."[21]

Of course, if one still thinks of class in vulgar Marxist terms, then this argument makes no sense. It is certainly not the case that a historically determined group, the proletariat, will inevitably overthrow the bourgeoisie and that philosophy is the weapon that it will use. However, it is the case that there is a relation between the role that one performs in the economy, the geographic area that one lives in, the school and mosque that one attends, the political party that one votes for, and the values that one cherishes. These affiliations can be observed, abstracted, and generalized. It is also the case that these values and practices come into conflict with those of others and that these antagonisms can be described not only in their singularity but also in terms of the conflicts between groups of people who maintain certain common practices against other groups of people who do not. As ideology runs deep and because it guides and allows social practice and affiliation, its critique by philosophy can be particularly powerful politically.[22] By marking out some parts of a discourse as correct and scientific from other parts that are incorrect and ideological, philosophy gives "ammunition" to that group of people whose practices are guided by science and it erodes the ideological fortifications of those guided by prejudice.

Looking at a nearly completed "struggle" may provide a clearer example of philosophy's potential effect than its mere abstract description. Take as an example the battle fought these last few centuries in journals, lecture halls, courtrooms, and kitchens over the notions of "primitive" and "civilized." It now seems clear that these concepts are untenable because cultures do not progress linearly from simple to complex, from primitive to civilized. Though now obvious, much anthropological research in the late nineteenth and early twentieth century was dedicated to observing indigenous cultures and to locating each somewhere on the grand historical path to civilization. By calling attention to the complexity of indigenous cultures and by developing a notion of culture as plural in works like *The Mind of Primitive Man* (1911), Franz Boas made it less possible to be a respectable social scientist and to still claim that some races and some cultures are more advanced than others. Though well beyond the scope of this book, it can be argued that this and complementary interventions buttressed, supported, and—in some ways—made possible the indigenous, civil, and cultural rights movements that followed in their wake.[23] Marking as ideological the thesis that some races or cultures are more advanced than others takes the force out of the argument that—because a culture is primitive—there is reason for it to be assimilated, removed, patronized, or just treated differently. Of course, one philosophical intervention is not enough to change complex, interrelated, and self-sustaining ideological, economic, and political practices. However, combined with other changes, it can make a difference and it can do so by "clarifying or obscuring the reality and stakes of [a] struggle."[24]

But does philosophy always get it right; does it mark the "division between the sciences and the ideologies" exactly and in every case?[25] Certainly, it does not. As the positions that philosophy defends are always conceptual, this can mean that philosophy can defend ideological error, it can "obscure the stakes of a struggle." In fact, for Althusser and with few exceptions, the defense of the dominant historical ideology constitutes the history of philosophy. However, Marx changed all that by providing a check on ideology. With his inauguration of the science of history, it became possible to recognize such philosophical defenses as ideological and erroneous; one could now analyze the objective social conditions that caused specific ideologies to emerge. What's more, this theoretical practice made it possible to continue with this type of analysis in the present, separating correct materialist concepts based on the real from ideological concepts that are erroneous.[26]

With the case of Monod and the noosphere, an example of this technique is given above in terms of an intervention in the physical sciences. Here, philosophy was mustered to defend against "idealist" assumptions about the origins of human culture and to demand that human culture be studied in its autonomy and integrity, not reduced to or explained by concepts developed for biology. Though this example dealt with the "hard" sciences, there is no reason that this technique cannot be applied to the social sciences as well. This is so because—like the physical sciences—the human sciences are concerned with real objects and real practices.[27] Not surprisingly given his background, most of Althusser's philosophical interventions are in the human sciences. For instance, critiquing Lévi-Strauss in a text from 1966, Althusser notes that the French anthropologist makes a classically idealist move when he takes one social system and its structure of kinship relations as the basic model for all cultural relations.[28] Contra this conclusion, Althusser argues that Marx's science of history has enabled us to understand that social relations change with each mode of production and that there is no "basic structure" or "structural constant" that explains each of these transformations or all formations. What there is is only the actual transformation of real structures in real history. As he writes, "The pertinent question is . . . the following: why is it *this possibility* and not another which *has come about, and is therefore real?*"[29]

To go beyond the description of these actual structures as they are or as they have become is to go beyond the purview of science and to slide into idealism. It is the task of Marxist philosophy to point this out and to make a distinction between ideological notions and those based upon scientific observation and study. Correspondingly, it is the task of Historical Materialism to research and understand the material relations that produce specific historical effects. Of course, because we are ourselves always within an ideology, we can never be one hundred percent certain of the distinctions we make nor of the conclusions that any science draws. Nonetheless, because there is a real that determines us and because this can become an object of study, we have the ability to correctly differentiate ideological knowledges from scientific knowledges. This is how philosophy intervenes politically in the field of science.

Marxist philosophy does not, however, stop at making political interventions in the field of science. According to Althusser, it also has the complementary role of representing "scientificity in politics."[30] Marxist philosophy and philosophy in general is thus understood as something of a referee. It is neither science, nor is it politics. However, by dogmatically declaring its theses, it makes theoretical interventions in each and may affect the way in which these practices play out.[31] As suggested above with examples drawn from anthropology and biology, for science, this means pointing out what in a discourse is ideological and what is scientific. For politics, however, this theoretical intervention means taking a side in the class struggle from the perspective of the Marxist science of Historical Materialism. This, Althusser indicates, is not a "(new) philosophy of *praxis*, but a new practice of philosophy."[32]

An example of this "new practice of philosophy" and its operation is (not coincidentally) Althusser's own intervention into Marxist theory in the early 1960s.[33] Though *Lire le Capital* and the articles which comprised *Pour Marx* fell short of their goal of securing a firm and unassailable foundation for Marxist philosophy and for science, they did draw upon the resources of Historical Materialism to reconfigure debates about the status of Marxist philosophy such that, for a time, people were led to think beyond Stalinism and Humanist Marxism. The results were not earthshaking; no revolution was made possible by Althusser's intervention. This, however, is consistent with his conclusions about the

status and role of Marxist thought. Althusser's intervention made clear
that Marxist philosophy could no longer be understood as a dialectical
formula for realizing political goals but must instead be understood as
the articulation and deployment of a materialist critique that may have
the effect of "assist[ing] in the transformation of the world."[34] This is
certainly a downgrading of the status of Marxist philosophy and one that
puts it worlds away from a formula for revolution or from a theory of
human liberation. In fact, it puts it much closer to the position of cultural
critique. However, with its realism and concomitant ability to correct
ideological errors, Althusser goes a long way to restoring or re-
configuring Marxist philosophy as a practice that is able to suggest,
given present realities, what events are possible.

What Remains of Marx's Philosophy?

The irony has certainly been pointed out before that the dustbin of history that was supposed to contain the decaying bones of capitalist institutions is today overflowing with the remnants of Marxist-inspired political movements. Orthodox, Revisionist, Spartacist, Bolshevist,
Trotskyist, Maoist, and most Western Marxisms have apparently had
their day. Even Structural Marxism, the most radical rethinking of
Marxism of its day, shows signs of serious wear. Emphases on such concepts as "structural causality" and "historical problematic" mark it as
much a product of 1960s France as do "Yé-Yé" girls and New Wave cin-
ema.[35] Though Françoise Hardy, Jean-Luc Godard, and analyses of
Ideological State Apparatuses all have a place in the twenty-first century,
it is also the case that they cannot have the same import or effect that
they did then and that we must consider what their meaning is today.
     Though pop culture shows a remarkable ability to recycle its old
formulas, it is apparent that some routes for the interpretation and instantiation of Marx's philosophy have been closed off. Simply put, the theoretical and practical traditions of Marxism in general and French Marxism in particular have demonstrated that these interpretations are
untenable or that they lead to unfortunate and misguided political practices. With these main avenues of Marxist thought foreclosed, the question is begged: "What remains of Marxism that is worth retaining and
from which a political philosophy adequate to today's exigencies might
be reconstructed?" As argued in the first part of this chapter and in the

one that precedes it, Althusser's intervention into the traditions of French Marxism and the subsequent revision of his preliminary conclusions provide clues as to how to proceed in this effort.

In the remainder of this book and in order to begin such an assessment, it may be helpful to look back at the traditions of French Marxism in order to observe what positions are no longer tenable. Specifically, this next section will consider that which now appears anachronistic in French Intellectual Marxism's and French Communism's take on the relationship between philosophy and science and between philosophy and history. Finally, the book as a whole will conclude with some thoughts about what Marxist philosophy can now be, given that a retreat to past formulations is foreclosed. With this consideration, it is hoped that an indication might be given of that which remains of Marx's philosophy such that it may prove to have contemporary philosophical and political value.

Philosophy and Science

Not many French Intellectual Marxists before Louis Althusser concerned themselves with the relationship between philosophy and science. The exceptions to this rule were those philosophers and scientists associated with *La Cercle de la Russie Neuve* in the 1930s.[36] As they were basically the only ones who did serious work on the subject and because the work that they did was consonant with the general theoretical conclusions of the French Communist Party, it is not worth considering either their work or the greater tradition of French Intellectual Marxism for any distinctive take on the relationship between philosophy and science. However, both Althusser and PCF theorists had much to say on this matter. Therefore, it is worth considering their conclusions regarding the status of science vis-à-vis philosophy (Marxist and otherwise) in order to ascertain what, if any, is a tenable position on the relationship between the two. In the process, these reflections should also help to clarify the status of the "Marxist science" of Historical Materialism both in relation to science in general and to Marxist philosophy in particular.

As we have seen, the consistent position of the PCF with to the relationship between philosophy and science is that, with Marx, philosophy had been superseded by science. With his discovery of the dialectic, a law that applied to and could explain all phenomena and all processes (be they cosmological, natural, biological, mental, social, or historical), the PCF argued that Marx left philosophy behind and pioneered a method by which the world could be scientifically understood and then transformed. The dialectic was thus not only a formula for revolution and total political transformation; it was also a formula that could explain phenomena as mundane as water freezing or as esoteric as nuclear reactions.

Regarding the hard sciences, much has already been said in this work about the absurdity of a formulation that reduces every phenomenal change to quantitative increases that precipitate sudden qualitative transformation. The poverty of this conception has been demonstrated not only by research in physics, biology, and chemistry (each of which demonstrate that changes in nature do not all conform to this pattern), but also by the fact that—in practice—the supposition that the motor of change in nature is dialectical has led to both deleterious political consequences and to bad science. One extreme example, despite a perceived urgent need in the 1950s to engineer crops that could feed its populations and survive harsh Russian winters, Soviet biologists researching plant husbandry were forbidden from incorporating the basic insights of Mendelian genetics and Darwinian evolution into their studies of plant reproduction. This left Soviet scientists in the unfortunate situation of trying to create Lamarckian evolutionary "leaps" by stressing crops and it led Soviet bureaucrats to prohibit the use of grain hybrids developed in the West using Mendelian insights.[37] Bad science was one result of this narrow application of the dialectic formula but the other was famine in areas where agricultural practices could have benefited from the incorporation of advances allowed by non-dialectical genetics.

With regards to political and social sciences, the results of the reduction of Marx's philosophy to a methodological formula were even worse. This is perhaps because, in the social sciences, the phenomena to which one applies such a formula are susceptible to manipulation and harm in a way that physical matter is not. Obviously, despite its misconceptions, Soviet science was good enough to develop a successful space program and to engineer massive building projects. However, it approached the engineering of the political body in much the same way as it did these other projects: identifying what social phenomena stood in the way of dialectical transformation (such as Kulaks, Yiddish intelligentsia, Socialists, etc.), and eliminating them. Though the results of this approach to social engineering were much more horrific in the Soviet Union than they were in France, it is also the case that a French Communist Party in pursuit of "theoretical and revolutionary purity" seriously undermined its ability to effect change in the socioeconomic structure, the goal that was ostensibly its reason for existence.

In retrospect, the Marxist-Leninist reductions of philosophy to science and science to the application of a crude dialectical formula appears ridiculous. Experience has made it clear that not only does this reduction do violence to the integrity of philosophy and science, but also that it is capable of doing violence to people. The universe does not run according to dialectical formulas and, even if it did, it is nowhere apparent that (as the Communist Party maintained) a certain population would be privy to this truth and able to understand and manipulate the world toward its natural conclusion. This kind of reductivism is simply impossible to entertain anymore.

With the theory that science is a privileged discourse that infallibly guides practice foreclosed, the alternative notion that science has no privilege at all, that it is just another form of ideological rhetoric, rears its head. In a rough formulation, this is the response of "postmodern" theorists to the excessive claims of Marxists, social engineers, and technocrats from the first part of this century regarding the power and privilege of science.[38] However, this response is, in its own way, excessive. That it echoes the Stalinist position of the "Two Sciences" with regard to the fact that all knowledge is judged to be ideological is reason enough to be suspicious of such claims. However, there is another reason to be suspicious of arguments that emphasize the exclusively cultural production of knowledge and which deny the ability of science to discover knowledge of the real. This is because the fact is repeatedly demonstrated in practice that science does not merely reflect and support cultural biases but that it produces knowledge that is theoretically and empirically verifiable and that is distinct from ideological knowledge.[39] Given this fact, what is called for is not the total rejection of science's privileged position in knowledge production, but a different understanding of what science is actually capable of doing granted its relative autonomy from ideological knowledge.[40]

If there is a lesson from Marxism-Leninism's treatment of the relationship between philosophy and science, it is that the notion that Marxism provides us with any formula to understand the world needs to be abandoned. It is now no more possible to say that dialectical processes govern the transformations of social structures than to say unequivocally that they govern the transformation of monkey into man.[41] Does this mean that Marxist philosophy has nothing to say about science and that science has nothing to say about the way in which the world is constituted physically and politically? This is not a necessary conclusion. Given that we live in a capitalist system and that science is one of its engines, the direction of science is invariably affected by the society that allows and supports it. Conversely, the society that allows, encourages, and validates science's discoveries is also always affected by that science's results. This reciprocal relationship is often not acknowledged but it seems to be the case that at least as much "bad science" is done with the goal of stoking the economic engines of capitalism as was ever done in the name of proving the truth of Dialectical Materialism and the superiority of communism. In this sense, the need for Marxist philosophy as a conceptual tool that provides for the possibility of the critique of "scientific" knowledge is as apparent now to us as it was to Althusser in the 1960s. What other critical apparatus is capable of explaining why so much scientific capital is now being expended in developing non-reproductive seed hybrids while research into sustainable farming is of interest primarily to members of a cultural elite who want to make sure that their morning caffeine rush is provided by an organic delivery vehicle?

Even though contemporary capitalist science is no less ideological than communist science was (and as much in need of critique), this does not mean that the knowledge science produces is exclusively in the service of class interests and that it is therefore ideological. As was indicated in this chapter's discussion of Althusser's realism, science does have its own integrity. As a material practice, it resists the ideological notions that are invariably a part of its theoretical constitution and it produces knowledge of the real world. This holds for the physical sciences as well as for the human sciences. This is the case because society consists of a system of practices that exhibit regularities and tendencies that manifest their relations to the socioeconomic totality.[42] As such, these phenomena are subject to scientific analysis. It is, however, a mistake to think that the "laws" that hold true for the physical sciences are the same as those that hold for the social sciences. As demonstrated in this work's study of the PCF, analyzing society exclusively according to dialectical law as a struggle and unity of opposites led the French party over and over again to misdiagnose the "revolutionary" potential of the French proletariat and, indeed, to misidentify the proletariat, its needs, and its potential. As Althusser pointed out in regards to the structural anthropology of Claude Lèvi-Strauss, the attribution of any social law not based on concrete analysis of actual social structures is apt to miss or occlude the specific factors that characterize and allow a given socioeconomic formation.

But what does all this mean for the science that Marxists have long held to be Marx's most significant contribution, that of Historical Materialism? It is obvious that this science can no longer be identified solely with the dialectic of history and with the description of this dialectic's unfolding. Just because Historical Materialism is not identified with the proof of this law does not mean that it is no longer a science. Obviously, physics did not cease to be a science when quantum theory replaced atomic theory. This is because the object that it studied did not change.

Like physics and like every other science, Historical Materialism has an object that it studies and for which it attempts to provide an abstract account of how this object functions. The object of Historical Materialism is the actual development of socioeconomic structures in history. It should not however be expected that this science will discover a universal "law of development" that governs the development and transformation of every socioeconomic structure. As historians have taken pains to point out, the feudal world was not ordered exclusively by the demands of non-mobile capital (as caricatures of Marx's analyses would have it).[43] Put differently, the Catholic Church did not exist only in order to ensure that starving peasants would think twice about storming the keep and demanding bread. Instead, the medieval world, as well as the contemporary, must be acknowledged as much more complex than this. This does not mean that they cannot be studied and understood but that, if we are to understand them, we are not helped and in fact are hindered by reducing their actual diversity to the multiple phenomenal manifestations of a proscribed law. Properly pursued as a study of actual socioeconomic formations in their integrity and diversity, the science of Historical Materialism allows us to understand social structures for what they have done and what they can do. However, it will always stop short of proscribing what they invariably will do.

Philosophy and History

Both the French Communist Party and most variants of French Intellectual Marxism subscribe to the notion that one of the most distinctive features of Marxism is the incorporation of a philosophy of history into its political philosophy.[44] Little has been said in this conclusion about what this philosophy of history consists of for French Intellectual Marxists. However, in discussing the relationship of the dialectic to the science of Historical Materialism, what this philosophy of history is for PCF theorists has been mentioned. It is probably best to review the PCF's understanding of Marx's philosophy of history before covering how it was understood differently by French Intellectual Marxists. After this is accomplished, we should then be able to point out that which is problematic in each of these formulations and to suggest a different way of conceiving the relationship of Marxist philosophy to history, one that avoids these errors.

For the most part, PCF theorists assumed that, with his philosophy of history, Marx had identified the fundamental logical structure that determines the transformation of economic structures in history. For them, this philosophy provided the conceptual tools to understand how and why class divisions and class struggle provide the motor for all historical development. The transformation of agrarian communities into feudal societies, feudal societies into capitalist societies, and capitalist societies into a communist one were all seen as determined by the logic of the economic formations themselves, by the logic of history. Therefore, from the first furrow that was cut into the earth, history had a trajectory. The final result or goal of this process was destined to be the instantiation of a communist mode of production, the formation of a classless society, and the end of history. For its part and for a good fifty years, the Communist Party was reasonably sure that it was the vehicle destined to achieve this goal.

No less than PCF theorists were French Intellectual Marxists convinced that history had a goal. However, intellectual Marxists like Cornu, Lefebvre, and Merleau-Ponty differed from PCF dogma in what they believed to be the means history used to reach this goal. They also differed in regards to what exactly the goal of history is. Not far removed from the Hegelian understanding of history as a dialectical process toward self-understanding, they argued that it was actually man and his thought about the world that drove the advance of history. Though Marxist enough to specify that the mode of production was (in the last instance) determinative, theirs was not an economic determinism but a conceptual one: culture and thought were described as the motor of historical transformation.

Although it was perceived as the political order that would allow history's realization, the goal of all these transformations wrought by man was not necessarily the communist state. Instead, for many French Intellectual Marxists, the goal of historical development was the end of alienation for human beings. Perhaps because of this conclusion, French Intellectual Marxists were much more flexible about how they believed this goal could be reached than were PCF theorists. Because of the PCF's belief in economic determinism and its acceptance of certain formulations of Marx, Engels, and Lenin as dogma, the organization was theoretically rigid in its conception of how a communist revolution would take place: capitalist production and the upward transfer of capital would increase class tensions, the rebellion of the working class would be directed by the party, proprietors would be expropriated, new political institutions would be put into place, and these institutions would smooth the transition to a classless society. In contrast to this rigid schema, French Intellectual Marxists held that the goal of history could be realized in any number of ways. Lefebvre, for instance, hints that the revolution might be cultural and artistic, Merleau-Ponty that it may have an entirely different vehicle for its realization than the Communist Party, Sartre that it will be achieved when individual members of the working class find meaning in communal political action. However, each of these analyses promises the same end to the process of history: the unalienated human being. In the sense that all promise this end and see the process or "reason" of history as inexorably leading to this supervenience and human liberation, French Intellectual Marxism is no less teleological than French Political Marxism.

Though the problems with ascribing a reason and purpose to history are more obvious in the PCF's philosophy of history than they are in the philosophy of history shared by the various strains of French Intellectual Marxism, the case can be made that both are damaging to Marxism conceived of as a theoretical and political practice intended to change the world. For the PCF, Marx's philosophy of history became a formula for social transformation. If all the material and economic criteria for a transformation of society were met, then the PCF reasoned that such a transformation would inevitably occur. The result of this belief was the PCF's identification with the Soviet Union and with revolution as the only means to achieving the end of history. Discovering the link between economic determinism and historical determinism proved not to be as simple as this identification; no matter how much economic and ideological

practices were forced to conform to what the Marxist model for successful revolutionary practice was thought to be, the actual world seemed
unwilling to be directed in such a fashion. The result was that the world
suffered for this forced transformation.

That the revolution and its end cannot be predicted or implemented
according to a philosophical understanding of the necessary economic
determination of history does not mean that Marx's theory of economic
determination, his "general theory of history," should be abandoned. This
theory has much explanatory power, albeit less than Marxist-Leninists
believed it to have. How else are we to understand the past horrors of
colonialism and the present expansion of global capital that are so deleterious to the environment and to human beings except as they are seen to
be motivated by a force that is greater than that of bourgeois morality?
To abandon the assumption that the demands of the economy somewhat
determine our actions and thoughts is to abandon the power of the critique that such an assumption enables.[45] However, to maintain the assumption that this determination necessarily entails a philosophy of history can create just the same or even worse violence than capitalism is
capable of on its own.

With the exception of Merleau-Ponty and Sartre, whose violences
were mostly rhetorical, the brutality associated with the forced realization of Marxism's philosophy of history did not hold for French Intellectual Marxism. This does not mean that the ascription of a telos to history by academic Marxists such as Lefebvre and Cornu is without its
own problems. With its emphasis on the power of thought and ideas to
realize revolutionary change, it is apparent that French Intellectual
Marxists for the most part missed or ignored Marx's point from the *Theses on Feuerbach* that one cannot think one's way to revolution. Just because a person realizes that she is alienated and even despite the fact that
she can now describe how this alienation happened does not mean that
she is now liberated from the tyranny of ideology. Althusser indeed
seems correct in his contention that one is alienated by and according to
one's place in the socioeconomic structure and that, in this sense, one is
overdetermined. Like it or not, ideology, will not change until the socioeconomic structure that produces it changes. In order for this to happen,
more is necessary than an artistic or intellectual "revolution." What is
necessary is the actual transformation of socioeconomic practices and
institutions. As Marx argued a century and a half ago, this requires political and not just conceptual action.

If there is a lesson to be learned from Althusser's critique of Hegelian Marxism in regard to its philosophy of history, it is that the dream of an end to alienation and an end to ideology should be abandoned. It should be abandoned because it is an unrealistic goal and because the specification of this goal often occludes the real factors that are determinative of ideologies: namely the interrelations of economic and social structures. Instead of being seen as some obstacle to true knowledge that can be overcome, ideology must be seen simply as the conceptual medium in which we function. This is not to say that present ideologies cannot be critiqued or that better and different ideologies are not possible. In fact, the conceptual critique of specific ideologies may be productive of new and better ideologies, ones that are not predicated upon oppressive economic relationships. However, it would have to be the case that this ideological critique is both allowed by contradictions in the socioeconomic totality and that its potential effect is recognized as limited by this structure. This does not mean that we cannot envision a society without class tensions, but that its actual realization can only be seen as possible when socioeconomic relations have changed such that a society like this *is* possible.

The Limits of Marxist Philosophy and Its Potential

In a somewhat obtuse formulation, Althusser often characterizes philosophy as a "void."[46] What he means by this is that, because philosophy has no status apart from that of critique, it is able to move around in conceptual space that is already occupied by ideology and by other practices. This is philosophy's virtue and its strength. However, it is not apparent to Althusser that philosophy, even Marxist philosophy, can fully explain the world or that it can radically change it. When philosophy attempts to do the former, it always falls short and ends up merely justifying an ideological and political position. When it attempts to do the latter, it likewise takes up a political position. However, because philosophy has the ability to look at what is and suggest what may be, it potentially has the power to affect and change conceptual and ideological structures and to intervene in the world of politics. For the most part, philosophy's interventions have been limited to justifying the world as it is or (what perhaps is worse) to arguing for a world as it should be. However, in certain instances like that when Machiavelli argued in the early

sixteenth century from the perspective of a "new Prince in a new princi-
pality," philosophy has also asserted its privilege to suggest what may
yet be based upon what is.[47] It seems that, with Marx, philosophy also
intervened in this way. However, unlike Machiavelli who did not yet
have the science of history on his side, Marx founded a practice of philosophy worth preserving whereby an analysis of the contemporary socioeconomic situation may at last allow the materialist philosopher to
suggest, given present realities, what events are possible. This is a much
more modest project than that undertaken by Marxism's past, but it is
also less dangerous and more realistic. It is also a project worth pursuing.

Notes

1. For instance, in *Althusser and the End of Leninism?*, Margaret Majumdar
characterizes this revision as a total failure. She states that it is a repudiation of
anything he had accomplished in his earlier work. See Margaret Majumdar, *Althusser and the End of Leninism?* (London: Pluto, 1995), 164. Perhaps Althusser's most eloquent defender, Étienne Balibar also comes to such a conclusion (later revised), arguing in "Tais-Toi encore-Althusser!" (1988) that his later
work constitutes a "self-annulment" of his earlier writings. See Étienne Balibar,
Écrits pour Althusser (Paris: Éditions la Découverte, 1991), 59-90.
2. Eric Hobsbawm, "The Structure of Capital," in *Althusser: A Critical
Reader*, ed. Gregory Elliot (Cambridge, MA: Blackwell, 1994), 9.
3. Gregory Elliot, "Analysis Terminated, Analysis Interminable," in *Althusser: A Critical Reader*, 187; and Étienne Balibar, "Althusser's Object," *Social Text* 39 (1994): 157-88.
4. In a very explicit instance of this strategy one finds Althusser in a letter
to party Secretary Waldeck Rochet condemning the resolutions made by the
Central Committee regarding humanism and urging the party to take note that:
"Nous possédons de nombreux textes de Marx, Engels, Lénine parfaitement
explicites [sur la non-validité des concepts humanistes]. Les recherches que j'ai
poursuivies dans ce domaine avec d'autres camarades philosophes ne représen-
tent que *l'approndisement* théorique de thèses que nous trouvons dans les classiques. Dans cette situation très particulière, où il y a effectivement recherche,
mais à l'intérieur de *connaissances marxistes déjà établies*, le Comité Central
pouvait retenir son jugement sur la partie effectivement "ouverte" de la recherche : il avait en revanche le devoir de réaffirmer les principes et les connaissances marxistes *déjà* acquises, dans la partie achevée du recherché." {We pos-
sess numerous texts of Marx, Engels, and Lenin that are perfectly explicit [about
the non-validity of humanist concepts]. The research that I have pursued with
other communist philosophers in this domain represents only the theoretical

enrichment of theses that we find already in the classics of Marxism. In these particular situations where there is *ongoing research but along already established lines* of Marxist thought, the Central Committee should hold back the judgment that it is open to any and all research. It has, on the contrary, the job of reaffirming the already acquired and established principles of Marxist science.} Louis Althusser, Unpublished typescript, "Lettre à Comité Central d'Argenteuil [March 11-13, 1966]," ALT2 A42.01, Fonds Althusser, Institut Mémoire de l'Édition Contemporaine, Paris, France, 6-7.

5. Consistently maintained, perhaps the best exposition of this position is to be found in "Textes sur la philosophie marxiste [1975-1976]," ALT2. A22.01.02, Fonds Althusser, Institut Mémoire de l'Édition Contemporaine, Paris, France.

6. Robert Paul Resch, *Althusser and the Renewal of Marxist Social Theory* (Berkeley: University of California Press, 1992), 160. For many of the points that I make in this and subsequent paragraphs I am indebted to Resch's work.

7. Louis Althusser and Étienne Balibar, *Reading Capital* (New York: Verso, 1970), 161.

8. Geoffrey M. Goshgarian, introduction to *The Humanist Controversy and Other Writings* (London: Verso, 2003), xi-lxii. In this introduction, Goshgarian provides a detailed account of the transformation of Althusser's thought between the summer of 1966 and 1968. Pulling not only from Althusser's published and unpublished theoretical writings but also from letters, notes, newspaper accounts, PCF archival materials, and interviews, he provides a convincing argument that it was Althusser's political experience battling with the PCF over humanism that fundamentally changed his thinking about the status of philosophy in relationship to politics and ideology. In that he takes into account the Maoist influence on Althusser's thought as well as Althusser's increasing reliance on Leninist concepts, Goshgarian's argument can be seen as complementary to those of Gregory Elliot in *The Detour of Theory* (New York: Verso, 1987), 196-210, and Sunil Khilnani, *Arguing Revolution: The Intellectual Left in Postwar France* (New Haven, CT: Yale University Press, 1993), 105-17, with the important exception that these earlier accounts overstate the importance of one influence on Althusser's thought to the exclusion of others.

9. Louis Althusser, "Justesse et Philosophie," *La Pensée* 176 (August 1974): 3-8.

10. Louis Althusser, "Philosophy and the Spontaneous Philosophy of the Scientists," in *Philosophy and the Spontaneous Philosophy of the Scientists* (London: Verso, 1990), 103.

11. Althusser and Balibar, *Reading Capital*, 161.

12. Resch, *Althusser*, 183.

13. Althusser, "Spontaneous Philosophy,"106.

14. Critiquing such a philosophy of science (in this case as articulated by fellow party member and philosopher of mathematics J. M. Desanti), Althusser

argues in unpublished class notes from the *Cours de Philosophie pour Scienti-fiques* that scientists never actually cede prerogative to philosophy even when they seem to be using philosophical categories to describe their research. Rather, they draw on philosophical vocabularies which are *"substitutes proviso ire"* while they work out the new categories or laws through their research. Later, scientists abandon philosophical categories and for good reason: they can now describe the reality that orders the appearance of certain phenomena more exactly. Thus, according to Althusser, one would expect certain philosophical categories used by physicists like "determinism" and "indeterminism" to be replaced by a more correct description of material behavior. Louis Althusser, "Sur Desanti et les pseudo-problémes de troisième espece [December 12, 1967]," ALT2. A12.02.01, Fonds Althusser, Institut Mémoire de l'Édition Contemporaine, Paris, France, 6-7.

15. Althusser, "Spontaneous Philosophy," 106.

16. Louis Althusser, "Ideologie et appareils idéologiques d'état (notes pour une recherche)," *La Pensée* 151 (1970): 3-38.

17. Althusser, "Appendix: On Jacques Monod," in *Philosophy and the Spontaneous Philosophy of the Scientists* (London: Verso, 1990), 145-65.

18. Althusser, "Appendix: On Jacques Monod," 150.

19. Althusser, "Appendix: On Jacques Monod," 151.

20. Louis Althusser, *Essays in Self-Criticism* (London: New Left Books, 1976).

21. Balibar, "Althusser's object," 173.

22. Louis Althusser, "The Historical Task of Marxist Philosophy," in *The Humanist Controversy*, 215.

23. Claudia Roth Pierpoint, "The Measure of America: How a Rebel Anthropologist Waged War on Racism," *New Yorker* (March 8, 2004), 48-63.

24. Warren Montag, *Althusser* (New York: Palgrave, 2002), 153.

25. Goshgarian, introduction to *The Humanist Controversy*, liii. The fact that Franz Boas may have falsified some of the data used to support his thesis about the plurality of culture marks another potential problem with philosophy rushing to the defense of scientists or to the critique of their hypotheses. See Constance Holden, "Going Head to Head over Boas' Data," *Science* 298 (November 2002): 942-43.

26. Louis Althusser, *Lenin and Philosophy, and Other Essays* (London: New Left Books, 1971), 61.

27. For a discussion of this possibility, albeit one clouded by Althusser's early theoreticism, see "Philosophie et sciences humaines (1963)," in *Solitude de Machiavel et autres textes*, ed. Yves Syntomer (Paris: PUF, 1998), 43-58.

28. Louis Althusser, "On Lévi-Strauss," in *The Humanist Controversy*, 28-29.

29. Louis Althusser, "On Lévi-Strauss," 26.

30. Althusser, *Lenin and Philosophy*, 65.

31. Althusser, "Spontaneous Philosophy," 74-75.

32. Althusser, *Lenin and Philosophy*, 68.

33. It should be added that this provides a performative example as the results were not intended on Althusser's part. At the time, Althusser did not conceive of philosophy as primarily strategic. Rather, he believed himself in the early 1960s to be in the process of "converting the party to Theory's [Truth]." Althusser as quoted in Goshgarian, introduction to *The Humanist Controversy*, xxxii.

34. Althusser, *Lenin and Philosophy*, 68.

35. Luc Ferry and Alain Renaut, *La Pensée 68: Essai sur l'antihumanisme contemporain* (Paris: Gallimard, 1985), 200.

36. Another exception—though not a prominent one—is Henri Lefebvre. His work on this area, *À La Lumière du materialisme dialectique, Tome II: Methodologie des sciences* (Paris: Éditions Sociales, 1940) was destroyed by PCF censors and, if read at all, had very little influence. It has recently been reissued as *Méthodologies des sciences* (Paris: Anthropos, 2002).

37. For more on this and other problems with Soviet science see J. Vadim Birstein, *The Perversion of Knowledge: The True Story of Soviet Science* (Boulder: Westview Press, 2001). Unproven rumors have it that crops were stressed by being forced to sit through endlessly repeated performances of social realist melodramas.

38. For examples of such positions see Ernesto Laclau, "Building a New Left: An Interview with Ernesto Laclau," *Strategies* (Fall 1988); and Richard Rorty, *Contingency, Irony and Solidarity* (New York: Cambridge University Press, 1989). For an argument that Jacques Derrida treats the sciences as exclusively sociocultural phenomena see Joseph Zycinski, "Postmodern Criticism of the Rationality of Science," *Studia Philosophiae Christianae* 30, no. 2 (1994): 299-312. For an argument supporting the position that Foucault undermines science's claim to progress and truth production due to his relativism see P. Dews, "Foucault and the French Tradition of Historical Epistemology," *History of European Ideas* 14, no. 3 (May 1992): 347-63.

39. In line with Robert Paul Resch and Andrew Collier, I second Roy Bhaskar's arguments from *A Realist Theory of Science* (Brighton: Harvester Press, 1978) and *The Possibility of Naturalism* (Atlantic Highlands, NJ: Humanities Press, 1979) defending scientific realism and would argue that it accords with Althusser's notion of reality and of science's role in producing an understanding of it. Like Resch but unlike Collier, I would suggest that immanent rather than transcendental realism suffices for a reconstructed Althusserian Marxism and, further, that an immanent realism is the only type that his description of "actually existing" practices allows.

40. Lest science's abilities be over- or misrepresented here, the "relative" in "relative autonomy" should be emphasized. As Jack Amariglio points out, the overdetermination of a subject by socioeconomic processes makes it very hard

to sort out ideological from scientific knowledge. What appears "scientific" to one person or a group of persons may appear so only by dint of a specific ideological bias. This does not mean that a distinction between science and ideology cannot be made, but that *knowing* that the distinction is correct is very difficult. Amariglio, "Marxism Against Economic Science," *Research in Political Economy* 10 (1987), 193.

41. Georges Cogniot, "Esquisse d'une histoire de la pensée scientifique," *Les Cahiers de l'université nouvelle* 414 (March 15 1966): 23.

42. Andrew Collier, *Scientific Realism and Socialist Thought* (Hertfordshire, Great Britain: Harvester Wheatsheaf, 1989), 178.

43. Roger S. Gottlieb, "Feudalism and Historical Materialism: A Critique and Synthesis," *Science and Society* 48, no. 1 (1984), 1-37.

44. Sartre is here perhaps the exception. While he believed that history gave meaning to an individual's struggle and provided the possibility for his liberation, it is not apparent that this struggle in Sartre is wedded to the notion of a necessary dialectical development for history. Rather, history and social structures just comprise the contingent situation within which the individual is able to act.

45. In "Theories, Practices and Pluralism," James Bohman makes a proposal for what a critical social science might look like once it gives up grand notions like that of traditional Marxism's philosophy of history. Viewing Bohman's proposal to judge critical social theories by their effect on the social sphere as Althusserian in spirit, a future paper will develop the thesis that Historical Materialism's standing as a critical social science can be judged according to the ability of its conclusions to be adopted and realized. For more on this pragmatic criterion see Bohman, "Theories, Practices and Pluralism: A Pragmatic Interpretation of Critical Social Science," *Philosophy of the Social Sciences* 28, no. 4 (December 1999), 459-80.

46. François Matheron, "The Recurrence of the Void in Louis Althusser," *Rethinking Marxism* 10, no. 3 (Fall 1998): 22-27.

47. Louis Althusser, "The Solitude of Machiavelli (1977)," in *Machiavelli and Us,* trans. Gregory Elliot (New York: Verso, 1999), 118. See also pages 124 and 129.

Bibliography

Adereth, Maxwell. *The French Communist Party: A Critical History (1920-1984): From Comintern to the Colours of France.* Manchester: Manchester University Press, 1984.

Althusser, Louis. *Essays in Self-Criticism.* London: New Left Books, 1976.

———. *For Marx.* Translated by Ben Brewster. London: New Left Books, 1977. Originally published as *Pour Marx* (Paris, Maspero, 1965).

———. *The Humanist Controversy and Other Writings.* Translated by Geoffrey M. Goshgarian. London: Verso, 2003.

———. "Idéologie et Appareils idéologiques d'État (notes pour une recherche)." *La Pensée* 151 (1970): 3-38.

———. *Lenin and Philosophy, and Other Essays.* Translated by Ben Brewster. London: New Left Books, 1971.

———. *Machiavelli and Us.* Translated by Gregory Elliot. New York: Verso, 1999.

———. *Montesquieu, la politique et l'histoire.* Paris: PUF, 1959 (augmented re-edition, Paris: La Découverte, 1996).

———. *Philosophy and the Spontaneous Philosophy of the Scientist and Other Essays.* Translated and with introduction by Gregory Elliot. London: Verso, 1990.

———. *Solitude de Machiavel et autres textes.* Edited by Yves Sintomer. Paris: PUF, 1998.

———. "Sur Raymond Polin, '*La Politique Morale de John Locke.*'" *Revue d'histoire moderne et contemporaine* 9, no. 2 (April-June 1962): 150-55.

———. *Sur la Reproduction.* Paris: PUF, 1995.

Althusser, Louis, and Étienne Balibar, *Reading Capital*. Translated by Ben Brewster. New York: Verso, 1970.

Amariglio, Jack. "Marxism against Economic Science: Althusser's Legacy." *Research in Political Economy* 10 (1987): 159-95.

Anderson, Kevin. "Lenin, Hegel and Western Marxism." *Studies in Soviet Thought* 44, no. 2 (Spring 1992): 79-126.

Anderson, Perry. *Considerations on Western Marxism*. London: New Left Books, 1976.

Angrand, Cécile. Introduction to *Cours de Philosophie*. Paris: Éditions Sociales, 1945.

Archard, David. *Marxism and Existentialism: The Political Philosophy of Sartre and Merleau-Ponty*. Belfast: Blackstaff Press, 1980.

Aron, Raymond. *D'une sainte famille à l'autre*. Paris: Gallimard, 1969.

Atkinson, D. "The Anatomy of Knowledge: Althusser's Epistemology and Its Consequences." *Philosophical Papers* 13 (October 1984): 1-19.

Balibar, Étienne. "Althusser's Object." *Social Text* 39 (1994): 157-88.

———. *Écrits pour Althusser*. Paris: Éditions la Découverte, 1991.

———. "From Bachelard to Althusser: The Concept of Epistemological Break." *Economy and Society* 7, no. 3 (1979): 24-47.

———. *Philosophy of Marx*. Translated by Chris Turner. New York: Verso, 1995.

Baugh, Bruce. *French Hegel: From Surrealism to Postmodernism*. London and New York: Routledge, 2003.

———. "Limiting Reason's Empire: The Early Reception of Hegel in France." *Journal of the History of Philosophy* 31, no. 2 (1993): 259-75.

Becker, Jean-Jacques. *The Great War and the French People*. Translated by Jay Winter. Dover, NH: Berg Publishers, 1985.

Bell, David, and Byron Criddle. *The French Communist Party in the Fifth Republic*. Oxford: Clarendon Press, 1994.

Benton, Ted. *The Rise and Fall of Structural Marxism: Althusser and his Influence*. London: McMillan, 1984.

Bhaskar, Roy. *The Possibility of Naturalism*. Atlantic Highlands, New Jersey: Humanities Press, 1979.

———. *A Realist Theory of Science*. Brighton: Harvester Press, 1978.

Birstein, J. Vadim. *The Perversion of Knowledge: The True Story of Soviet Science*. Boulder: Westview Press, 2001.

Blume, Daniel, et al. *Histoire du Réformisme en France depuis 1920.* Paris: Éditions Sociales, 1976.

Boas, Franz. *The Mind of Primitive Man.* New York: Macmillan, 1911.

Bohman, James. "Theories, Practices and Pluralism: A Pragmatic Interpretation of Critical Social Science." *Philosophy of the Social Sciences* 28, no. 4 (December 1999): 459-480.

Bourderon, Roger. *La Négociation: Été 1940, Crise au PCF.* Paris: Éditions Syllepse, 2001.

Bourdin, Jean-Claude. "The Uncertain Materialism of Louis Althusser." *Graduate Faculty Philosophy Journal* 22, no. 1 (2000): 271-87.

Bowd, Gavin. *L'Interminable Enterrement: Le communisme et les intellectuels français depuis 1956.* Paris: Digraphe, 1999.

Burkhard, Bud. *French Marxism Between the Wars: Henri Lefebvre and the "Philosophies."* New York: Humanity Books, 1999.

Callinicos, Alex. *Althusser's Marxism.* London: Pluto Press, 1976.

Casanova, Laurent, Francis Cohen, Jean Desanti, Raymond Guyot, and Gérard Vassails. *Science bourgeoise et science prolétarienne.* Paris: Éditions de La Nouvelle Critique, 1950.

Caute, David. *Communism and the French Intellectuals: 1914-1960.* New York: Macmillan, 1964.

Chiodi, Pietro. *Sartre and Marxism.* Brighton: Harvester Press, 1976.

Clero, Jean-Pierre, and Olivier Bloch. "Maurice Merleau-Ponty et la Guerre; Philosophie en France (1940-1944)." *Revue Philosophique de la France et de l'Etranger* 3, no. 127 (2002): 315-31.

Coeuré, Sophie. *La Grande lueur á l'Est: les Français et l'Union Soviétique, 1917-1939.* Paris: Éditions du Seuil, 1999.

Cogniot, Georges. *La 'Dialectique de la Nature,' Une Oeuvre Géniale de Friedrich Engels.* Éditions Sociales, 1953.

———. "Esquisse d'une histoire de la pensée scientifique." *Les Cahiers de l'Université Nouvelle* no. 414 (March 15, 1966).

———. "L'Histoire du parti bolchévik, conférence faite par Georges Cogniot sur le *Précis* d''l'Histoire du Parti Communiste de l'U.R.S.S.'." *Ce Que Nous Enseigne* (April 12, 1939).

———. *L'Histoire du parti bolchevik et ses enseignements actuels.* Paris: Éditions Sociales, 1949.

———. *Karl Marx notre contemporain.* Paris: Éditions Sociales, 1968.

———. "La loi économique fondamentale du socialisme." *Apprendre* no. 22 (February/March 1953): 4-23.

————. "Staline, Homme de Science." *La Pensée* (November-December 1948): 3-15.

Collier, Andrew. *Scientific Realism and Socialist Thought.* Hertfordshire: Harvester Wheatsheaf, 1989.

Cooper, Barry. *Merleau-Ponty and Marxism: From Terror to Reform.* Toronto: University of Toronto Press, 1979.

Cornu, Auguste. *Karl Marx et Friedrich Engels*, 3 vols. Paris: Éditions Sociales, 1955.

————. *Karl Marx et la pensée moderne: contribution à l'étude de la formation du marxisme.* Paris: Éditions Sociales, 1948.

————. "Karl Marx et la pensée romantique allemande." *Europe* (October 15, 1935): 199-216.

Cornu, Auguste, and Félix Armand. "Critique et Auto-Critique." *La Pensée* (September-October 1949): 84-88.

Courtois, Stéphane, and Marc Lazar. *Histoire du Parti Communiste Français.* Paris: PUF, 1995.

————. *Histoire du Parti Communiste Français dans las Lutte pour la Paix, 1914-1947.* Paris: S. Arslan, 2000.

Cranston, M. "The Thought of Roger Garaudy." *Problems of Communism* 19, no. 5 (September/October 1970): 11-18.

Desanti, Jean-Toussaint. *Introduction à l'Histoire de la Philosophie.* Paris: Bibliothèque nationale de France, 1956.

————. *La Philosophie Silencieuse ou Critique des Philosophies de la Science.* Paris: Éditions du Seuil, 1975.

Dews, Peter. "Althusser, Structuralism, and the French Tradition of Historical Epistemology." In *Althusser: A Critical Reader*, edited by Gregory Elliot, 104-42. Oxford: Blackwell, 1994.

————. "Foucault and the French Tradition of Historical Epistemology." *History of European Ideas* 14, no. 3 (May 1992): 347-63.

Duménil, Gérard. *Économie Marxiste du Capitalisme.* Paris: Éditions La Découverte, 2003.

Elliot, Gregory. *Althusser: The Detour of Theory.* New York: Verso, 1987.

————. "Analysis Terminated, Analysis Interminable." In *Althusser: A Critical Reader*, edited by Gregory Elliot, 177-202. Oxford: Blackwell, 1994.

Emerson, Michael. "Althusser on Overdetermination and Structural Causality." *Philosophy Today* 29 (Fall 84): 203-214.

Engels, Friedrich. *Herr Eugen Dühring's Revolution in Science (Anti-Dühring)*. New York: International Publishers, 1939.

———. *Socialism: Utopian and Scientific* [1889]. Marx/Engels Archive, 1993. marxists.org/archive/marx/works/1889/soc-utop/index.htm (accessed July 21, 2004).

Fauvet, Jacques. *Histoire du Parti Communiste Français*. Paris: Fayard, 1977.

Ferry, Luc, and Alain Renaut. *La pensée 68: Essai sur l'antihumanisme contemporain*. Paris: Gallimard, 1985.

Fonds Althusser [Althusser Archives], Institut Mémoire de l'Édition Contemporaine. Paris, France.

Furet, François. *Le Passé d'une illusion: essai sur l'idée communiste au XXéme siécle*. Paris: Robert Laffont/Calman-Lévy, 1995.

Gadamer, Hans-Georg. *Philosophical Hermeneutics*. Berkeley: University of California Press, 1977.

Garaudy, Roger. "À propos de la position de parti dans les sciences." *Cahiers de Communisme* no. 5 (May 1955): 590-611.

———. "Humanisme et dialectique." *Semaine de la pensée marxiste (7-14 Decembre 1961)*. Paris: CERM, 1962.

———. *Humanisme Marxiste*. Paris: Éditions Sociales, 1949.

———. *Le Marxisme et la Personne Humaine*. Paris: Éditions Sociales, 1948.

———. *Perspectives de l'homme*. Paris: PUF, 1960.

Gedö, András. "The Irrevocable Presence of Marxist Philosophy in Contemporary Thought." In *Nature, Society and Thought*. vol. 7, no. 2 (1987): 133–53.

Geerlandt, Robert. *Garaudy et Althusser: le débate sur l'humanisme dans le Parti Communiste Français et son Enjeu*. Paris: Presses Universitaire de France, 1978.

Gerratana, Valentino. "Althusser and Stalinism." Pt. 1. *New Left Review* 101/102 (1977): 110-21.

———. "Stalin, Lenin and Leninism." Pt. 2. *New Left Review* 103 (1977): 59-71.

Glucksmann, André. "Un Structuralisme ventriloque." *Les Temps Modernes* no. 250 (1967).

Glucksman, Miriam. *Structuralist Analysis in Contemporary Social Thought*. London: Routledge, 1974.

Goldmann, Lucien. *The Hidden God: A Study of Tragic Vision in the* Pensées *of Pascal and the Tragedies of Racine*. New York: Humanities Press, 1964.

Goshgarian, Geoffrey. "Introduction." In *The Humanist Controversy and Other Writings*, by Louis Althusser, xi-lxii. London: Verso, 2003.

Griese, Anneliese, and Gerd Panelzig. "Why Did Marx and Engels Concern Themselves With Natural Science?" *Nature and Social Thought* 8, no. 2 (1997): 125-37.

Guterman, Norbert, and Henri Lefebvre. *La Conscience mystifiée*. Paris: Gallimard, 1936.

Harnecker, Marta. "Althusser and the Theoretical Anti-Humanism of Marx." *Nature, Society, and Thought* 7, no. 3 (1994): 325-29.

Hazareesingh, Sudhir. *Intellectuals and the French Communist Party: Delusion and Decline*. Oxford: Oxford University Press, 1991.

Hegel, G. W. F. *Morceaux choisis de Hegel*. Translated and selected by Norbert Guterman and Henri Lefebvre. Paris: Gallimard, 1938.

Hess, Remi. *Henri Lefebvre et l'aventure du siècle*. Paris: Éditions A.M. Métailié, 1988.

Hobsbawm, Eric. "The Structure of Capital." In *Althusser: A Critical Reader*, edited by Gregory Elliot, 1-9. Oxford: Blackwell,1994.

Holden, Constance. "Going Head to Head over Boas' Data." *Science,* no. 298 (November 2002): 942-43.

Hughes, H. Stuart. *The Obstructed Path: French Social Thought in the Years of Desperation*. New York: Harper & Row, 1968.

Hyppolite, Jean. *Genèse et structure de la phénoménologie de l'esprit de Hegel*. Paris: Aubiers, 1946.

———. "Le 'scientifique' et l' 'idéologique' dans une perspective marxiste." *Diogène* 64 (1968).

"Idéologie, direction et organisations homogènes (à l'occasion du prochain Congrès national de Paris)." *Cahiers du bolchevisme* (November 28, 1924): 65-67.

Jay, Martin. *Marxism and Totality: The Adventures of a Concept from Lukács to Habermas.* Berkeley: University of California Press, 1984.

Jose, Pierre, ed. *Tractes surréalistes et declarations collectives, Tome 1 (1922-1939)*. Paris: Terrain Vague, 1979.

Judt, Tony. *Marxism and the French Left: Studies in Labour and Politics in France, 1830-1981*. Oxford: Clarendon Press, 1986.

Juquin, Pierre. *Autocritiques*. Paris: Grasset, 1985.

Kautsky, Karl. *Les Trois sources du Marxisme: l'oeuvre historique de Marx* [1907]. Paris: Spartacus, 1947.

Kelly, Michael. "Hegel in France to 1940: A Bibliographic Essay." *Journal of European Studies* 11, no. 1 (March 1981): 19-52.

————. *Modern French Marxism.* Oxford: Blackwell, 1982.

Khilnani, Sunil. *Arguing Revolution: The Intellectual Left in Postwar France.* New Haven, CT: Yale University Press, 1993.

Kivisaari, Marja. "The Decline of the French Communist Party: The Party Education System as a Brake to Change, 1945-90." Ph.D. diss., University of Portsmouth, 2000. Abstract in *Communist History Network Newslettter On-Line*, Issue 12 (Spring 2002). http://les1.man.ac.uk/chnn/CHNN12PCF.html (accessed August 1, 2004).

Kojève, Alexandre. *Introduction to the Reading of Hegel.* New York: Basic Books, 1969.

Kriegel, Annie. *Aux Origines du Communisme Français, 1914-1920: Contributions à l'histoire du Mouvement Ouvrier Français.* 2 volumes. Paris: Mouton, 1964.

————. *Les Communistes français dans leur premier demi-siécle: 1920-1970.* New edition, augmented with the collaboration of Guillaume Bourgeois. Paris: Seuil, 1985.

Kruks, Sonia. *The Political Philosophy of Merleau-Ponty.* Atlantic Highlands, NJ: Humanities Press, 1981.

Kurzweil, Edith. *The Age of Structuralism.* New Brunswick, NJ: Transaction Publications, 1996.

Laclau, Ernesto. "Building a New Left: An Interview with Ernesto Laclau." *Strategies* (Fall 1988): 10-28.

Laclau, Ernesto, and Chantal Mouffe. *Hegemony and Socialist Strategy: Towards a Radical Democratic Politics.* London: Verso, 1985.

"La Lutte sur les deux fronts." *Cahiers de Bolchevisme* (September 1930): 850.

Langevin, Michel. "L'Enrichissement du Marxisme à partir des resultats du developpement des sciences de la nature: 'la dialectique de la nature.'" In *Esquisse d'une Histoire de la Pensée Scientifique* 412. Paris: Cahiers de l'Université Nouvelle, 1966.

Lazarus, Sylvain, ed. *Politique et Philosophie dans l'oeuvre de Louis Althusser.* Paris: PUF, 1993.

Lecourt, Dominique. *Lyssenko: histoire réelle d'une science prolétarienne.* Paris: Maspero, 1976.

Lee, Donald. "Althusser on Science and Ideology." *Southwest Philosophical Studies* 7 (April 1982): 68-74.

Lefebvre, Henri. *À la lumière du matérialisme dialectique, Tome I: Logique formelle, Logique dialectique.* Paris: Éditions Sociales, 1947.

————. *À la lumière du materialisme dialectique,* Tome II: Methodologie des sciences. Paris: Éditions Sociales, 1940. Reprinted as *Méthodologies des sciences.* Paris: Anthropos, 2002.

————. "Auto-Critique: contribution à l'effort d'èclaircissement idéologique." *La Nouvelle Critique* 4 (March 1949): 41-57.

————. *Contribution à l'esthétique.* Paris: Éditions Sociales, 1953.

————. *Dialectical Materialism.* Translated by John Sturrock. London: Jonathan Cape, 1968. Originally published as *Le Matérialisme dialectique* (Paris: PUF, 1940).

————. *L'existentialisme.* Paris: Editions du Sagittaire, 1946.

————. Introduction to *Recherches Philosophiques sur l'essence de la liberté humaine* by Friedrich von Schelling. Translated by Georges Politzer. Paris: Rieder, 1926.

————. *Le langage et la société.* Paris: Gallimard, 1966.

————. *Le Marxisme.* Paris: PUF, 1974 (1948).

————. *La somme et le reste.* Paris: Bélibaste, 1973.

————. "Sur une interpretation marxiste." *L'Homme et la société* 4 (1967)

————. *Le temps des méprises.* Paris: Stock, 1975.

————. *La vie quotidienne dans le monde moderne.* Paris: Gallimard, 1968.

Lefranc, Georges. *Les Gauches en France.* Paris: Payot, 1973.

Lenin, Vladimir. *Cahiers de Lénine sur la dialectique de Hegel.* Translated and introduced by Norbert Guterman and Henri Lefebvre. Paris: Gallimard, 1938.

————. *Materialism and Empiriocriticism.* 1908. Lenin Internet Archive, 1993. www.Marxists.org/archive/lenin/works/1908/mec/ 01.htm (accessed August 11, 2004).

————. *Philosophical Notebooks, Collected Works.* vol. 38. Moscow: Progress Publishers, 1972.

————. *The State and Revolution* [1917]. Lenin Internet Archive. 1993. www.marxists.org/archive/lenin/works/1917/sep/staterev/ index.htm (accessed August 11, 2004).

————. "The Three Sources and Three Component Parts of Marxism [1913]." *Collected Works*, vol. 19. Moscow: Progress Publishers, 1970.

Lewis, John. "The Althusser Case." *Marxism Today* (January and February 1972).

Lichtheim, George. *Marxism in Modern France*. New York: Columbia University Press, 1966.

Majumdar, Margaret. *Althusser and the End of Leninism?* East Haven, CT: Pluto Press, 1995.

Marx, Karl. *Capital*. 3 vols. London: Lawrence and Wishart, 1960.

————. *Capital: A New Abridgment*. Edited by David McLellan. Oxford: Oxford University Press, 1995.

————. *Economic and Philosophical Manuscripts of 1844*. Edited by Dirk J. Struik. New York: International Publishers, 1964.

————. *Karl Marx, oeuvres et choisies Tome 1 et 2*. Translated and introduced by Norbert Guterman and Henri Lefebvre. Paris: Gallimard, 1934.

————. "The Law on Thefts of Wood." *Selected Writings*. Edited by David McLellan. Oxford: Oxford University Press, 1977.

————. *Selected Correspondence, 1846-1895*. Translated by Dona Torr. Westport, CT: Greenwood Press, 1975.

Marx, Karl, and Friedrich Engels. *The Communist Manifesto*. New York: International Publishers, 1948.

————. *The German Ideology*. London: International Publishers, 1989.

Matheron, François. "The Recurrence of the Void in Louis Althusser." *Rethinking Marxism* 10, no. 3 (Fall 1998): 22-27.

Maublanc, René. "La Philosophie du marxisme et l'enseignement officiel." *Les Cahiers de Contre-Enseignement Prolétarien* 19. Paris: PCF, Bureau d'Éditions (July 1935).

Mazower, Mark. *Dark Continent: Europe's Twentieth Century*. New York: Vintage Books, 2000.

Merleau-Ponty, Maurice. *Adventures of the Dialectic*. Translated by Joseph Bien. Chicago: Northwestern University Press, 1973.

————. *Humanism and Terror: An Essay on the Communist Problem*. Boston: Beacon Press, 1969.

————. *Phénoménologie de la perception*. Paris: Gallimard, 1945.

————. *Sens et Non Sens*. Paris: Nagel, 1948.

Monod, Lucien. *Élements de philosophie marxiste*. Cannes: E. Cruvés, 1927.

Montag, Warren. *Althusser*. New York: Palgrave, 2002.

Murphy, Francis J. "Marxism in Continental France." *Studies in Soviet Thought* 37 (Fall 1989): 159-67.

Nancy, Jean-Luc. "Marx et la philosophie." *Esprit* 349 (1966).

Nielsen, Kai, and Robert Ware, editors. *Analyzing Marxism—New Essays on Analytical Marxism*. Calgary: University of Calgary Press, 1989.

Norris, Christopher. "Deconstruction, Ontology and Philosophy of Science: Derrida on Aristotle." *Revue Internationale de Philosophie* 52, no. 205 (1998): 411-49.

Nugent, Neill, and David Lowe. *The Left in France*. New York: St. Martin's Press, 1982.

Parti Communiste Français. *La Crise économique et les Partis Politiques*. Les Dossiers de l'Agitateur 2. Paris: Editions du PCF, 1932.

———. *Six cours élémentaires d'éducation communiste*. Paris: Section d'Agitation-Propagande du PCF, 1928.

Payne, Michael. *Reading Knowledge: An Introduction to Barthes, Foucault and Althusser*. Malden, MA: Blackwell, 1997.

Pierpoint, Claudia Roth. "The Measure of America: How a Rebel Anthropologist Waged War on Racism." *The New Yorker* (March 8, 2004): 48-63.

Plekhanov, George V. *Fundamental Problems of Marxism*. New York, International Publishers, 1969.

Politzer, Georges. *Principes élémentaires de la philosophie*. Paris: Éditions Sociales, 1968 (1945).

Poster, Mark. *Existential Marxism in Post-war France: from Sartre to Althusser*. Princeton, NJ: Princeton University Press, 1975.

———. *Sartre's Marxism*. Cambridge: Cambridge University Press, 1982.

Poulantzas, Nicos. "Ver une théorie marxiste." *Les Temps Modernes* 240 (1966).

Racine, Nicole, and Louis Bodin. *Le parti communiste français pendant l'entre-deux-guerres*. Paris: Presses de la Fondation Nationale des Sciences Politiques, 1982.

Resch, Robert Paul. *Althusser and the Renewal of Marxist Social Theory*. Berkeley, CA: University of California Press, 1992.

Roberts, Marcus. *Analytic Marxism: A Critique*. London: Verso, 1996.

Rorty, Richard. *Contingency, Irony and Solidarity*. New York: Cambridge University Press, 1989.

Rousset, Bernard. "Althusser: la question de l'humanisme et la critique de la notion de sujet." In *Althusser Philosophe*, edited by Pierre Raymond. PUF: Paris, 1997, 137-54.

Santamaria, Yves. *L'Enfant du malheur: le Parti Communiste Français dans la lutte pour la paix, 1914-1947*. Paris: S. Arslan, 2002.

———. *Histoire du Parti Communiste Français*. Paris: Éditions La Découverte, 1999.

Sartre, Jean-Paul. *Being and Nothingness*. Translated by Hazel Barnes. New York: Washington Square Press, 1966.

———. *Existentialism and Humanism*. London: Methuen, 1948.

———. *Nausea*. Translated by Lloyd Alexander. Norfolk, CT: New Directions, 1964.

———. *Search for a Method*. Translated by Hazel Barnes. New York: Knopf, 1963.

———. *Situations I-VI*. Paris: Gallimard, 1964.

Sée, Henri. *Matérialisme historique et interpretation économique de l'histoire*. Paris: Marcel Giard, 1927.

Sève, Lucien. *Marxisme et la théorie de la personnalité*. Paris: Éditions Sociales, 1969.

Shandewyl, Eva. "Tensions Between Scientific Ethos and Political Engagement: Belgian University Professors and the Lysenko Case." Lecture, 19th International Congress of Historical Sciences, Oslo, Norway, 11 August 2000. www.oslo2000.uio.no/univhist/presentation.html (accessed August 11, 2004).

Smith, Steven. *Reading Althusser: An Essay on Structural Marxism*. Ithaca, NY: Cornell University Press, 1984.

Souvarine, Boris. *Le Stalinisme: ignomie de Staline*. Paris: R. Lefeuvre, 1972.

Stalin, Joseph. *Deux Mondes (Rapport au XVIIeme congrès de Partie Communite de l'U.R.S.S.)* Paris: PCF Bureau d'Editions, 1933.

———. "Dialectical and Historical Materialism." In *The Essential Stalin: Major Theoretical Writings, 1905-1952*. New York: Anchor Books, 1972.

———. "The Foundations of Leninism." In *Problems of Leninism*. Moscow: Foreign Language Publishing House, 1947.

———. "Marxism and Linguistics." In *The Essential Stalin: Major Theoretical Writings, 1905-1952*. New York: Anchor Books, 1972.

————. "Two Camps." *The Essential Stalin: Major Theoretical Writings, 1905-1952.* New York: Anchor Books, 1972.

Subise, Louis. *Le Marxisme aprés Marx, 1956-1965: quatre marxistes dissidents français.* Paris: Aubiers, 1967.

Thèses directrices sur la tactique de l'Internationale communiste dans la lutte pour la Dictature du Prolétariat. Geneva: La Nouvelle Internationale, 1920-1921.

Thompson, Edward P. *The Poverty of Theory.* New York: Monthly Review Press, 1978.

Thorez, Maurice. *Le Fils du Peuple, Oeuvres, Tome 14.* Paris: Éditions Sociales, 1937.

Thorez, Maurice, and Roger Garaudy. "Les Taches des philosophes communistes et la critique des erreurs philosophiques de Staline." Supplement to *Cahiers du Communisme* no. 7-8 (July/August 1962).

Tiersky, Ronald. *French Communism 1920-1972.* New York and London: Columbia University Press, 1974.

Tran Duc Thao. "Le 'noyau rationnel' dans la dialectique hégélienne." *La Pensée* (January-February 1965): 6-23.

Tucker, Robert C. *Philosophy and Myth in Karl Marx.* Cambridge: Cambridge University Press, 1972.

Valéry, Paul. "La Crise de l'Esprit." *Nouvelle Revue Française* 71 (August 1919): 322.

Verdès-Leroux, Jeanine. *Le réveil des somnambules: le Parti Communiste, les intellectuels et la culture (1956-85).* Paris: Fayard/Minuit, 1987.

Wallon, Henri. *A la lumiére du Marxisme, essais.* Paris: Éditions Sociales Internationales, vol. 1, 1935. Vol. 2, 1937.

Wheen, Francis. *Karl Marx: A Life.* New York: Norton, 2000.

Willard, Claude. *Socialisme et Communisme Français.* Paris: Armand Collin, 1967.

Wolff, Richard. "A Note on Althusser's Importance for Marxism Today." *Rethinking Marxism* 10, no. 3 (Fall 98): 90-97.

Zycinski, Joseph. "Postmodern Criticism of the Rationality of Science." *Studia Philosophiae Christianae* 30, no. 2 (1994): 299-312.

Index

About the Author

William S. Lewis is currently an Assistant Professor of Philosophy at Skidmore College in Saratoga Springs, New York. He specializes in the History of Political Philosophy and in American Pragmatism. Articles by him have appeared in *The Journal of Speculative Philosophy*, *Rethinking Marxism*, *The American Journal of Semiotics*, and *Studies in Social and Political Thought*. He holds a Ph.D. in Philosophy from the Pennsylvania State University.